Edith Wharton's Letters from the Underworld

Fictions of Women and Writing

Candace Waid

The University of North Carolina Press

Chapel Hill and London

The Frederick W. Hilles Publication Fund of Yale University
provided a subvention to aid in the publication of this work.

© 1991 The University of North Carolina Press

Library of Congress Cataloging-in-Publication Data

Waid, Candace.
    Edith Wharton's letters from the underworld : fictions of
women and writing / by Candace Waid.
        p.   cm.
    Includes bibliographical references and index.
    ISBN 0-8078-1938-7 (cloth : alk. paper).—
    ISBN 0-8078-4302-4 (pbk. : alk. paper)
    1. Wharton, Edith, 1862–1937—Criticism and interpretation.
2. Women and literature—United States—History—20th
century.   3. Authorship in literature.   4. Women in literature.
I. Title.
PS3545.H16Z89   1990
813'.52—dc20   90-41588
                                                                    CIP

A portion of Chapter 4 appeared in a different version as the Introduction to Edith Wharton, *The Custom of the Country* © 1989 New
American Library. Used by permission.

The paper in this book meets the guidelines for permanence and
durability of the Committee on Production Guidelines for Book
Longevity of the Council on Library Resources.

Design by April Leidig-Higgins

Manufactured in the United States of America

95   94   93   92   91   5   4   3   2   1

Frontispiece: *Portrait of Mrs. Lloyd* by Sir Joshua Reynolds
(courtesy The Royal Academy of Arts)

For my parents

Harriet Jones,

Donald Waid,

& Billie Waid

Contents

ix   Acknowledgments

1   Introduction:
The American Persephone

15   *One*
Women and Letters
(*The House of Mirth*)

51   *Two*
The Woman Behind the Door
(*Ethan Frome*)

85   *Three*
Wharton and Wilkins:
Rereading the Mother
(*Summer*)

127   *Four*
The Devouring Muse
(*The Custom of the Country*)

173   *Five*
Pomegranate Seeds:
Letters from the Underworld
(*The Touchstone* and *Ghosts*)

205   Notes

231   Index

Acknowledgments

Anyone who works on Edith Wharton is in the debt of R. W. B. Lewis. Throughout the research and writing of this book, I had the good fortune to benefit not only from his scholarship and critical example but also from his guidance and support. This book would not have been begun or completed without the early and continuing encouragement of Jean-Christophe Agnew. My friends and colleagues Jennifer Wicke, Margaret Ferguson, Alan Trachtenberg, and Patricia Meyer Spacks also read versions of these chapters, offering valuable criticism and providing a community in which to write. I am also grateful to Harriet Chessman and Brigitte Peucker for participating in the intellectual and personal dialogue that this book represents. To Allen Tullos, who has been a reader for many years, I owe my introduction to the life of the mind and a debt of spirit and imagination.

Others who offered essential encouragement, support, and education include: Virginia Praytor, David Lowe, Miriam Hansen, Susan Allein, Harriet Swift, Phil Teague, Ellen Dawson Sutton, Norton Batkin, Paul Fry, Richard Brodhead, Laura Kalman, Jean Edmunds, Dorothy Tullos, Rolf Tullos, Augusta Harper Cunningham, Andrea Kaufman, Elizabeth Sicelof, Rhoda McGraw, Robert Yuran, Alice Parker, Helene Marshall, Arthur Marshall, Leslie Agnew, Thelma Levine, Elizabeth Meese, Judy Babbitts, Susan Smulyan, Lee Howard, George Lord, and Rose Gladney.

I would like to thank Bill Murray, Dawn Murray, and Will Murray, for their special efforts on my behalf. Pat Saik, Kathleen Bagley Tanner, and Sue Bullard offered important encouragement. I thank Harriet Jones, Donald Waid, Billie Waid, Allen Tullos, and Donna Waid Murray for sharing the will to narrate. For standing with me among what Wharton thought of as the pots and pans of language, I thank David Marshall, who has been the other voice in a dialogue that shaped the argument of this book. His dedication and inspiration have made the book possible.

In its early stages this project was supported by a fellowship from the American Association of University Women. A fellowship from the Georges

Lurcy Trust allowed me to spend a year in residence at the Whitney Humanities Center at Yale. I am grateful to Peter Brooks and the Fellows of the Whitney Center for their conversation and interest. I am also grateful for a Morse Fellowship from Yale University for support while the final revisions were completed. Kate Nickerson helped prepare the manuscript with scholarly care. I would like to thank Iris Tillman Hill and Kate Torrey for their interest and patience. The Beinecke Rare Book and Manuscript Library at Yale provided generous assistance and permission to quote from unpublished materials in the Wharton Collection. I am grateful to Mr. William Royall Tyler for granting permission to cite from Edith Wharton's unpublished manuscripts. The Royal Academy of Arts facilitated the reproduction of Sir Joshua Reynolds's *Portrait of Mrs. Lloyd*. Duncan Robinson and Malcolm Cormack of Yale's British Art Center also provided helpful advice. Finally, I would like to thank Bruce Covey for his assistance in proofreading, and Brian Edwards for his careful and intelligent work on the index.

Edith Wharton's
Letters from the
Underworld

Introduction
The American
Persephone

I trod the confines of death and the threshold of Proserpine; I was swept around all the elements & back again; I saw the sun shining at midnight in purest radiance; *Gods of heaven & Gods of hell I saw face to face & adored them.*—Apuleius, *The Mysteries of Isis* (transcribed by Edith Wharton in the planning notebook for her unfinished novel, "Literature," 1914)

In 1913 Edith Wharton wrote to her publisher, "Plus je vais, more and more it becomes the essential thing for me that anyone who writes should be able to say 'Gods of heaven and Gods of hell have I looked on face to face, and adored them.'" At the close of *Hudson River Bracketed*, the young writer Vance Weston evokes these same lines at a moment of revelation about his literary calling.[1] Wharton quotes at greater length from Apuleius's *The Mysteries of Isis* in the planning notebook for her unfinished novel, "Literature": "I trod the confines of death and the threshold of Proserpine; I was swept around all the elements & back again; I saw the sun shining at midnight in purest radiance; *Gods of heaven & Gods of hell I saw face to face & adored them.*"[2] For Wharton it is the woman writer in particular who must have eaten the seed of the pomegranate and crossed the threshold of Persephone.

The readings of Wharton's fiction in the chapters that follow will be informed by Wharton's identification with the daughter who chooses to leave the world of the mother and dwell in the underworld of experience. As R. W. B. Lewis has noted, Wharton had a "lifelong obsession" with "Persephone and her sojourn in the underworld."[3] Wharton often writes (especially in her ghost stories) about characters who cross the threshold between life and death; these characters are often women writers, and in more than one story they share with Wharton the distinction of authoring a text entitled "Pomegranate Seed."[4] This book is not, however, a study of classical motifs or allusions, or even a study devoted primarily to the importance of the Persephone myth in Wharton's work. Wharton's early stories, *The House of Mirth*, *Artemis to Actaeon and Other Verse*, *Ethan Frome*, *Summer*, *The Custom of the Country*, *The Touchstone*, and *Ghosts* do not all contain specific allusions to pomegranate seeds and the figure of Persephone. This figure is a touchstone in my readings, but I am interested in it here only insofar as Persephone is Wharton's figure for the woman writer. This book is about Wharton's attempts to imagine the place of the woman writer.

In locating this figure, I am partly concerned with the biographical and public identity of a woman who was a remarkably successful, accomplished, and nationally recognized author for more than forty-five years. I am more concerned, however, with the perhaps paradoxical recurrence throughout Wharton's work of failed artists, unfinished texts, and anxieties about silence, inarticulateness, and suffocation. My focus on *women and writing* in Wharton's fiction is meant to suggest the interrelations of two major areas of emphasis in Wharton's work: a self-conscious attention to writing and the conditions of art and a deeply ambivalent preoccupation with women and the conditions of female identity. This book does not seek to find either heroines or martyrs in Wharton's fiction; Wharton was more likely to critique women than to celebrate them, and if she was concerned with the ways in which society contributed to the destruction of women, she also was likely to see certain modes of female identity as a threat to society. I argue that a consideration of Wharton's ambivalent view of women must take into account her preoccupation with writing and the very possibility of the woman writer. Most of her works do not depict characters who are authors or artists, of course—although a surprising number of them do, and even more of them repeatedly describe difficult and often conflicted acts of writing. Rather than focusing solely on female characters who are writers, I am concerned with both male and female characters who dramatize Wharton's concerns in a variety of texts that can be read as meditations on and even allegories about women, art, and letters.

Wharton's recurrent efforts to imagine the *place* of the woman writer address the problem of women's position in social and gender hierarchies. They also consider the problem of place in a geographical sense—not just the imaginary geography that divides Persephone's underworld from the world of the mother but also the actual place of country and region. As the title of this introduction suggests, I am interested in the predicament of an *American* Persephone, the figure of a woman writer who must conduct, in Elizabeth Ammons's fine phrase, an "argument with America."[5] From the beginning of her career, Edith Wharton was presented to the reading public as a female Henry James. Like James, Wharton often analyzed the world of high society, defining herself and her art through her relation to European traditions. Although she did not give up her American citizenship, as James did, Wharton spent the last twenty-six years of her life in France, returning to America only twice for brief visits.

James's first known comment about Wharton refers to the question of her place. In a letter written shortly after he read *The Valley of Decision*, the novel she published in 1902 about eighteenth-century Italy, James advised restraint; he wrote to Wharton's sister-in-law, who had sent him the novel, that the young author "*must* be tethered in native pastures, even if it reduces her to a backyard in New York."[6] A decade later, James sensed that Wharton had become "elegiac" in *The Reef*, a quality that suggested to him his friend's estrangement and (what seemed particularly poignant in 1912) her lack of a sense of place. "Your only drawback," he wrote, "is not having the homeliness and the inevitability and the happy limitation and the affluent poverty of a

Country of your Own." James, who himself had been ruthlessly satirized in the American press as a "man without a country," added parenthetically, with less irony than truth, *"comme moi, par exemple!"*[7]

James senses Wharton to be without a country when she is most Jamesian, both in style and subject; *The Reef* is a novel about Americans living in France. For James, however, settled in England and his art, America appears to have been less of a problem than it was for Wharton. She is by far the more estranged from her history—both her family and her native land. Having left America for the first time in her infancy, she returned at the age of ten to find herself a foreigner. She often complained to her friends of the difficulties of returning to America after being in Europe, speaking of "the curse of having been brought up" with the traditions and aesthetic sensibilities of Europe and "having it ineradically in one's blood."[8] In 1912, as she began her permanent exile from America and from marriage, Wharton seemed particularly unsettled. James had referred to Wharton previously as "the great and glorious pendulum," a reference to her yearly habit of Atlantic crossings;[9] but although she was well traveled internationally, she was limited in her firsthand knowledge of America.[10] Ironically, these adventures were left to the sedentary James, who crossed the length and breadth of the United States by train, visiting his brothers in California and Florida and gathering material for his 1907 book, *The American Scene*.

James, however, wrote primarily of Americans abroad, while Wharton continued to set most of her work in America long after her departure from her "homeland." She insisted on her knowledge of American society, especially when critics chastised her for her ignorance of the traditional and contemporary customs practiced outside of the province of Old New York. Wharton claimed that the accuracy of her perceptions was not diminished by living abroad; and indeed, this was true insofar as she always had been careful to describe herself as a person apart from both life and literature in America. In her unpublished autobiography, "Life and I," Wharton declared that from the time she was ten years old she never felt "otherwise than as in exile in America."[11] In 1934, writing in *A Backward Glance*, she described the publication of her first book of fiction in terms of a different kind of nationalism: "I felt like some homeless waif who, after trying for years to take out naturalization papers, and being rejected by every country, has finally acquired a nationality." However, although Wharton could claim that the "Land of Letters was henceforth to be my country, and I gloried in my new citizenship," the question of her place continued to be a source of anxiety.[12]

In 1962, Diana Trilling wrote that it still remained "for criticism to show Mrs. Wharton her proper place in the mainstream of American literature."[13] A decade earlier, Blake Nevius found Wharton "the least American of our important authors." Unlike James, who wrote a book about Hawthorne, Wharton herself insisted on her position outside of any indigenous American tradition. Nevius asserts that the whole of Wharton's work would not have been significantly different if nineteenth-century American literature had never existed.[14]

Wharton herself encouraged this view in her autobiographical and critical writings. Her critical statements on nineteenth-century American authors, with the exception of her comments on James and Whitman, rarely rise above superficial dismissals;[15] her assessments appear to have remained unrevised during the course of her career. Provoked by the rising critical recognition of Melville in the 1920s, she was pleased to go against the tide to proclaim her belief that Melville wasted his time depicting cannibals in drawing rooms.[16] This statement from late in her life indicates Wharton's high ground of exile and isolation and her resistance to any effort to recognize or celebrate a tradition of American literature.

Wharton did read American authors. From the closely censored reading of her childhood, she recalled (among other favorites) Twain's *Innocents Abroad*, Bret Harte's "parodies of novels," and the humorous narratives of the Chicago philosopher in Irish dialect, "Mr. Dooley." Yet even as a child, Wharton remembered, she was taught to keep these books at a distance. They were appreciated for their expression of fresh American idiom, for the "picturesque terms" which were a source of vitality and humor to the New York circle. At the same time, Wharton's mother, Lucretia Jones, insisted that her daughter and family speak only the purest English. Idioms were to be treated as slang, appropriate in conversation only if framed as if the speaker were using quotation marks. To Wharton's ear, even the flat Dutch tones of her father placed him outside of the approved family practice (*BG*, 50–51).

Just as Wharton was taught to keep Americanisms at a distance—she shared James's worry that the English language was becoming soiled by careless, everyday usage—she used her critical writing to position herself at a distance from recognized American authors (*BG*, 51).[17] Her apparent lack of interest in authors such as Twain, Melville, and Hawthorne is reflected by the near absence of those authors as forces in her fiction. Traces of a Hawthornian aesthetic have been found in the unrelenting symbolism of *Ethan Frome* (which Nevius takes to be Wharton's most indigenous work); the names of Wharton's characters Ethan and Zeena echo the names of Hawthorne's characters Ethan Brand (from the story "Ethan Brand") and Zenobia (from *The Blithedale Romance*).[18] However, if Wharton is anxious about the influence of fathers, the result among other things of a rearing so careful that even the voices of her father's family seemed tainted by foreignness, her brief acceptance of Hawthorne appears to be little more than a gesture meant to establish the primacy in American literature of the dark and stylized view she promoted of New England. It is a slight yet significant bow which works to obscure a deeper anxiety about other American authors.

Indeed, in her development as an artist it was more important for Wharton to distinguish herself from what Hawthorne called "the damned mob of scribbling women" than from any of America's recognized male authors.[19] Wharton did not dislike all women writers. Although she particularly respected the English authors George Eliot, Jane Austen, and Emily Brontë, American women writers were another story. Wharton claimed to be grateful that her mother prohibited her from reading novels—a prohibition that neither her mother nor her aunts observed in their own reading. This saved her, she felt, from the distorted and sentimental books which fill the imaginations of her own novels' heroines with feminine illusions. (Such illusions lead to the destruction of Lily Bart in *The House of Mirth* and in *The Custom of the Country* offer Undine Spragg a language of sentimental sophistry with which she can justify her destruction of others.) Wharton claims that she hungered for books of philosophy, imagining that logic might release her from the confusion of the "dark, trackless region 'where ignorant armies clash by night.'" She hoped that a more systematic knowledge might save her from the fate of being a "mere 'little girl'" (LI, 27, 33).[20]

Wharton's first attempt at a novel, "Fast and Loose," written when she was fifteen years old, displays her early self-consciousness about writing fiction. This private effort was accompanied by a series of mock reviews, attributed to various prominent English and American periodicals, which excoriate the supposedly male author of the novel. The review which she attributed to the *Nation* complained: "The English of it is that every character is a failure, the plot a vacuum, the style spiritless, the dialogue vague, the sentiments weak &

the whole thing a fiasco." The author is compared to "a sick-sentimental school-girl who has begun her work with a fierce & bloody resolve to make it as bad as Wilhelm Meister, Consuelo, & 'Goodbye Sweetheart' together." Another review claims that "the hero evaporates into a vacillating sentimentalist."[21] Wharton was aware of condescending attitudes toward sentimentalism, just as she was aware of her mother's distaste for the commonness of a successful female author such as Mrs. Stowe (*BG*, 68).

All of Wharton's references to American women writers imply the taint (often pastel) of an unacceptable sentimentalism. (She made no distinctions between local colorists and sentimentalists.) For Wharton, whose views of women writers reflected her views of women's lives in general, it was as women writing *for women* that they were most disadvantaged. Wharton felt that the limitations of a female audience hindered the growth of all women. In *French Ways and Their Meaning* (published in 1919), she writes: "It is because American women are each other's only audience, and to a great extent each other's only companions, that they seem, compared to women who play an intellectual and social part in the lives of men, like children in a baby school." Her contrasting description in the same volume of a "man's woman," the woman who is less spiteful because she "breathes a freer air,"[22] indicates the privileged position in relation to her sex that Wharton reserves for women among men such as George Eliot and herself. As we shall see, "breath" in Wharton's private symbolism figures voice, especially artistic voice.

"Real living" was the term Wharton reserved for the "close and constant and interesting and important relations between men and women." According to Lewis, Wharton's phrase "real life" was a euphemism for eroticism.[23] In her view, men lived lives closer to "reality"; she expressed a preference for men that she claimed went back as far as her childhood affection for "little boys and puppies" and her conscious dislike of the "negligible" and "despised" alternatives such as little girls, dolls, and canaries (LI, 12, 15). Realism and the real were associated with men; women in Wharton's view were protean and deceptive. Both the lives and the fiction of women were diffuse and formless, lacking the stable structure that would make them "real." Thus, when Wharton selects Sarah Orne Jewett and Mary Wilkins as her literary adversaries in her defensive discussions of her New England novels, her complaints about their writings ostensibly are based on an argument about realism; but for Wharton, realism and the real are more than literary categories. They are gender-related and often sexually charged terms. What becomes increasingly apparent throughout Wharton's writings is her tendency to stress structure and plot as the formal requirements of the real while denouncing a feminine aesthetic that focuses on surfaces.

This feminine aesthetic is one of decoration and ornamentation that substitutes description for structure. By describing the surfaces, writers can create the illusion of continuity through the blurring of disjunctures and differences. Wharton fears the diffusion she associates with the descriptive sketch and the loosely grouped stories characteristic of the work of the local colorists. In *A Backward Glance*, Wharton recalls the fears of structural inadequacy she felt when she was a young writer: "My idea of a novel was something very different, something far more compact and centripetal, and I doubted whether I should ever have enough constructive power to achieve anything beyond isolated character studies, or the stringing together of picturesque episodes" (*BG*, 205).

It is entirely appropriate, then, that Wharton's first book was *The Decoration of Houses* (coauthored with the architect Ogden Codman and published in 1897). It is a principle of this book, which seeks to rescue interior design from the dressmaker's art and elevate it to the realm of architecture, that structure and symmetry are to be valued over ornamentation. Wharton's warning to would-be decorators about the dangers of description contains a concise statement of her literary hierarchies. She writes:

> It is well, as a rule, to shun the decorative schemes concocted by the writers who supply our newspaper with hints for "artistic interiors." The use of such poetic adjectives as jonquil-yellow, willow-green, shell-pink, or ashes-of-roses, gives to these descriptions of the "unique boudoir" or "ideal summer room" a charm which the reality would probably not possess. The arrangements suggested are usually cheap devices based upon the mistaken idea that defects in structure or design may be remedied by an overlaying of color and ornament.[24]

For Wharton, the language of description and those writers who practice description are suspect; neither the poetic adjectives in print nor the pastel paints which cover the walls can efface the reality of structural flaws. Indeed, the presence of color or ornamentation suggests an underlying inadequacy.

Writing to Robert Grant in 1907 about his response to her novel *The Fruit of the Tree*, Wharton addresses the relations of architecture, gender, and writing in a description of her "congenital" difficulties as a writer:

> I am very much pleased that you like the construction of the book, & I more than agree with you that I have not been able to keep the characters from being, so to speak mere *building material*. The fact is that I am beginning to see exactly where my weakest point is.—I conceive my subjects like a man—that is, rather more architectonically & dramatically than most women—& then execute them like a woman; or rather, I sacrifice, to my desire for construction & breadth, the small incidental effects that women have always excelled in, the episodical characterization, I mean. The worst of it is that this fault is congenital, & not the result of an ambition to do big things. [L, 124]

Wharton contrasts her tendency, when approaching a subject "from the novel-angle," to "see it in its relation to a larger whole" with a "smaller realism" that she associates with the success of her "short stories." She continues:

> This is the reason why I have always obscurely felt that I didn't know how to write a novel. I feel it more clearly after each attempt, because it is in such sharp contrast to the sense of authority with which I take hold of a short story.—I think it ought to be a warning to stop; but alas, I see things more & more from the novel-angle, so that I'm enclosed in a vicious circle from which I suspect silence to be the only escape. [L, 124]

By Wharton's own account, from the beginning of her conscious life she was concerned with an opposition between truth and appearance. In her unpublished memoir "Life and I," Wharton chooses the phrase "moral tortures" to describe her feeling of being caught between opposing and irresolvably differing sets of expectations. She writes: "For years afterward I was never free from the oppressive sense that I had two absolutely inscrutable beings to please— God & my mother—who while ostensibly upholding the same principles of behaviour, differed totally as to their application. And my mother was the most inscrutable of the two." Her mother required politeness, she writes, and God required the "truth." Wharton confesses, "Nothing I have suffered since has equalled the darkness of horror that weighed on my childhood in respect to this vexed problem of truth-telling, & the impossibility of reconciling 'God's' standard of truthfulness with the conventional obligation [the word "necessity" is crossed out here] to be 'polite'" (LI, 6, 7).

The truth, associated with an invisible God, seems to be realized through its opposition to politeness, a decorum of behavior which existed entirely in the realm of visible appearances. Truth, if it was unpleasant, was not to be spoken, yet Wharton felt compelled to speak it out of fear of being "punished by the dark Power I knew as God." One measure of the truth was the amount of disapproval she expected from her mother. Wharton describes "two means of escape from this chronic moral malady." "One," she writes, "was provided by my love of pretty things—pretty clothes, pretty pictures, pretty sights—& the other by my learning to read" (LI, 7). These two escapes from her moral tortures correspond to the opposing powers that divide her world: the women's realm of surface and appearance and the realm of truth represented by God and books.

To Wharton, reading and writing represented the masculine and adult province of knowledge and power. Through the possession of books, particularly books of philosophy, Wharton felt she could escape being "that helpless blundering thing a mere 'little girl'" (LI, 33). Not surprisingly, the only expressions of vocational desire Wharton recalls from her early life are first to be the best-dressed woman in New York, like her mother, and later to be a writer. For Wharton, then, the world of appearances and the visible was feminine. She writes, "I always saw the visible world as a series of pictures more or less harmoniously composed, & the wish *to make the pictures prettier* was, as nearly as I can define it, the form my feminine instinct of pleasing took" (LI, 1–2).

Color, surface, ornamentation, structure, beauty, and *reality* are key terms in the aesthetic debate that Wharton conducts with both others and herself throughout her work. Wharton struggles against a feminine aesthetic represented by both her mother and, at times, those she describes as her literary "predecessors," Mary Wilkins and Sarah Orne Jewett. Her need to define herself against such authors and the culture they represented to her informs *Ethan Frome* and *Summer* and is related to the struggle against others through which Wharton defines herself as an individual and an artist. Although it is inscribed within a literary context, this aesthetic debate goes beyond merely literary terms—or rather, it depends upon a broader conception of the literary which includes constructing a life as well as writing fiction. In *The House of Mirth,* which was in early versions titled "A Moment's Ornament" and "The Year of the Rose," Lily Bart's fate is related to her ornamental and floral identity. In *The Custom of the Country,* the struggle against a feminine aesthetic has implications for the fate of the American artist and American society as well. In these novels it is the marriage of capitalism and sentimentalism that embodies Wharton's most apocalyptic vision of America.

Near the beginning of her 1934 autobiography, *A Backward Glance*, Wharton explains that her decision to write the story of her life was motivated by her sense of the disappearance of the New York that she had once known—a place that no longer existed in a world seemingly divided by a great abyss. Looking back, she writes, the old New York that existed prior to 1914 seemed to have a "pathetic picturesqueness" (*BG*, 6). She explains elsewhere in *A Backward Glance* that in writing *The Age of Innocence*, the 1920 novel which looks back to the New York of the 1870s, she "found a momentary escape in going back to . . . childish memories of a long-vanished America" (*BG*, 369). Wharton was fifty-eight when she published *The Age of Innocence*. The novel closes with a fifty-seven-year-old Newland Archer looking back over his life as he sits on a park bench in Paris looking up at the window of the apartment of the Countess Ellen Olenska, whom he once loved. Archer has not seen Ellen Olenska for almost thirty years, since the dinner that consecrated their separation, when "a deathly sense of the superiority of implication and analogy over direct action, and of silence over rash words, closed over him like the doors of the family vault."[25] Visiting in Paris, instead of seeing Ellen Olenska himself Archer sends up his son—who is said to "take after him"—because he does not want to see the richness of her life. "For nearly thirty years, her life—of which he knew so strangely little—had been spent in this rich atmosphere that he already felt to be too dense and yet too stimulating for his lungs."[26]

In Wharton's original plans for *The Age of Innocence*, Archer "falls in love" with Ellen Olenska and decides that "life with May Welland, or any other young woman who has not had Ellen's initiation, would be unutterably dull." In Wharton's outline, Ellen Olenska "shocks him deeply by proposing that they should 'go off for a few weeks' so that he can be sure he is not making a mistake." When Archer "reproaches her," Ellen Olenska "begins to feel ashamed of having made the suggestion" and begins to think that "the 'Europe-an corruption' has tainted her soul." They marry, in part to "efface this impres-sion from her own mind and his," but Ellen Olenska soon realizes that she cannot remain in America with Newland Archer. Wharton writes, "She realizes that for the next 30 or so years they are going to live in Madison Ave. in winter and on the Hudson in the Spring and autumn, with a few weeks of Europe or Newport every summer." Her "whole soul recoils and she knows at once that she has eaten of the Pomegranate Seed and can never live without it."

In Wharton's scheme, Europe is the underworld of experience where Ellen Olenska has a "real life." The America of Newland Archer is the place where "nothing ever happens to him again."[27] This idea is carried through in the published work even if the plot is drastically changed. In *The Age of Innocence*, Archer marries the American woman May Welland who shares with her countrywomen a "factitious purity, so cunningly manufactured by a conspiracy of mothers and aunts and grandmothers and long dead ancestresses."[28] This is the world that Wharton escaped from by leaving both her marriage and her mother country and going to live in Europe. In 1911 after her separation from her husband Teddy she wrote to Morton Fullerton, the man who was in effect her first lover: "If I didn't feel the irresistible 'call' to write I should give up the last struggle for an individual existence & turn into a nurse & dame de compagnie for Teddy" (*L*, 261). She had just published *Ethan Frome*, which envisions characters caught in an interminable cycle of caretaking.[29] By the time she wrote *The Age of Innocence*, Wharton had also "eaten of the Pomegranate Seed." As Lewis notes, the eating of the pomegranate seed represents erotic experience for Wharton;[30] it represents everything that has initiated Ellen Olenska, everything that she cannot give up to return to her mother country.

Yet the pomegranate seed also names the world that Wharton escapes to by becoming a writer. The pomegranate seed represents the experience of the writer, the world of experience to which Wharton as a writer could escape. Several of the books discussed in the chapters that follow depict America and are written during the period of separation from America that Wharton describes in her autobiography as "Widening Waters"; but in general in placing Wharton and the female artist she figures throughout her work, I will be more concerned with Wharton's tendency to imagine her life divided into two worlds: the worlds of Europe and America, men and women, experience and innocence, truth and the artifice of surface appearance, decoration, and the trivial realities of everyday life. In locating "the sources of my story-telling" in a process that "takes place in some secret region on the sheer edge of consciousness," Wharton speaks of "my two lives, divided between these equally real yet totally unrelated worlds"—one the everyday world of "real happenings" and the other "as real and tangible . . . often more so . . . as intense, and with as great an appearance of reality" (*BG*, 205). The chapter in *A Backward Glance* devoted to a discussion of her writing and "the making of my books" (*BG*, 197) is suggestively titled "The Secret Garden." Wharton also recalls in "Life and I" the "almost tangible presences" of words, which had "faces as distinct as those of the persons among whom I lived. And like Erlkönig's daughters, they sang to me so bewitchingly that they almost lured me from the wholesome noonday air of childhood into the strange supernatural region where the normal pleasures of my age seemed as insipid as the fruits of the earth to Persephone after she had eaten of the pomegranate seed" (LI, X).

The end of *The Age of Innocence* seems to return to the conclusion of *The House of Mirth*, Wharton's first novel set in America. In each of these works the male protagonist finds himself looking up at a window behind which he imagines the woman he loves. Newland Archer sends his son through "the vaulted doorway" while he stays on a bench to watch the windows of Ellen Olenska's building until the shades are drawn.[31] Lawrence Selden, who has "found the one word he meant to say to" Lily Bart, looks up at the windows of Lily's boarding house, where "only one blind was down" and the "door-step had suddenly become the threshold of the untried"; he enters the building but, of course, he finds Lily Bart dead.[32] Both novels end with the returned lover looking up at the window and learning that it is too late to cross the threshold from which he had earlier retreated. Both Archer and Selden represent men with literary interests who at crucial moments in their lives have pulled back from the threshold of the women they associate with art and poetry.

In *The Age of Innocence*, as we have seen, the woman behind the window has eaten the pomegranate seed; like "the new Persephone" Wharton imagines in an unpublished poem called "The New Litany," in living a *real life* this woman is "goddess of the living as the dead."[33] The woman behind the window in *The House of Mirth*, however, is simply dead; Lily Bart is what Wharton calls in another poem a "lifeless blossom in the Book of Life."[34] Here the realm of death does not appear to be the underworld of Persephone. The difference between these two moments suggests the dangers of being the woman that the would-be writer must cross the threshold to possess—or embody. It might remind us that Wharton's novels recurrently picture characters who sit at their writing desks and then choose suicide. The woman writer in the underworld is not necessarily seated on a throne, and Wharton's attempts to imagine the place of the woman writer can only be attempts to imagine her possibility. The figure of Persephone suggests the dangers in the divisions that Wharton delineates and the place of the writer who must "die to purchase life."[35]

Women and Letters

(The House of Mirth)

But all its chief delight was still
On roses thus its self to fill,
And its pure virgin limbs to fold
In whitest sheets of lilies cold:
Had it lived long, it would have been
Lilies without, roses within.
—Andrew Marvell, "The Nymph
Complaining for the Death of Her Faun"

Fond lovers, cruel as their flame,
Cut in these trees their mistress' name:
Little, alas! they know or heed,
How far these beauties her's exceed!
Fair trees! wheres'e'er your bark I wound,
No name shall but your own be found.
—Andrew Marvell, "The Garden"

In an important analysis of *The House of Mirth* as Wharton's condemnation of "the pervasive influence of the art of femininity" and "femininity as the art of 'being,'" Cynthia Griffin Wolff has described the novel as Wharton's "first *Künstlerroman*." Suggesting that *The House of Mirth* "takes art and the artist for its subject," Wolff reads the tragedy of Lily Bart as "the psychological disfigurement of any woman who chooses to accept society's definition of her as a beautiful object and nothing more." According to Wolff, if Wharton "could not conveniently chronicle her own coming of age as an artist, she could turn her fury upon a world which had enjoined women to spend their artistic inclinations entirely upon a display of self." Wolff's discussion of the novel insightfully accounts for the social and psychological tragedy in which Lily Bart's brilliant success embodying a work of art in the famous *tableau vivant* scene sets the stage for suicide as Lily seeks to escape the problems of a "real" woman by becoming the idealized decorative woman of Art Nouveau. Wolff points to the "satiric vein" of a *Künstlerroman* that condemns society for allowing women the role of "self-creating artistic object" but not the role of "productive artist." Reading the novel as a tale told by its ending, Wolff rightly concludes that the heroine must be sacrificed because she cannot be a productive artist.[1]

Pursuing this question, I would like to suggest another way to understand the novel's concern with art and the artist and indeed the character of Lily Bart. I will argue that Wharton's heroine figures the predicament of the woman artist as the novel tells the story of a crisis about the place and the possibility of the woman writer. *The House of Mirth*, the breakthrough work in which Wharton could be said to have invented herself as a novelist, is a complex allegory about women and art. It represents Wharton's first sustained interrogation of the relation between women and writing—a question that would preoccupy her in her most important works.

Explicit depictions of female authors or artists are rare in Wharton's fiction; yet this was not true in 1904 and 1905 as Wharton was writing *The House of Mirth*. The stories that Wharton wrote before *The House of Mirth* often focused on the complexities of art and, in particular, the telling experiences of the artist. These stories describe dilemmas of novelists, painters, intellectuals, and lecturers. Wharton's first collection of stories, *The Greater Inclination*, published in 1899, opens and closes with stories that delve into the origins of art: "The Muse's Tragedy" and "The Portrait." Wharton's decision to exclude "The Fullness of Life" and "The Lamp of Psyche," two early stories that emphasize dissatisfaction in marriage, and her last-minute addition of "The Portrait" as the book's concluding story, shifted the focus of the collection from painfully revelatory depictions of the troubled relations between men and women to more indirectly autobiographical reflections about the problems of representing these relations.[2]

Presented as a dramatic monologue of a painter within the frame of the first-person account of a writer, "The Portrait" tells the story of a famous artist who decides to fail in painting the portrait of a notorious political boss. Recognized for his unerring ability to select the "real" aspect of his subject "as instinctively as a detective collars a pickpocket in a crowd," the painter first sees the boss as a "lath-and-plaster bogey" who is "vulgar to the core."[3] However, he becomes obsessed with the political boss's daughter and her mystified illusions about her father. The daughter becomes the muse of willful artistic failure as the painter becomes seduced by his desire to protect her from seeing her fallen father. In the end, instead of a scathing exposé, he denies his public a painting that would provide "post-mortem 'revelations'" or stand as "an incriminating document"; he conceals the villain in the portrait of a "pseudo-gentleman" (*C*, 175). The boss ultimately commits suicide on the first day that the painting is exhibited, suggesting the fatal consequences of the art of concealment as well as the art of revelation.

"The Muse's Tragedy," the opening story of Wharton's collection, describes the illusions of art from the point of view of a woman who ostensibly is the subject of the artist. Mrs. Anerton has become a character in literary circles because the public has come to think of her as the Silvia of the *Sonnets to Silvia*, the woman who is thought to have been the lover and inspiration of the great poet Vincent Rendle. In the story, she is supposed to have prepared Rendle's letters for publication. In circumstances that partially recall James's *The Aspern Papers*, Danyers, a scholar and poet who admires Rendle, comes to know "the Mrs. A. of the *Life and Letters*" (*C*, 67). As they converse, he begins to feel that "in a certain sense Silvia had herself created the *Sonnets to Silvia*" (*C*, 72), and in the end she writes a letter in which she confesses her actual role in the poet's texts.

In Danyers's view, Mrs. Anerton has been most discreet in transcribing Rendle's letters to her, keeping the "*détails intimes*" of their relationship from the public eye and inserting lines of asterisks where the letters seem to be growing "warmer." Yet Mrs. Anerton confesses that the asterisks indicating that something has been left out "were a sham" (*C*, 75)—they conceal the fact that there were no intimate details to omit. In love with Rendle, she never received any affection from him beyond the bounds of intellectual friendship. Distinguishing herself from "Silvia," Mrs. Anerton insists that she did not plan ("like a woman in a book") the romantic "episode" (*C*, 77) in which she led Danyers to fall in love with her. In the letter that concludes the story, the tragic muse tells the young man who has provided her in life with the experience she had known only in fiction: "It was so good, for once in my life, to get away from literature" (*C*, 78).

"The Portrait" and "The Muse's Tragedy" describe four male artists (one painter and three writers), but they end by focusing on female figures who transform the face of art. Both the boss's daughter and the poet's correspondent begin as intimate audiences, but they end up as the authors of fictions in which the men they love are idealized characters. These early stories show women intervening in art to preserve the remnants of a sentimental story, even as they become conscious of the deception. (It is appropriate that just before *The Greater Inclination* went to press Wharton replaced "The Lamp of Psyche," a story about a wife's sudden disillusionment with her husband, with a story about a portrait that masked the crimes of the father.)[4] In "The Pelican," another story from the same collection, Wharton also relates women to the sentimental and the art of concealment, but here the woman figures not as muse but rather as author.

In this comic portrait, Mrs. Amyot is not so much a writer as a performer of a story in which she herself becomes the main character. In the course of a thirty-year career as a public lecturer, she has presented herself in the guise of a retiring widow who has been forced to face the public because of debts left by her late alcoholic husband and the necessity of supporting "the baby" (*C*, 88). Although Mrs. Amyot lectures on subjects such as the influences of "Turner on Ruskin, of Schiller on Goethe, of Shakespeare on English literature" (*C*, 95), her audiences come to hear a sentimental autobiography that remains the same throughout her career. Mrs. Amyot's appeal as a lecturer is founded on the repetition of her formulaic story. "Mrs. Amyot's art" is described as "an extension of coquetry: she flirted with her audience." In particular it is her "art of transposing secondhand ideas into firsthand emotions that so endeared her to her feminine listeners" (*C*, 92, 91).

Although the mystifying muses of "The Portrait" and "The Muse's Tragedy" are granted a certain pathos despite their romantic illusions, Mrs. Amyot is portrayed with devastating comedy. She places herself in a female literary tradition of "geniuses" that includes her mother, who is the author of a poem called "The Fall of Man" and who is supposedly described by N. P. Willis as "the female Milton of America" (*C*, 90). In two other stories about female writers, Wharton includes herself in the satire of a female literary genealogy. The first novels of Theodora in "April Showers" and Mrs. Fetherel in "Expiation" each allude to "Fast and Loose," the novel Wharton wrote at the age of fifteen.[5] The idea of a feminine literary tradition seems comic in these stories, but in two other fictions from this period, "Copy" and *The Touchstone*, Wharton describes successful women novelists who author works with the same title that Wharton would later use for two of her own works: "Pomegranate Seed."[6]

Despite differences in tone—"Copy" is sharply witty and *The Touchstone* verges on melodrama—in these fictions, Wharton imagines the situation of the woman writer in ways that might be considered monitory. "Copy" is written as a dialogue between a successful woman novelist and her former lover, a famous poet, who meet after twenty years to struggle over the meaning and the ownership of their love letters. The woman, who claims to have "died years ago," describes herself as "the figment of the reporter's brain—a monster manufactured out of newspaper paragraphs, with ink in its veins." "A keen sense of copyright," she adds, "is *my* nearest approach to an emotion" (*C*, 278). *The Touchstone*, Wharton's first published novella, is about a woman novelist who is already dead. In order to get money so he can marry, Stephen Glennard decides to publish the letters he had received from Margaret Aubyn, the deceased novelist who had loved him years before. By publishing letters that originally had "exhausted his slender store of reciprocity,"[7] he belatedly becomes the intimate reader Margaret Aubyn had sought but never found in him during her life.

"Copy," *The Touchstone*, "The Muse's Tragedy," and even "The Pelican" extend Wharton's depictions of artists and intellectuals to focus on the emotional sacrifices required of women who aspire to literary accomplishment. In variations of the stories of concealment associated with the feminine muse, these stories center on the revelation of the private stories of public women. Furthermore, despite her suspicions of the sentimental story she associates with a female literary tradition, here Wharton tries to imagine the isolation of women artists. When Stephen Glennard prepares to publish Margaret Aubyn's letters, he seeks out collections of "women's letters" at the library, chafing at "his own ignorance of the sentimental by-paths of literature." Here, rather than meeting characters such as "the female Milton of America," we are offered a list of authors that includes Hannah More, "Miss Martineau," Eloise, George Sand, Mlle. Aïssé, Madame de Sabran, and George Eliot—as well as women who (like the fictitious Mrs. Anerton) received letters from famous male writers.[8]

In addition to suggesting a history of women's writing in which she might imagine her characters as well as herself, *The Touchstone* underlines Wharton's fascination with the story of women's letters. The fascination displayed in "Copy," *The Touchstone*, and "The Muse's Tragedy" is also evident in later stories, such as "His Father's Son," "The Letters," "Mr. Jones," and "Pomegranate Seed"—all of which center on the significance of women's letters. The early stories in particular are concerned with the public fate of private letters—and it is in this context that we must read *The House of Mirth*. The plot of *The House of Mirth* turns on the question of whether a woman's private letters will be made public. Wharton's early stories about art, women, writing, and letters provide a narrative context that allows us to recognize this 1905 novel as a crucial moment in Wharton's chronicle of the woman writer and the question of women and letters.

That *The House of Mirth* turns on the problem of a woman's letters is perhaps too obvious to have been fully appreciated. Wharton's short fiction, particularly the work composed prior to 1905, provides a system of internal reference that suggests the significance for her of a packet of a woman's private love letters. This context should alert us to the importance in *The House of Mirth* of Bertha Dorset, the author of the letters at the center of the plot of the novel. Although Bertha is often on the margins of the narrative, she is crucial to any understanding of Lily Bart and the place of writing in the novel. From the moment Bertha Dorset first appears in the second chapter of *The House of Mirth*, walking into a railway car and wondering aloud whether she can have Lily Bart's place, questions concerning place, displacement, poses, and positions are at issue between the two women. (Known for her "restless pliability of pose," Bertha Dorset discovers "that the seat adjoining Miss Bart was at her disposal" and she is said to possess "herself of it with a farther displacement of her surroundings.")[9]

Ostensibly, the rivalry between these fashionable society women is the result of their competition over men. In the train scene we see Bertha interrupting Lily's pursuit of Percy Gryce, a wealthy book collector whom Lily is plotting to marry. More important, in the course of the novel Lily is drawn to Lawrence

Selden, with whom Bertha has had an affair with "a long history" (101). This triangle is first set in motion at Bellomont, where we see Lily, Bertha, and Selden together in a library; the antagonism between the two women displayed in these scenes is the force that structures the plot of much of the novel.

Yet *The House of Mirth* cannot be reduced to a story about a personal rivalry or a romantic triangle. Bertha's centrality to both the plot and the allegory of the novel originates in her identity as the author of the love letters to Lawrence Selden—the letters that set so much of the plot in motion. When the charwoman Mrs. Haffen finds the letters that Selden has carelessly discarded, she sells them to Lily Bart in the mistaken belief that Lily is the author. Although Lily ultimately refuses to make the letters public or to use them to blackmail or even influence Bertha, Lily's possession of the letters gives her a power which may be the source of the fear that causes Bertha to conduct her campaign to drive Lily from the social stage. Bertha's relentless campaign seems to lead in the end to Lily's suicide. The importance of these letters to the plot is finally overdetermined, however. In addition to motivating the plot, they point to Bertha's role as an author and the potential power of letters in the world of *The House of Mirth*.

In addition to being the literal author of the letters that determine the plot of the novel, Bertha Dorset is associated with writing and literature throughout *The House of Mirth*. She has been involved, of course, with Selden, who represents "the republic of the spirit" (65) and who is associated by Lily with "literature" (62). Bertha is known for her penchant for "clever fellows," described by her husband as "bores" and "intellectual ones" with "long hair" (116); her past fancy for musicians has given way to "sentimental experiments" with a would-be poet "who had meant to live on proof-reading and write an epic" (53). Speaking of his wife and her "clever fellows," George Dorset declares, "She could write better than any of 'em if she chose" (116). In Monte Carlo Selden imagines Bertha's dress being described as worthy of "'the literary style'" (210).

Bertha's most important literary style appears in the stories she tells about Lily Bart. To thwart Lily's plan to marry Percy Gryce, Bertha tells "some story" (73) about money borrowed from a man as well as other misleading stories that turn him against her. Later in the novel Rosedale tells Lily, "I don't believe those stories about you. . . . I don't believe those stories—I believe they were all got up by a woman who didn't hesitate to sacrifice you to her own convenience";

but in answer to Lily's insistence that the situation is altered if the stories "are not true," Rosedale insists: "I believe it does in novels; but I'm certain it don't in real life" (250–51). Throughout the novel Bertha is responsible for "horrors" (73, 246), "falsehood" (294), and an "allusive jargon that could flay its victims without the shedding of blood" (107).

Bertha Dorset is not just the author of well-placed stories that frame Lily as a disreputable woman, she is also the powerful scripter of scenes in which Lily Bart is cast as a character. What will be a carefully staged production is set in motion in the final lines of Book 1 when Bertha sends a telegram to Lily inviting her to "join us on a cruise in Mediterranean" (176). This brief written text authored by Bertha is a prelude to the more elaborate scenario that Bertha authors in Monte Carlo. Here Lily is manipulated into distracting Bertha's husband and screening Bertha's infidelities, only to be set up as a "sacrifice" (237)—banished in an invented scandal to protect Bertha's marriage and reputation.

The series of scenes which seal Lily's fate take place in Monte Carlo as "the chief performers" assemble before Lawrence Selden's eyes in a setting that recalls a "closing *tableau*." As he watches, the intensity of light signals the "last moments of the performance [which] seemed to gain an added brightness from the hovering threat of the curtain." To Selden,

> Their appearance confirmed the impression that the show had been staged regardless of expense, and emphasized its resemblance to one of those "costume-plays" in which the protagonists walk through the passions without displacing a drapery. The ladies stood in unrelated attitudes calculated to isolate their effects, and the men hung about them as irrelevantly as stage heroes whose tailors are named in the programme. [178]

These are not simply tableaux of conspicuous consumption. Lily assumes that she has been invited to play a supporting role in the story of Bertha's affair, but she eventually senses that she is "involved in the crash, instead of merely witnessing it from the road" (197). When Bertha stays out all night with her young poet, her husband describes their subsequent confrontation to Lily as a "*dénouement*." Lily suggests that this is "too big a word for such a small incident" (196), but she does not realize that the *dénouement* is (or will be) her own. Forced to make an exit "like some deposed princess moving tranquilly to exile" (214), she finds herself "publicly branded as the heroine of a 'queer' episode," the main character in a "story" (228) orchestrated by Bertha.

These scenes are played out before "the watchful pen of Mr. Dabham" (211)—the author of the column called "Society Notes from the Riviera" (193)—as if they were being staged for this amanuensis of society. As Selden watches Lily during the dinner party, he fears what might show itself through the fissure in the social surface that he and Lily have worked so hard to conceal; he wonders "what part Miss Bart had played in organizing the entertainment," noting the "bright security" of her bearing: "Never had she appeared more serenely mistress of the situation" (211). Yet as she plays her designated role, Lily doesn't realize that the story has taken a different turn. Selden has noted that Bertha's "literary style" dress "had been almost too preoccupying to its wearer; but now she was in full command of it, and was even producing her effects with unwonted freedom" (210). When Bertha abruptly announces that "Miss Bart is not going back to the yacht" (212), Lily finds herself the heroine of a story destined for the gossip columns.

Lily's early desires to replace Bertha at Bellomont are translated into monstrous proportions in the fiction of replacement that Bertha stages in Monte Carlo. After bringing along Lily as a stand-in who will temporarily take her place with her husband, Bertha accuses Lily of being her rival for her husband's affections in order to obscure her own affair with the poet Ned Silverton. In a play of double indemnity that has its poetic justice, Bertha accuses Lily of fulfilling the role Bertha assigned to her; and Lily assumes Bertha's place as she takes the blame for Bertha's infidelities in what is later described as a "sacrifice." Although on the level of melodrama the entire novel might be said to be motivated by Lily and Bertha's shared desires for the same man, these scenes suggest that what is most interesting about Lily and Bertha's apparent rivalry is a doubling or interchangeability that is related to a confusion of identities.

Indeed, the crux of the plot of *The House of Mirth*—the acquisition by Lily of Bertha's letters—depends on a case of mistaken identity in which Lily is taken for Bertha and assumed to be Selden's intimate correspondent and lover. In the very first chapter of the novel, Lily finds herself stared at by Selden's charwoman Mrs. Haffen, whose "persistent gaze implied a groping among past associations" (12). Only later, when Mrs. Haffen tries to blackmail Lily with the torn love letters she has found in Selden's wastepaper basket, does Lily realize that she has been confused with Bertha Dorset: "Mrs. Haffen supposed her to be the writer of the letters" (102). Examining a letter, Lily recognizes "a large disjoint-ed hand, with a flourish of masculinity which but slightly disguised its ram-bling weakness. . . . The letter before her . . . told a long history—a history over which, for the last four years, the friends of the writer had smiled and shrugged, viewing it merely as one among the countless 'good situations' of the mundane comedy" (101).

In the comedy of the novel Mrs. Haffen has made a mistake in assuming that the discarded letters appealing to Selden "for the renewal of a tie" are from Lily; but on another level Mrs. Haffen is an astute reader. Just as she takes a "letter [that] was torn in two" and "with a rapid gesture . . . laid the torn edges together and smoothed out the page" (101-2), Mrs. Haffen has put two and two together. Lily agrees to buy the letters—meeting Mrs. Haffen's price with "a counter-offer of half the amount" (103)—but Lily's decision is based on more than a desire to have power over the woman who might be called her other half. By becoming the "possessor" (101) of the letters, Lily in a sense *owns* them. Faced with "the irony of the coincidence" (102) of Mrs. Haffen's mistake, Lily does not deny authorship of the letters; in more senses than one she assumes responsibility for them, as if she were accepting the role of Bertha's double rather than her rival.

In the subterranean plot of the letters that drives the narrative forward, the ironic coincidence whereby Lily is mistaken for Bertha and given the letters is fundamental to the allegory about women and writing that Wharton plays out in *The House of Mirth*. In a sense the novel turns on the significance of the act of mistaken identity in which Mrs. Haffen supposes Lily "to be the writer of the letters" (102). We have seen that in her sinister way Bertha Dorset acts as an author in the novel: telling stories, arranging scenarios, setting up people as characters in fictions destined for publication, and actually writing texts that turn up as key props in the plot. We also have seen that Lily Bart doubles Bertha in the formulaic story that repeatedly juxtaposes them as almost inter-changeable rivals. Mrs. Haffen's inadvertent insight puts the halves together and places Lily Bart in the line of literary inheritance that, beginning with Wharton's early works, joins together women writers—particularly female authors of letters. To understand *The House of Mirth* we must understand Lily Bart as a writer. We must understand the significance of the supposition that she is the author of the letters and the ways in which she might double Bertha not just in the formulaic rivalry over men but in a larger struggle over authority and textual control. In the end, the dramatic tension of the novel turns on the question of whether Lily will play the role of the writer.

Although there are some passing references to professional writers ("representatives of the press" who appear "notebook in hand" [84]), Lily Bart is the only character in *The House of Mirth* who is shown in the act of writing. Early in the novel, among the "horrors" that Judy Trenor asks Lily to assist her with when her secretary is gone are "notes and dinner-cards to write" and "the monotony of note-writing" (37–38). As Lily sits at Judy Trenor's "writing-table" (38) listening to comparisons of herself with Bertha, she "writes in silence" (42). (The presence of writing tables is noted at various times in the novel, but Lily is the only one who actually uses one to write.) Later, she appeals to Judy Trenor: "You must have some letters for me to answer" (75). Toward the end of the novel, approaching the nadir of her social descent, she actually becomes the secretary to Mrs. Hatch (Wharton's prototype for *The Custom of the Country's* Undine Spragg) although her duties are "restricted by the fact that Mrs. Hatch, as yet, knew hardly anyone to write to" (269). At the end of Book 1 and in the penultimate chapter of Book 2 (which is the end of Lily's life), we see Lily Bart seated at a table writing.

From the opening chapters of *The House of Mirth*, the men that Lily Bart is interested in are associated with books. Percy Gryce, whom Lily looks upon as a potential husband, is a book collector, although as a wealthy collector of Americana he is more interested in the "ugly badly-printed book that one is never going to read" (9). Selden's apartment, which Lily visits in the first chapter, is described as "a small library, dark but cheerful, with its walls of books" and "littered desk" (4). Selden insists: "I'm not really a collector, you see; I simply like to have good editions of the books I am fond of" (9). Lily associates Selden with literature. As she talks with him at Bellomont, we read that "Lily, who prided herself on her broad-minded recognition of literature, and always carried an Omar Khayam in her travelling-bag" is attracted to Selden's ability "to look his part," to have "the air of belonging to a more specialized race, of carrying the impress of a concentrated past" (62–63).

Despite her early determination to be to Percy Gryce "what his Americana had hitherto been: the one possession in which he took sufficient pride to spend money on" (47), Lily makes an appeal for Selden's friendship: "'You don't know how much I need such a friend,' she said. 'My aunt is full of copy-book axioms. . . . I always feel that to live up to them would include wearing book-muslin with gigot sleeves'" (7). At least when she is with Selden, Lily would prefer to be a "good edition" rather than a collector's item. When she finds herself "scanning her little world through his retina" (52) at the dinner table at Bellomont—in a vision that she associates with Selden's "republic of the spirit" (65)—she abandons the roseate vision that Wharton ascribed to sentimental-ism: "It was as though the pink lamps had been shut off and the dusty daylight let in." To Lily's altered eyes the guests have become "dreary and trivial," mundane social texts that seem to embody a trivialization of the written word. Carrie Fisher is said to have the "general air of embodying a 'spicy paragraph.'" The would-be poet "Silverton, who had meant to live on proof-reading and write an epic," has become a man who "lived on his friends and had become critical of truffles," while Alice Weatherall is described as "an animated visiting-list, whose most fervid convictions turned on the wording of invitations and the engraving of dinner-cards" (52–53).

Lily herself seems to embody literature most explicitly in the famous *tableau vivant* scene of Chapter 12. In the newly constructed Bry mansion where "the whole *mise-en-scène*" compels one "to touch the marble columns to learn they were not of card-board," Carrie Fisher induces "a dozen fashionable women to exhibit themselves in a series of pictures" (127–28) based on paintings by Botticelli, Goya, Titian, Van Dyck, Kauffmann, Veronese, Watteau, and oth-ers.[10] Arranged by the "organizing hand" of the portrait painter Paul Morpeth, "the participators had been cleverly fitted with characters suited to their types" (130). The culmination of these *tableaux vivants* occurs when Lily Bart appears on stage to "break the spell of the illusion" with her representation: "So skilfully had the personality of the actors been subdued to the scenes they figured . . . even the least imaginative of the audience must have felt a thrill of contrast when the curtain suddenly parted on a picture which was simply and undis-guisedly the portrait of Miss Bart" (131).

The *tableau vivant* that Lily performs is the portrait of Mrs. Lloyd by Sir Joshua Reynolds, but the audience clearly responds to Lily's representation of herself.

The unanimous "Oh!" of the spectators was a tribute, not to the brush-work of Reynolds's "Mrs. Lloyd" but to the flesh and blood loveliness of Lily Bart. She had shown her artistic intelligence in selecting a type so like her own that she could embody the person represented without ceasing to be herself. It was as though she had stepped, not out of, but into, Reynolds's canvas, banishing the phantom of his dead beauty by the beams of her living grace. [131]

As readers have noted, this scene shows Lily Bart embodying a work of art. In the *tableaux vivants* that provide "magic glimpses of the boundary world between fact and imagination" (130), Lily alone crosses the boundary between illusion and reality. Miss Bart alone seems not to portray art but to be art.

However, Lily personifies more than a painting in this performance. Unlike the others, who are directed by the portrait painter Morpeth, Lily Bart becomes the active artist of a self-portrait. Earlier in the novel Selden calls Lily a "wonderful spectacle" but he also recognizes her as an artist. He says: "Your taking a walk with me is only another way of making use of your material. You are an artist and I happen to be the bit of colour you are using today" (63). In the *tableau vivant* Lily is herself the material of her art; but if we are to recognize her as what Wolff calls a "self-creating artistic object," we must recognize that a self-portrait must be a self-portrait of the artist. Reynolds's *Mrs. Lloyd* is a portrait of a woman writing.[11] Wharton's narrative describes Lily's portrayal of the portrait: "Her pale draperies, and the background of foliage against which she stood, served only to relieve the long dryad-like curves that swept upward from her poised foot to her lifted arm. The noble buoyancy of her attitude, its suggestion of soaring grace, revealed the touch of poetry in her beauty that Selden always felt in her presence" (131). Despite its descriptive detail, the narrative does not note that the portrait of Mrs. Lloyd is the figure of a woman engaged in writing. Reynolds's portrait depicts the young Joanna Leigh at or near the time of her marriage to Richard Lloyd standing in a vaguely classical dress next to a tree in a wood. Holding a penlike instrument, she appears to be carving the letters of her husband's name in the bark of the tree. One can make out two *L*'s and the *O* that she is in the process of completing.[12]

The topos of a lover writing verses and the name of the beloved on a tree is familiar.[13] In *As You Like It* Orlando declares:

> these trees shall be my books,
> And in their barks my thoughts I'll character,
> . . . .
> Run, run, Orlando, carve on every tree
> The fair, the chaste, and unexpressive she.

Marvell's speaker in "The Garden" laments:

> Fond Lovers, cruel as their flame,
> Cut in these trees their mistress' name:
> . . . .
> Fair trees! wheres'e'er your bark I wound,
> No name shall but your own be found.[14]

However, the pictorial tradition behind Reynolds's painting favors the female lover who writes on trees. Reynolds himself apparently painted a depiction of Angelica and Medora, borrowing Ariosto's account in *Orlando Furioso* of a woman who carves her lover's name on a tree. The subject was popular in Italian baroque painting and throughout the eighteenth century, attracting the attention of Ricci, Boucher, Giambattista Tiepolo, Giandomenico Tiepolo, Luti, and West, among others. *Mrs. Lloyd* may have been more directly influenced by Francesco Imperiali's depiction of Ermina from Tasso's *Gerusalemme Liberata*: "Unto her knight she songs and sonnets made, / And them engrav'd in bark of beech and bays."[15]

Reynolds's painting uses this motif as a witty and elegant device to commemorate a marriage. Lily Bart uses the painting as a vehicle to display her "unassisted beauty": "She had purposely chosen a picture without distracting accessories of dress or surroundings" (131). After having earlier vowed to be the "mystically veiled figure occupying the centre of attention" at a wedding rather than "a casual spectator" (84), Lily gets her wish as she represents the draped bride in a *tableau vivant*. In posing Lily as Reynolds's Mrs. Lloyd, however, Wharton constructs an allusion that places her heroine in a tradition of representations of women writing. As she assumes an attitude that reveals the "touch of poetry in her beauty" (131), Lily stands as an emblem of the woman as poet.

In the centerpiece of Wharton's allegory of women and art, the curtain parts to reveal a woman writing. After having been accused of being the author of letters, in this crucially overdetermined scene Lily poses as a writer of letters. We read that Lily "had thought for a moment of representing Tiepolo's Cleopatra" (131), who dies by taking her own life. While Tiepolo's Cleopatra holds the pearl that she will destroy in a glass of wine in a notorious act of conspicuous consumption,[16] Lily as Mrs. Lloyd holds an implement of writing in her hand. Earlier when Selden insists that "one has to know how to read" the "sign-posts" to "the republic of the spirit," Lily declares, "Whenever I see you, I find myself spelling out a letter of the sign" (65–66). In the *tableau vivant*, as she "break[s] the spell of the illusion" (131), Lily spells out letters and herself embodies the sign. As Mrs. Lloyd spells out the letters of her new name, Lily—whom Rosedale sarcastically accuses of "collecting autographs" (252)—almost signs her name. As she composes her self-portrait the letters are transformed: presumably her audience can see the resemblance between the first two letters on the tree (*LL*) and the first two letters in Lily's name (*LI*)—as it responds to "the portrait of Miss Bart" writing the letter *O* with a "unanimous 'Oh!'" (131).

The scene of Lily's *tableau vivant* might be read as the signature piece in Wharton's allegory of women and art. Wharton's representation of the richly allusive self-portrait in which Lily poses herself as a woman writing might be seen in the genre of Artemisia Gentileschi's *Self-Portrait as the Allegory of Painting*, a painting in which the female artist represents herself as an artist and not merely as the traditional allegorical personification of her art.[17] However, what will separate Lily from her author is Lily's refusal to play the role that she seems to accept when she tacitly accepts the identity of the author of Bertha's letters and when she poses as the writer of letters in the *tableau vivant*. Although Mrs. Haffen senses Lily's authority in "a vision of the elaborate machinery of revenge which a word of this commanding young lady's might set into motion" (103) and although Lily herself consciously embodies a vision of a lady who might command words, like the scrivener Bartleby, Miss Bart spends the second half of the novel preferring not to.

Just before Mrs. Haffen comes to Lily with the letters, Lily acknowledges that there is something wrong with her story. She realizes that her society friends "would welcome her in a new character, but as Miss Bart they knew her by heart. She knew herself by heart too, and was sick of the old story" (97). Only if she marries can Lily escape the old story of a twenty-nine-year-old *"jeune fille à marier"* (66)—and subsequently the new story in which she is framed by Bertha Dorset as the familiar character of the fallen woman. The letters from Bertha Dorset to Selden provide Lily with the means to change her story and appear as a new character. After suffering in silence the fate of being the questionable "heroine" in Bertha's scenarios, Lily has the power to change the plot of her life and, in effect, the plot of the novel.

In Chapters 5, 6, and 7 of Book 2, Carrie Fisher, George Dorset, and Simon Rosedale each meet with Lily twice to talk to her about her status as a sacrificial victim and to plead with her to turn the tables on the woman who has told horrible stories about her; they insist that she use what she knows to regain her social position. Each of Lily's advisers suggests a story that ends in marriage. Carrie Fisher, who is particularly surprised by Bertha's persistent efforts to crush Lily, speculates that "there's only one reason for being afraid of you; and my own idea is that, if you want to punish her, you hold the means in your hand" (246). She suggests marriage with George Dorset. When Dorset himself comes to plead with Lily to expose Bertha, promising that "there wouldn't be a hint of publicity—not a sound or a syllable to connect you with the thing," Lily thinks that "the power to make him" hers "lay in her hand—lay there in a completeness that he could not even conjecture. Revenge and rehabilitation might be hers at a stroke" (239).

Rosedale, however, is the only one who has discovered that the power in Lily's hands lies in "the secret of the letters"—a realization that leaves Lily "speechless" in a "temporary loss of self-possession" (251). Insisting that "we're neither of us such new hands that a little plain speaking is going to hurt us" (249), and acknowledging that "some people say you've got the neatest kind of answer in your hands," he warns against an answer that would lead to marrying George Dorset: "In a deal like that nobody comes out with perfectly clean hands" (252). Rosedale proposes a shift in plot in which he would become Lily's husband: "She had only to put to [Bertha] the latent menace contained in the packet so miraculously delivered into her hands" (253). He tells Lily: "The wonder to me is that you've waited so long to get square with that woman, when you've had the power in your hands. . . . I know how completely she's in your power. That sounds like stage-talk, don't it?—but . . . I don't suppose you bought those letters simply because you're collecting autographs" (251–52).

To the frustration of her friends (and the reader) Lily will not make use of the power in her hands. She will not assert her authority by making the letters public (or even threatening their publication). As the possessor of the letters, Lily has the power to rewrite the ending of the novel, to "get Bertha Dorset into line" (252) by taking control of the narrative away from her. After standing in for Bertha in accepting the "autographs," Lily refuses the role of Bertha's double; she refuses a writing of the self that would put her in the place of the powerful female author. Despite her pose as the writer of letters standing with pen in hand in the *tableau vivant*, Lily will never be Mrs. Ambrose Dale, the successful novelist of "Copy"; she will not even be Mrs. Rosedale, the potentially powerful authority in the novel Wharton once titled "The Year of the Rose."[18]

Lily's refusal to use the power in her hands to tell her story by publishing Bertha's story is part of her devotion to social fictions. Throughout the novel she is dedicated to the art of concealment that Wharton associated with the sentimental artist. In Monte Carlo, Lily practices the social arts at her command in order to cover Bertha's indiscretions; she builds up "again and again, the crumbling structure of 'appearances'" (204). In these crucial chapters at the opening of Book 2, Lily views herself as Bertha's accomplice in a cover story, although she is increasingly puzzled by Bertha's rejection of her "rescuing hand" (205). Lily writes only a few letters of her own in *The House of Mirth*; one of the most important is the telegram that she sends to Selden at this point to ask for his assistance. Denying "any special relation to the case," he joins forces with Lily to counter Bertha's "reckless disregard of appearances" (203) and to "spare [Lily] the embarrassment of being ever so remotely connected with the public washing of the Dorset linen" (203).

For Selden, the "message" of Lily's telegram "necessarily left large gaps for conjecture; but all that he had heard and seen made these but too easy to fill in" (203). However, Selden is interested in maintaining the gaps, not in filling them in. After Lily sends George Dorset to consult with Selden, Selden reflects:

> If anything came out at all, it would be such a vast unpacking of accumulated moral rags. . . . But nothing should come out; and happily for his side of the case, the dirty rags, however pieced together, could not, without considerable difficulty, be turned into a homogeneous grievance. The torn edges did not always fit—there were missing bits, there were disparities of size and colour, all of which it was naturally Selden's business to make the most of in putting them under his client's eye. [203]

The language of Selden's thoughts—the "dirty rags" with "torn edges" and "missing bits" that might be "pieced together"—recalls the dirty sheets of Dorset linen that Lily possesses: the whole story of the letters that Lily receives from Mrs. Haffen "wrapped in dirty newspaper" (99). These letters—which Selden himself "tore . . . in little bits," and which are presented to Lily with "torn edges," "in small fragments," "torn in half," and "pieced together with strips of thin paper"—comprise the record of the "long history" (100–103) in which Selden himself is the correspondent as well as the potential corespondent. Both Selden and Lily choose to keep these stories in pieces and they collude in a conspiracy of silence.[19]

Refusing to tell the story, they try to convince each other that there is no story to tell. When Lily asks Selden, "What has happened?" and more urgently, "What *will* happen?" as the dénouement of Monte Carlo threatens to veer out of their control, Selden replies, "Nothing as yet—and nothing in the future, I think" (205). Soon after, Lily again asks him, "What has happened?" and to Selden's reply, "Nothing," Lily seems to reassure herself by saying, "Nothing will" (208–9). As their conversation continues, in a "private word" with Lily after he almost resorts to "the unsatisfactory alternative of writing" (208), Selden joins Lily in an anxious chorus: "'Oh, well, nothing *will* happen,' he said more for his reassurance than for hers; and 'Nothing, nothing, of course!' she valiantly assented" (209).

When George Dorset pleads with Lily to tell on his wife, insisting "there's nothing to keep you back," he begs Lily to fill in the blanks, the "missing bits" in the story: "All I need is to be able to say definitely: 'I know this—and this— and this'"; but Lily, who "could have filled up the blanks," insists, "There's nothing in the world that I can do" (238–39). Dorset later appeals to her, "It's just a word to say, and you put me out of my misery!" and again, with "the sheer force of reiteration," Lily refuses to say a word: "'I know nothing; I saw nothing,' she exclaimed," continuing "to repeat, as if it were a charm: 'I know nothing—absolutely nothing'" (242). Although she has become the victim of Bertha's vengeful stories, Lily refuses to tell the story that would make her Bertha's equal rather than her sacrificial double. She refuses to admit that she has a story to tell, that she secretly possesses the power of letters.

For one brief moment Lily does appear willing to exercise this power. After she has been driven by Bertha from even the outer circle of society, after she has been shamed by Selden from her position as a secretary to a parvenue divorcée and dismissed from her job as a hatmaker, Lily makes a radical decision to alter the plot of her life and the novel. She makes her decision to assert her narrative authority in what might be described as a tearoom of muses. Attracted to a restaurant by a "long perspective of white tables," Lily finds herself surrounded by "women, with their bags and note-books and rolls of music"; they are "engrossed in their own affairs" or "busy running over proof-sheets or devouring magazines" while "Lily alone was stranded in a great waste of disoccupation." It may be a sign of Lily's social descent that she envies "sallow preoccupied women" who have occupations—but with their music, notebooks, proof-sheets, and magazines, these otherwise unexplained women seated at white tables seem to be arranged in an allegorical (if unglamorous) tableau that represents women and the arts. It is here, "shut out in a little circle of silence," that Lily "unconsciously arrived at a final decision" (296): to take up the power of letters.

Lily returns home, takes out the packet of letters, and writes a letter of her own: a "note" to Bertha Dorset "which she meant to send up with her name" (297), a sort of forward to the possible publication of the letters that will gain her an audience with her rival and write her way back into society. However, as she proceeds in her plan to take control of the narrative of her life story, Lily finds herself on the street in front of Selden's apartment. She is returned to the scene of the first chapter of the novel and the scene where she is first taken for the author of the letters. Seized with a "vision" of "the bookshelves, and the fire on the hearth" in the "library" (298) of the man whom Lily has associated with literature, she interrupts her errand of survival. Instead she goes up to Selden's apartment and burns the letters.

Finding that the "scene was unchanged," and recognizing "the row of shelves from which she had taken down his La Bruyère," Lily "pause[s] near his writing-table" (299). Here she retreats from her decision to take a hand in the story. After Lily refers ominously to "whatever happens," Selden asks, in a reversal of their previous roles, "What is going to happen?" and Lily echoes their former chorus of reassurance: "Nothing at present." Selden watches as she kneels by his hearth "for a few moments in silence; a silence which he dared not break," but he doesn't understand that she is burning a packet of letters. "His faculties seemed tranced, and he was still groping for the word to break the spell" (304).

Lily decides once again to choose silence and insists on saying nothing; she irrevocably alters her "final decision" (296) about the question that haunts the novel: whether it is better to publish or to burn. In doing so, Lily ostensibly recoils from the realization that "to attain her end, she must trade on [Selden's] name, and profit by a secret of his past" (298). This reluctance to soil Selden's name has restrained Lily from using the letters to clear her own name and get even with Bertha. However, the motives of protection and revenge—which have never been adequate to explain Lily's behavior—seem particularly thin by this point in the plot as Lily moves toward self-destruction. What happens at the end of *The House of Mirth* is less the tragedy of star-crossed lovers than a scene of sacrifice devoted to rituals of writing and erasure.

Immediately following her decision to tell the story, Lily Bart returns as if by accident to the scene of the first chapter of the novel. Surrounded by books in Selden's apartment, she performs the first of several rituals that lead to her fatal conclusion. By burning the letters, Lily gives up the power in her hands; she sacrifices the power of letters for the impossible hope of erasing the preceding scenes of the novel. By burning the letters where Selden first discarded them, Lily seeks to rewrite the beginning and thus the ending of the novel. In the logic of fiction and imagination she is not so much protecting Selden as enacting the scene that would have made much of the novel unnecessary, a preemptive act that would have prevented Lily from being mistaken for an author by either Mrs. Haffen or Bertha Dorset. In burning the letters, Lily destroys the force that has driven the plot of the novel. However, it is too late to perform the magic of erasing the fiction (particularly one that has been appearing in serial publication). The ending is inevitable and—as the burning of the letters signals—fatal.

In attempting to go back to this impossible beginning, Lily is giving up the power to change the ending of the novel. The letters are the means to reinscribe herself in the society from which Bertha has exiled her; but they are also scripts, formulaic or exemplary letters addressed to Selden expressing the desire for the "renewal of a tie" (102). These are the words of desire that Lily cannot utter to the man she loves, the words that (were she able to author them) might have led to the happy ending that readers of the serialized publication of the novel requested from Wharton. Lacking the power to erase the story, to make it come to nothing, Lily destroys the words that in her hand rather than in Bertha's might have saved her. She interrupts her plans to announce herself to Bertha with a note and her name and instead chooses a future filled with "the emptiness of renunciation" (314). Facing Selden, "the power of expression failed her suddenly" and "the words would not come out more clearly" (300–301). The "words died on her lips." As she "broke off suddenly," she "touched the packet" of letters "in the folds of her dress" and "the words died on her lips" (302). Following the burning of the letters, "her will-power seemed to have spent itself in a last great effort, and she was lost in the blank reaction which follows on an unwonted expenditure of energy"; she anticipates "the silence of her cheerless room—that silence of the night" (305).

On the way to her death, Lily is offered the vision of another ending for the story of her life. She is discovered and brought home by Nettie Struther, the working girl whose life she had saved with Gus Trenor's money. Here Lily enters the familiar world of the sentimental novel and witnesses the invigorating power of maternity. Nettie embodies the romantic alternative of the fallen woman saved by a man who accepts her despite his knowledge of her past. This exemplary story suggests an alternate ending for Lily's story, but in the language of the novel Nettie Struther also seems to be an embodiment of the letters Lily has just burned. Like the letters purloined from Selden's wastebasket, Nettie is saved from the "refuse heap," and, like the letters, her life is purchased by Lily with Trenor's money. She once appeared to Lily as "one of the superfluous fragments of life"; she still seems to be little more than a "frail envelope" (307) who has "found [the] strength to gather up the fragments of her life" (314). By the example of her life, Nettie represents the possibility of "renewal" (314). From the "fragments," the working mother has made a "nest" which like the envelope of her body has a "frail" but "audacious permanence." Nettie Struther has made a "shelter" from "a mere wisp of leaves" but her simple story has "scant margin for . . . mischance" (314).

In their conversation about collecting books in Chapter 1, Selden speaks to Lily of picking up "something in the rubbish heap" (8). Moments before she burns the letters, Lily tells Selden, "You don't know what it's like in the rubbish heap" (302). Faced with the torn fragments of her own life, Lily can't be like Nettie any more than she can be like Mrs. Haffen. Having destroyed the story she possessed, Lily cannot construct an autobiography from the fragments of her life. Nettie tells Lily: "I used to watch for your name in the papers, and we'd talk over what you were doing, and read the descriptions of the dresses you wore. I haven't seen your name for a long time, though, and I began to be afraid you were sick" (308). Just after she renounces the power of the letters, Lily encounters a reader who tells her that she is no longer a character in the story. Nettie's comment is prophetic, anticipating the imminent end of the novel. (With similar irony Wharton has Nettie name her daughter "Marry Anto'nette" [309] because an actress playing the queen reminded her of Lily.) It also is a reading of what already has happened. In burning the letters Lily already has written herself out of the story. The burning of the letters is the moment of Lily's death.

However, when Lily returns to her room, she still seems surrounded by letters. In the final chapter of her life, she reviews the possessions that represent the story of her past. Ritualistically making order of the fragments of her life, Lily sits at her "writing-desk . . . sorting papers and writing, till the intense silence reminded her of the lateness of the hour" (315). As she sits "pressing her hands against her eyes," Lily assumes the pose she held at the end of Book 1 where she sits over "a sheet of paper . . . with suspended pen" (176) trying to write the letter to Rosedale that would allow her to appear "in a new character" (97) and thus change the course of her life: "Her inspiration flagged . . . she laid the pen down, and sat with . . . her face hidden in her hands" (176). (It also recalls the posture of the failed poet Ralph Marvell shortly before he kills himself in *The Custom of the Country*.) Lily reads and writes as she fantasizes an ending: "If only life could end now—end on this tragic yet sweet vision of lost possibilities" (315).

Before Lily sits at her "writing-desk . . . sorting papers and writing," she opens the trunk where she had kept the letters and takes out dresses that seem to bring with them the power of recollection.

> The remaining . . . dresses still kept the long unerring lines, the sweep and amplitude of the great artist's stroke, and as she spread them out on the bed the scenes in which they had been worn rose vividly before her. An association lurked in every fold: each fall of lace and gleam of embroidery was like a letter in the record of her past. She was startled to find how the atmosphere of her old life enveloped her.

The dresses themselves seem to contain the scenes and stories of her life: "some gleam of light, some note of laughter" (311). Not only do lines and artist's strokes evoke scenes; each dress seems to hold letters, records of a past that in turn envelops her. Even before she tries to sleep and feels that "her whole past was reënacting itself at a hundred different points of consciousness" (316), Lily seems to be rereading her life, rereading the scenes of the novel. From the moment she returns to her room after destroying the letters that she carried "in the folds of her dress" (302), she is reviewing the letters of her past.

The most important of the dresses that seem to carry the power of letters is, of course, "the Reynolds dress she had worn in the Bry *tableaux*," the "heap of white drapery" in which she had represented a woman writing. The lines and letters contained in the folds of this dress, the story that envelops Lily as it reenacts itself, all set the scene for the final tableau of the novel. This time, however, the dress in which Lily triumphantly appeared as Mrs. Lloyd signing her name in the *tableau vivant* is folded away to clear the stage for the scene of a different sort of writing: the composition of a *nature morte*. As she closes "her trunk on the white folds of the Reynolds dress" (311), the story turns from the letters represented and alluded to by the dresses to an actual letter, "a belated letter" that is said to "break silence" with a communication from her aunt's executors. The enclosed check, with its "five figures dancing before her eyes," sets Lily to her last act of "book-keeping" (312). She authors the work that is later called "the book" (322), the checkbook in which she settles accounts with her creditors, especially Gus Trenor. After the burning of the letters, this settling of accounts is Lily's most explicit act of erasure. Once again, she insists that an account come to nothing, that motives for stories be counterbalanced and finally canceled. Lily burns the letters, rereads the scenes and stories of her life, folds away the dresses that read like letters, and closes out her accounts.

When Selden enters the room and sees Lily's dead body on the bed, we see a reenactment of the *tableau vivant* scene. In the later scene, however, he does not witness Lily "banishing the phantom of [Reynolds's] dead beauty"—that is, Mrs. Lloyd—"by the beams of her living grace" (131). In the Reynolds *tableau* he had seen in "the portrait of Miss Bart," "the real Lily Bart," what Gerty Farish calls "the real Lily" (131–32); here Selden tries to deny that he sees "her real self" in "the semblance of Lily Bart," but he finally acknowledges that in "the sleeping face which seemed to lie like a delicate impalpable mask over the living lineaments he had known . . . the real Lily was still there" (319–20). No longer writing letters, Lily lies next to the trunk that has been purged of the dirty rags of Dorset linen and closed on the dresses that hold letters and scenes from Lily's life in their folds. Her writing dress, the dress in which she appeared as Mrs. Lloyd, has been folded away and the trunk remains unopened. Yet despite Lily's attempt to break her staff and drown her book, Selden still is faced with Lily's writing. Lily is surrounded by the fragments that remain from her life: pins (a "rose-coloured pin-cushion" and "tortoise-shell hairpins") and paper; envelopes (addresses rather than dresses); a checkbook which is referred to as a "book" (321–22); and letters. Whereas in the *tableau vivant* the "real Lily Bart" seemed "divested of the trivialities of her little world" and invested with the "touch of poetry" (131), in this *nature morte* Lily's still life has been soiled by dirty sheets. Reading only the outside of an unsealed envelope that bears the name of Gus Trenor, Selden immediately senses defilement.

Lily lies before Selden with "mute lips" (323) that refuse to tell her story—as mute in death as they had been in life. After contemplating the mask that covers the once-living lineaments, Selden picks up two letters from the top of the desk. Putting aside the sealed letter addressed to the bank, he focuses on the "ungummed" (321) envelope on which Lily has written the name of someone else's husband, just as she wrote the name of someone else's husband while posing as Mrs. Lloyd. Despite Lily's efforts at erasure in the final hours she spends "writing and sorting papers," despite her effort as she sinks into death to remember a word to "tell Selden, some word she had found that should make life clear between them" (317), Lily leaves two words on the outside of a "letter" that for Selden "unhallowed the memory of that last hour, made a mock of the word he had come to speak, and defiled even the reconciling silence upon which it fell" (321). The words on the envelope— "Gus Trenor"—lead Selden to ask "why had she been writing" (321) to such a man. The defilement that Selden senses in reading a name and the "old doubts [that] started to life again at the mere sight of Trenor's name," make him want to withdraw his investment; he feels that "his personal stake" has been "annulled" (322). However, in his "examination of the papers" he discovers in Lily's writing two more names, two more signs of exchange that change his relation to the dead Lily.

First, he discovers the note that presumably bears his own name: "the note he had written her" ("When may I come to you?") on the day following Lily's performance as Mrs. Lloyd. Like Romeo, who arrives too late to save his apparently dead lover after a breakdown in correspondence, Wharton's "negative hero" arrives too late to save the dead heroine Wharton originally named "Juliet."[20] Next, Selden finds a name in the "book" Lily has left behind, the "cheque-book" that tells the story of settled accounts. A "page" of this book recording a check made out to "Charles Augustus Trenor" impresses him with "the taint of such a transaction" (322–23), but the same entry also (as Rosedale predicted) "cleans [Lily] out altogether" (287). The "magic formula" of "five figures dancing" (312) contained in the check for $10,000 from Mrs. Peniston's estate has been converted into a payment to Trenor that cleans Lily by cleaning out her account, reducing her balance to nearly nothing. Choosing not to read the contents of the unsealed envelope that he, in effect, has misread, Selden continues his audit of Lily's "book-keeping" (312) and his reconstruction of her accounts.[21]

Laying aside Lily's book, Selden sits down in the writing chair beside her desk and assumes the pose that Lily held as she ceased to write at the close of

Book 1 and at the close of the preceding chapter—the close of her life. Seated with "his elbows" on Lily's writing desk, hiding "his face in his hands" (322), Selden sits in the position that has come to signal the cessation of writing, a pose that in *The House of Mirth* as well as in *The Custom of the Country* also signals suicide. Selden, however, by assuming the position that is both the position of Lily and the pose of the author, is able to complete the story of the novel. Unable once again "to wash his hands of the sequel" (206), by taking Lily's place he continues to imagine Lily's life until "out of the very insinuations he had feared to probe, he constructed an explanation of the mystery." This construction, along with what "the contents of the little desk declared," amount to "all he knew—all he could hope to unravel of the story" (323). Although the "mute lips on the pillow refused him more than this, unless indeed they had told him the rest in the kiss they had left upon his forehead," Selden feels authorized to "read into that farewell all that his heart craved to find there" (323).

Like Mrs. Haffen, Selden stands ready to condemn Lily as the author of illicit letters, as both correspondent and corespondent in an adulterous liaison. Lily's attempts at erasure and closure fail and the barest traces of writing almost frame her. Even when Selden finally corrects his superficial misreading by reconstructing Lily's account, he does so through stories that he must create as well as unravel. Lily has attempted to burn letters, to hide letters away, to refuse the role of writer in which she has been cast by others and herself. She has wanted to settle accounts and have the story of her life "end now"; but the reading and writing remain. Selden becomes a spectator to a *tableau* in which Lily is framed in and by sheets, surrounded by written names and pieces of writing. The communion between Lily and Selden that ends the novel is mediated once again through writing, letters, and names and finally through the exchange of a single word that remains unspoken.

The mysterious word referred to at the close of each of the three chapters which comprise the conclusion of *The House of Mirth* is followed by the end of writing: in Chapter 12 the burning of letters, in Chapter 13 the suicide of the woman who refuses to write, and in Chapter 14 the deferred ending of the serialized novel itself. At the close of Chapter 12, just after Selden fancies that he sees Lily "draw something from her dress and drop it into the fire," just after she in fact burns the letters, Selden is pictured "still groping for the word to break the spell" (304). In the next chapter, as Lily sinks into what will be "a sleep without waking," she thinks of "something she must tell Selden, some word she had found that should make life clear between them. She tried to repeat the word, which lingered vague and luminous on the far edge of thought" (317). Finally, in the last chapter, Selden thinks that he has "found the word he meant to say to her. . . . It was not a word for twilight, but for the morning" (318–19).

The words on the envelope he finds after her death at first "made a mock of the word he had come to speak" (321), but after further reading explains away his sense of defilement, Selden seems to experience a moment of communion with Lily: "He knelt by the bed and bent over her, draining their last moment to its lees; and in the silence there passed between them the word which made all clear" (323). The only words that follow are "THE END." It remains unclear which "word" passes in silence between Selden, who "read into that farewell all that his heart craved to find there" (323), and the woman who found herself "spelling out a letter of the sign" and writing a word for all to see.

The conventions of the late nineteenth-century novel and its story of female sacrifice offer various possibilities for identifying the word that Lily and Selden imagine at the end of *The House of Mirth*. One possibility is the word that Selden speaks in the sequel to the *tableau vivant* in the conservatory. Selden, whom Lily earlier has avoided because seeing him "would have broken the spell" (132), says, "The only way I can help you is by loving you," to which Lily responds, "Ah, love me, love me—but don't tell me so!" (134). Lily sees "danger" in allowing this "episode" to have "a sequel" (136), but convention would suggest that "love" is the unspoken word communicated by "mute lips" in the deathbed scene that takes place in so many nineteenth-century novels. In the familiar sentimental formula, the woman or woman child (immortalized by Stowe's little Eva) dies a sacrificial death to redeem those who live.[22] Here, however, Lily is already dead, which suggests the inadequacy of reading *love* in "the word that made all clear." Selden decides that "the word he meant to say to her . . . was not a word for twilight, but for the morning" (318–19). Following the logic of Ecclesiastes, where the heart of the foolish is in the house of mirth and the heart of the wise in the house of mourning, the word for "morning" here must also be the word for *mourning*.[23] In her unfinished novel "Literature," Wharton's writer-protagonist Dickie Thaxter is awakened to poetry when he is moved by Whitman's lines from "Out of the Cradle Endlessly Rocking": "the low and delicious word death, / And again death, death, death, death."[24] The classic formula, of course, joins the words of "love" and "death," especially in the sentimental requirement of virgin death. In addition to evoking Juliet and Romeo, the final meeting of Lily and Selden evokes Desdemona and Othello, as Selden realizes that he has been wrong in believing the rumors about Lily's defilement.

Selden earlier asserts that there are "sign-posts" to the "republic of the spirit" but warns that "one has to know how to read them." Lily responds, "Whenever I see you, I find myself spelling out a letter of the sign" (65–66). As Selden stands before Lily's deathbed and tries to "read into" the unspoken word a "moment of love" (323), communion, reconciliation, and transcendence, we should remember that this book collector is a rather poor reader. Furthermore, the centerpiece of this novel about women's letters frames Lily in the act of writing a word, spelling out the letters of an interrupted sign. Assuming the pose and props of Reynolds's Mrs. Lloyd in the *tableau vivant*, Lily stands interrupted after having written the first three letters of a word—*Llo*—presumably the name that is or will be Joanna Leigh's married name. However, the presence of an unidentified word at the end of the novel, as well as Lily's stance as both writer and sign, ask the reader to speculate about what Lily is writing.

The topos of the lover writing letters on a tree suggests in the double *L* of "Lloyd" the initials that join Miss *Leigh* to Mr. *Lloyd*; when the writing instrument is in Lily's hand it also brings together the initials of *Lawrence* and *Lily*. While the joining and doubling of *L*'s is an act of signing that means marriage for Mrs. Lloyd, it adds up to *0* in Lily's writing. Yet if Lily cannot write her husband's name, if in fact she gets into trouble by writing the name of someone else's husband, there is also a sense in which she can be seen to be writing her own name when she stands posed as Mrs. Lloyd. We have seen that Lily's performance as Mrs. Lloyd is able to "break the spell of the illusion" of the *tableaux vivants* as "the curtain suddenly parted on a picture which was simply and undisguisedly the portrait of Miss Bart" (131). Standing as an emblem of the woman as poet in an allegory of women and art, Lily embodies a sign and spells out letters that almost sign her name: the vertical stems of the *L*'s inscribed on the tree might evoke both the *LI* as well as the double *L*'s of "LILY"—the traces of an autograph that would literally write the name of the self.[25]

Lily's *tableau* of Mrs. Lloyd is a self-portrait in part because it represents the signing of an autograph as well as an allusive self-portrait in which she poses as a woman artist. If Lily may be said to discover what she calls "my self" in spelling out the letter of this sign, it is also because the letters take on an autobiographical quality. Here the writing on trees (by the woman accused of collecting "autographs" [252]) is not merely a sign on nature but also the beginning of a *signature*. Furthermore, the audience is said to utter a "unanimous 'Oh!'" (131) as Lily is in the act of writing *O*—as if Lily is literally writing the novel, anticipating or rather scripting the audience's response as she poses as the self-portrait of the author.

If the *tableau vivant* represents the scene of a triumphant woman writing letters, spelling out a word, the deathbed scene that ends the novel frames Lily spelling out the letters of a signature, a sign of the self, only because she herself has become the word. As Susan Gubar suggests, Lily's body represents "the flesh made word."[26] Paradoxically, this final act of self-portraiture marks both the failure of writing and the failure of Lily to stop writing. Despite her efforts to clear the ledgers of her accounts and "tell Selden, some word she had found that should make life clear between them" (317), the final word that Lily embodies cannot be "the word which made all clear" (323). Lily laid out among her sheets, papers, letters, and books cannot stop being a text; Selden has the last word because he is left reading. His last-minute efforts at interpretation allow him to unravel the story and save him from totally misreading Lily's final *tableau*; but the word that ends the novel is far from clear, and the transcendence that Selden finds in the conventions of melodrama is hollow and tinged with irony.

There may be sentimentalism or melodrama in the reconciliation of Selden and the dead Lily Bart, and perhaps tragedy in Lily's death-mask reenactment of Mrs. Lloyd after "the power of expression failed her," "the words died on her lips" (300–302), and she burns the letters. However, there is a way in which for Wharton the woman writer has to die because her place is the underworld: the realm not only of death but also of experience. We have seen that Wharton's depictions of famous women novelists mainly appeared in the years preceding the publication of *The House of Mirth* in *The Touchstone* and "Copy." In the first narrative, Margaret Aubyn has died before the events of the novella take place; in the second, Mrs. Ambrose Dale claims to have "died years ago." In both texts there are disputes about the fate of the personal correspondence (the love letters) of these women authors. It is appropriate that each of these writers has published a novel entitled "Pomegranate Seed"; each, in some sense—like the letter writers Elsie Corder Ashby in Wharton's story "Pomegranate Seed" and Juliana in "Mr. Jones"—may be said to address her readers from the realm of the dead.[27]

In *The House of Mirth*, Bertha Dorset, the author of the love letters and the most explicit figure for the woman writer, is also associated with the underworld. Like Ellen Olenska as Wharton imagined her in her plan for *The Age of Innocence*, Bertha's "soul" seems "tainted" by "corruption"; Bertha represents a woman who has "eaten of the Pomegranate Seed and can never live without it."[28] Although she may seem too destructive to play the role of Persephone, she nonetheless represents the underworld of experience and the transgression of erotic knowledge. When Lily reads Bertha's love letter to Selden she is confronted with passion from the other side, the netherworld: "Now the other side presented itself to Lily, the volcanic nether side of the surface over which conjecture and innuendo glide so lightly till the first fissure turns their whisper to a shriek" (101). The "flourish of masculinity" that Lily sees in Bertha's handwriting links Bertha to Elsie Corder Ashby, the deceased author of letters in "Pomegranate Seed" whose pale writing is said to have "masculine curves."[29] Like the dead wife's letters to her remarried husband in the story, Bertha's "appeals" to Selden "for the renewal of a tie" (102) are apparently resisted. As with the second wife in the "Pomegranate Seed," Lily's illicit reading of a single letter seems to determine the fate of all. This letter, which Lily conjectures is one of "a dozen" (101) letters (recalling, perhaps, the months of the year represented by the seeds in the myth of Persephone), is the single seed that may be read as Lily's invitation to the netherworld.

Lily's initial acceptance of the position of the writer of letters that she is placed in by Mrs. Haffen leads to visits to the underworld. At the end of Book 1, as Lily sits over an unfinished letter to Rosedale, she receives a letter from Bertha inviting her to join the Dorsets on a cruise in the Mediterranean. It is on this trip that Lily is exposed to Bertha's dangerous liaisons and once again put in Bertha's place to take the blame for her indiscretions. When George Dorset tells her of his wife's infidelity, she has a glimpse of the other side through fissures in the social surface that recall the "flash of divination" (102) she experiences when she sees Bertha's letter to Selden. Her conversation with Dorset is described as "a dreadful hour—an hour from which she emerged shrinking and seared, as though her lids had been scorched by its actual glare. It was not that she had never had premonitory glimpses of such an outbreak;

but rather because, here and there throughout the three months, the surface of life had shown such ominous cracks and vapours that her fears had always been on the alert for an upheaval" (197).

The role of sacrificial victim that Lily assumes at the end of Book 2 is prefigured in the scene in which Lily visits the Trenor mansion. Here she seems to enter the actual realm of the underworld. Responding to the invitation that ostensibly came from Mrs. Trenor, Lily unexpectedly finds herself escorted by Gus Trenor into a deadly world of illicit eroticism.[30] As Lily descends into the "den" of Trenor's heated passions through "the shrouded hall," Trenor appears "on the threshold." Claiming that his wife has "a devil of a headache" and telling Lily, "you look deadbeat," he asks, referring to "this awful slippery white stuff" that wraps the furniture of the deserted house, "Doesn't this room look as if it was waiting for the body to be brought down?" (137–38). In a scene in which references to the body proliferate, Lily is the body that is brought down. She wishes to cut short "their *tête-à-tête*" while he insists that they "have a nice quiet jaw together" (139). Lily is finally spared when Trenor comes to himself like a "sleep-walker on a deathly ledge": "With his last gust of words the flame had died out, leaving him chill and humbled. It was as though a cold air had dispersed the fumes of his libations, and the situation loomed before him black and naked as the ruins of a fire" (144).

Although Lily escapes from the sexual demands that Trenor presses in his version of the inferno, she has not escaped the consequences of abduction to the underworld: "There was a great gulf fixed between today and yesterday. Everything in the past seemed simple, natural, full of daylight—and she was alone in a place of darkness and pollution" (145). She feels "the frightened self in her . . . dragging the other down" (142); she continues to experience a sense of self-division:

> She seemed a stranger to herself, or rather there were two selves in her, the one she had always known, and a new abhorrent being to which it found itself chained. She had once picked up . . . a translation of the *Eumenides*, and her imagination had been seized by the high terror of the scene where Orestes, in the cave of the oracle, finds his implacable huntresses asleep, and snatches an hour's repose. Yes, the Furies might sometimes sleep, but they were there, always there in the dark corners, and now they were awake and the iron clang of their wings was in her brain. [144–45]

Lily's realization that she has two selves is an acknowledgment of the double-ness that has haunted her steps from the opening chapter of the book when, thinking of herself as an "unwonted apparition" (12), she is first mistaken by Mrs. Haffen for Bertha, whom Lily thinks of in the next chapter as a "dis-embodied spirit" (21). Mistaken for Bertha, put in Bertha's place, Miss Bart appears as a stand-in, rival, and double for Bertha throughout the novel. Lily's image of her divided self also describes her increasingly tormented relation with Bertha; this is made explicit when she later imagines that "the pursuing furies seem to take the shape of Bertha Dorset" (290). Pursued by Bertha, Lily flees her relation *to* Bertha, the aspect of her self that is identified with Bertha. Her final fate as a sacrificial victim in some sense carries out the scheme Bertha set in motion on the yacht; her death seems both an escape from and a punishment for the dangerous eroticism of the underworld that Bertha seems to embody.

The appearance of "a translation of the *Eumenides*" and Lily's identification with Orestes in relation to her conception of Bertha as the Furies is puzzling and complex. Wharton was clearly preoccupied with these figures. She pub-lished a poem called "Eumenides" in 1909, and among her papers is a four-part poem called "The Oresteia," in which she tells the stories of Iphigenia, Aga-memnon, Clytemnestra, and Orestes. Wharton's Orestes is left hearing "the hum of Hell / And in my brain the clang of iron wings" just as Lily Bart imagines of the Furies that "the iron clang of their wings was in her brain" (145).[31] Wharton's translation of Greek myth in *The House of Mirth* involves a complex and ironic recasting of primal forces and primal stories. To identify Bertha with the Furies is to associate her with the embodiment of female vengeance. These chthonic deities, "Daughters of the Earth and the Shadow,"[32] are the attendants of Persephone and Hades who lived at the entrance to the underworld. In the *Eumenides*, the third part of Aeschylus's *Oresteia*, the Furies pursue Orestes after he has murdered his mother. Transformed by Athena from the dogs of hell into the more benevolent Eumenides, they become goddesses of marriage and childbirth.[33]

It is not surprising to see Bertha associated with relentless avengers, al-though there may be some irony in Bertha's association with these avengers of crimes against mother and daughter. The Furies seek to avenge the murdered mother, Clytemnestra, who has avenged the death of her virgin daughter. However, Bertha's adulterous intrigues align her with Clytemnestra, and her association with sexual knowledge aligns her with both marriage and child-birth. Marriage and motherhood are not necessarily associated with purity: the baby Lily imagines she is holding at the end of the novel belongs to Nettie Struther, a woman who has been seduced and abandoned and then saved by marriage. Marriage and childbirth belong rather to the realm of the blood rites that mark the body with earthly experience.[34] Lily's flight from Bertha is also a flight from this experience. By burning the letters Lily attempts to erase the signs of Bertha's erotic transgression as well as the illicit reading that seems to transport Lily herself to the underworld of eroticism.

By trying to go back to an earlier story and erase Bertha's writing to Selden, Lily also is trying to distinguish herself from Bertha. She burns the letters to destroy the forbidden fruit that has identified her with Bertha and identified her as Bertha. Despite the hallucination of motherhood that Lily has as she dies, she might be said to die so that she will not bear fruit. She dies in order to escape the underworld. Although Lily is both fearful of and attracted to the underworld that Bertha's letters tell of, she remains between worlds and there-fore without the fruits of her labor—neither a Demeter nor a Persephone. In Carrie Fisher's account of Lily's ambivalent pursuit of marriage, Lily is stymied by "despis[ing] the things she's trying for." The same Lily Bart who "works like a slave preparing her ground and sowing her seed" on "the day she ought to be reaping the harvest . . . oversleeps herself or goes off on a picnic" (183). Pursued by Trenor to the gates of hell and confronted with propositions from George Dorset and Rosedale that demand she act as Bertha would, Lily seeks to avoid defilement. "Everything in the past seemed simple, natural, full of day-light," she thinks after escaping from Trenor, finding herself "alone in a place of darkness and pollution" (145).

Here, paradoxically, Lily retreats from the role of the hero Orestes and tries to become Iphigenia. In one version of the myth, Iphigenia believes that she is brought to Agamemnon to be given in marriage and ends up as a sacrificed virgin instead. Lily embraces virgin sacrifice rather than marriage.[35] She es-capes the bloody rites of marriage and childbirth, of bodily change, fleeing the daughter of earth and shadow. Wharton's allegory of women and art tells the story of Lily Bart and Bertha Dorset. Lily *Bart*, the woman who would *be art*, flees *Bertha Dorset*, backs away from the *birth door* and the gates of eroticism: the grounding in the flesh that insists that women take their *being* from the *earth*.

In *The House of Mirth*, Wharton goes back to a myth of the house of Agamemnon that begins with virgin sacrifice and ironizes the plot of the nineteenth-century sentimental novel—which conventionally ends in virgin sacrifice. Lily fulfills her vow to be the "mystically veiled figure occupying the centre of attention" at a wedding rather than "a casual spectator" (84) when she represents "Mrs. Lloyd" in the *tableau vivant*; but her deathbed scene reminds us that we don't know whether Reynolds's painting portrays Mrs. Lloyd or Miss Leigh. The painting may display the young bride, but it may depict Joanna Leigh at the moment *before* her marriage.

Choosing to escape from the torment of "her whole past . . . reënacting itself at a hundred different points of consciousness" (316), Lily looks for "renewal" (290) in a bottle of "chloral" (305). She casts her lot with the most gentle of the underworld figures, Chlora, the goddess of flowers. (Wharton, of course, identified flowers with women and ornament). Lily takes the chloral in the hopes of entering the green and floral world of Elysium that lies beyond experience and the torment of reading and writing. By taking chloral, Lily attempts through the efflorescence of death to personify her name. (At different times Wharton considered calling her novel "The Year of the Rose" and "A Moment's Ornament.") As she sits at the writing desk after wishing, "If only life could end now—end on this tragic yet sweet vision of lost possibilities" (315), she drinks the dangerous hypnotic and blows "out her candle" (316). In this spell, as "an invisible hand" seems to make "magic passes over her," Lily seeks a peace that will take her beyond spelling across the river Lethe into what will be a "brief bath of oblivion" or "a sleep without waking" (316–17).

Lily's desire for the floral, the natural, the moment's ornament, is part of the desire described by Wolff to be an artistic object, to end her life as a tableau. However, Lily's choice of the chloral also represents a fierce decision to reject the world of writing and experience embodied by Bertha, to refuse the power in her hands. She rejects both Persephone and Demeter, both the daughter who crosses the threshold and the mother who would call her back. Lily would rather have the taste of chloral in her mouth as she dies than—like Emma Bovary—the taste of ink. Unlike Emma Bovary, she burns the letters that tell of adultery; but Selden, like Charles Bovary, still manages to find an apparently compromising envelope.[36] Finally, even in death, Lily cannot escape either the underworld of writing or the realm of erotic transgression. The envelope addressed to Trenor at least temporarily defiles her even in the reconciling silence: it reads as another letter that links a woman to illicit eroticism. The last three chapters frame Lily's final tableau with a proliferation of literal and figurative texts, envelopes, papers, letters, books, writing, and words. If the pose of the woman writer is finally untenable for Lily because becoming Mrs. Lloyd also means becoming Mrs. Dorset, Lily is still left as an author facing her less than adequate reader. Despite Wharton's success in writing *The House of Mirth*, the novel imagines two untenable places for the woman writer: the defiled underworld of experience and writing represented by Bertha Dorset, and the literal death that results from Lily Bart's refusal to use the power in her hands.

TWO

The Woman Behind the Door

(Ethan Frome)

Why should, of all things, man, unruled,
Such unproportioned dwellings build?
. . . .
No creature loves an empty space;
Their bodies measure out their place.
But he, superfluously spread,
Demands more room alive than dead;
And in his hollow palace goes,
Where winds, as he, themselves may lose.
—Andrew Marvell, "Upon Appelton House"

The gate clanged on him, and he went his
    way
Amid the alien millions, mute and grey,
Swept like a cold mist down an unlit strand,
Where nameless wreckage gluts the stealthy
    sand,
Drift of the cockle-shells of hope and faith
Wherein they foundered on the rock of death.
—Edith Wharton, "Orpheus"

In October of 1908 Wharton wrote to her publisher William Crary Brownell: "I have perversely and inexcusably taken to warbling again, instead of sticking to prose."[1] Wharton at this point had put aside the writing of *The Custom of the Country*, which had been begun the previous year and would remain unfinished until 1913. More and more preoccupied in 1908 and 1909 with her relationship with Morton Fullerton—the man who in effect was her first lover—Wharton wrote love letters, an intimate journal, and at least ten poems, most of which were addressed to Fullerton. Sometime in the spring of 1908 Wharton wrote to Scribner's to request a copy of a poem she had published with them in 1902 called "Artemis to Actaeon." It was one of the several provocative poems she had written in 1902—the year following her mother's death and the year in which she both published her first ghost story and completed her first novel. Wharton apparently read "Artemis to Actaeon" aloud to Fullerton and Henry James in May of 1908, and it became the title poem of the collection of poetry she published in April of 1909: *Artemis to Actaeon and Other Verse*. R. W. B. Lewis has suggested that Wharton found in the poems she had written six years earlier "an anticipation of her feelings about" Fullerton and that in general "for the expression of her own most private and vital emotions, she turned to poetry."[2] In the periods of her life when she was profoundly unsettled Wharton often turned to a genre that offered emotional immediacy at the same time it offered the distance of both formal structures and classical, mythic, and historical personae.

"Life," one of the poems that she wrote to Fullerton during this period, has much in common with the poems of 1902—not only "Artemis to Actaeon" but also "Vesalius in Zante" and "Margaret of Cortona." Wharton not only grouped these four poems together in *Artemis to Actaeon and Other Verse*; she also chose them to begin the volume. Lewis describes "Life" as "a high-spirited allegory of sexual and psychic arousal,"[3] and indeed this passionate and extravagant poem shares with the others both language and imagery that are erotically charged and often ecstatic. More strangely, however, all four poems tell stories about desire and carnal knowledge between women and men that turn upon bodily pain and acts of physical violation. These poems are filled with literal as well as figurative acts of penetration, wounding, and the rending of both veils and flesh. Furthermore, these poems share a characteristic that is rare in Wharton's work; composed as dramatic monologues, they are written in the first-person singular.

"Life," which contains the phrase "Life and I" that years later Wharton would use as the title for an unpublished autobiographical fragment, is written in the first person in the persona of a reed. It begins, "Nay, lift me to thy lips, Life, and once more / Pour the wild music through me—"; the apostrophized "Life" is an allegorical figure, referred to as "she," who brings the reed to voice. The poem describes the various songs that Life has played upon the reed, ranging from the mythic world in which trees become nymphs to cities in which "the heavy merchant" is "at his desk."[4] The initial description of the cutting of the reed suggests the violence that will characterize its union with Life:

> I quivered in the reed-bed with my kind,
> Rooted in Lethe-bank, when at the dawn
> There came a groping shape of mystery
> Moving among us, that with random stroke
> Severed, and rapt me from my silent tribe,
> Pierced, fashioned, lipped me, sounding for a voice, . . .
> [A, 7]

The voice that comes from being raptured from silence, "Severed," and "Pierced," goes on to tell an increasingly explicit story about the wounding pain of its art: its wounds are made into musical stops. Life "in my live flank dug a finger-hole, / And wrung new music from it." "Ah, the pain!" the reed continues, describing how Life "breathed and kissed me, stilling the dim need. / But evermore it woke, and stabbed my flank / With yearnings for new music and new pain." Life tells the reed: "Of every heart-wound I will make a stop, / And drink thy life in music, pang by pang." Finally, as the reed feels "beneath her hands / The stab of a new wound" the two are joined "In indistinguishable union bent, / Till she became the flute and I the player" (A, 9–12).

The moment of erotic communion that takes place in these songs of experience is simultaneously a moment of art and a moment of violation and pain. Passion is depicted as stabbing and wounding. These moments also are juxtaposed in "Margaret of Cortona," the 1902 poem in which Wharton gives voice to a fourteenth-century saint. Margaret of Cortona lived openly as the mistress to a nobleman but dedicated her life to penance and the care of the sick after her lover was murdered. Wharton follows *The Lives of the Saints* in placing Margaret's discovery of Christ in the discovery of her lover's mutilated body:[5]

> I found him lying in the woods, alive
> To gasp my name out and his life-blood with it,

As though the murderer's knife had probed for me
In his hacked breast and found me in each wound . . .
[*A*, 27; Wharton's ellipses]

In a monologue addressed to Fra Paolo recounting her spiritual struggles with earthly and divine love, Margaret describes her failures of faith in images of stabbing: "I have tried the saints' names and our blessed Mother's, / . . . And like a blade bent backward at first thrust / They yield and fail me" (*A*, 25). She recounts how she was taken by her lover in terms that anticipate the picking of the reed in "Life": seeing her, he wonders *"How grew so white a bud in such black slime, / And why not mine the hand to pluck it out?"* (*A*, 26). Margaret goes on to contrast the lover, who lifts her "Stem, root and all—ay, and the clinging mud—" (*A*, 27) with "Christ, the heavenly gardener." It is Christ who

Plucks flowers for Paradise (do I not know?)
He snaps the stem above the root, and presses
The ransomed soul between two convent walls,
A lifeless blossom in the Book of Life.
[*A*, 26]

Wharton's poem evoked an accusation of heresy from a Jesuit priest, who may have objected to the saint's defiant faithfulness to her lover. "Suppose my lover had not died," she says, "Think you I ever would have left him living, / Even to be Christ's blessed Margaret?" (*A*, 28). The poem describes both earthly and divine passion in the same figures of violence that Wharton would use in "Life"; the two seem to coincide in moments of stabbing, wounding, plucking, and severing. The story of this saint is a story of a life of female sacrifice. The male lover is punished with death for his desire, but the woman who seems to find herself in the wounds of the lover's Christ-like body becomes (in her own images) a flower cut off from life and preserved between the pages of a book.

The ecstatic paean of "Life" and the opposing desires of "Margaret of Cortona" pale in comparison with "Vesalius in Zante," perhaps the most shocking of Wharton's poems of 1902. (She wrote to her publisher in November of 1902 that "Vesalius in Zante" "has made me want to hide under the furniture ever since I've seen it in print".)[6] Based on historical personages and events, the poem is a monologue spoken by the sixteenth-century anatomist and surgeon Vesalius. In the only note contained in *Artemis to Actaeon*, Wharton explains on the closing page of the volume that Vesalius was "one of the first physiologists to dissect the human body" and the author of a "great work" entitled "The Structure of the Human Body" (*A*, 90).[7]

In the poem, which is concerned with competition between men and the question of who has received credit for the discovery of hidden knowledge, Vesalius has an imaginary conversation with Gabriel Fallopius, Vesalius's successor in the chair of surgery at Padua. The poem imagines the "tradition" that Vesalius's journey to Jerusalem "was a penance to which the Church condemned him for having opened the body of a woman before she was actually dead" (*A*, 90). Here the literal descriptions and metaphors of stabbing knives, violently fingered flesh, and wounded bodies that are present in the erotic and spiritual scenes of "Life" and "Margaret of Cortona" are mapped out in scenes of scientific discovery as the body of a woman is sacrificed under the surgical knife.

The extravagant desire for knowledge that is recounted in "Vesalius in Zante" is also deeply informed by the story of desire that is contained in the title poem of Wharton's collection of poetry, "Artemis to Actaeon." In this poem, Wharton constructs a monologue spoken by the virgin goddess of the hunt in which she tells Actaeon of her efforts to seduce him. Artemis begins: "Thou couldst not look on me and live: so runs / The mortal legend—thou that couldst not live / Nor look on me (so the divine decree)!" She then boasts how she "mocked" him "in every guise of life" and lured him "down the primal silences / Where the heart hushes and the flesh is dumb" (*A*, 3).

Describing the "veil" that hangs between them, the "myriad-tinted veil of sense," she imagines the character of some "rash votary" who might

> Break rank, fling past the people and the priest,
> Up the last step, on to the inmost shrine,
> And there, the sacred curtain in his clutch,
> Drop dead of seeing—while the others prayed!
> Yea, this we wait for, this renews us, this
> Incarnates us, pale people of your dreams,
> Who are but what you make us, wood or stone. . . .
> [*A*, 4–5]

It is Actaeon's desire to see Artemis, to see the goddess behind the curtain of the life that embodies her, to rend the sacred curtain so he can look on the inmost shrine, that leads to his death. The poem foretells Actaeon's death. Although the goddess proclaims, "*Because I love thee thou shalt die!*," we know from the myth that Actaeon will not precisely "drop dead of seeing" (*A*, 6, 4). Rather, he will be punished for his vision of Artemis by being turned into a stag and torn apart by hounds.[8] Like the reed in "Life" and both the lover and Christ in "Margaret of Cortona," the character addressed in "Artemis to Actaeon" is destined to die wounded, rent, mutilated, torn apart—in his case because of his desire to see.

In "Vesalius in Zante," a man also desires to see a woman, but here he is the one who tears the flesh of the body he seeks to know; she is the one who is rent apart by his desire to see, who drops dead of his seeing. In his defense of his decision to take the scalpel to a girl brought to him in "catalepsy," a "trance . . . not yet darkened into death" (*A*, 15), Vesalius insists:

> If my blade
> Once questioned living flesh, if once I tore
> The pages of the Book in opening it,
> See what the torn page yielded ere the light
> Had paled its buried characters—and judge!
> [*A*, 14]

Whereas Margaret of Cortona describes herself as a "lifeless blossom in the Book of Life," the body whose flesh is torn by Vesalius is figured here as a book; its interior is like a page and its buried characters are impaled as well as paled by the light of Vesalius's vision. In Vesalius's imagery the woman becomes blossom and book at once:

> Think what she purchased with that one heart-flutter
> That whispered its deep secret to my blade!
> For, just because her bosom fluttered still,
> It told me more than many rifled graves;
> Because I spoke too soon, she answered me,
> Her vain life ripened to this bud of death
> As the whole plant is forced into one flower,

All her blank past a scroll on which God wrote
His word of healing—so that the poor flesh,
Which spread death living, died to purchase life!
[A, 15]

Like the figure of Life in "Life," the scientist has wounded in his attempt to pluck this plant and know its song of experience. Like Actaeon and the votary figured in "Artemis to Actaeon," both Vesalius and his successor Fallopius wanted to "*rent the veil of flesh*"; all would have "*forced a way / Into the secret fortalice of life*" (A, 20).

Margaret of Cortona, who describes how she packed "empty days" with "Credos and Hail Marys / So close that not a fear should force the door," figures her life with her lover as "by Love, / The patient architect, so shaped and fitted / that not a crevice let the winter in" (A, 24, 29). Vesalius and Fallopius want to force the door and see the inmost shrine that is hidden inside. Vesalius, complaining that he has become "but the symbol of a man, / The sign-board creaking o'er an empty inn," imagines Fallopius's claim that he would have made his discovery even if unassisted by Vesalius's previous work:

"*Oh, give the door its due
I entered by. Only, I pray you, note,
Had door been none, a shoulder-thrust of mine
Had breached the crazy wall*"—he seems to say.
[A, 18]

In the imagined dialogue, Fallopius credits the author of *The Structure of the Human Body* as the one who first opened the door of the structure of the body, whose book first opened the living book that contains the buried characters and pages of life. Yet Vesalius imagines that Fallopius keeps "his eye upon the goal, / Cuts a straight furrow to the end in view, / Cares not who oped the fountain by the way" (A, 19). Fallopius has discovered the passage between the ovaries and the uterus. The discoverer of what we now call the fallopian tubes, he has followed the furrow to the fountain, the path that connects the buried characters to the inmost shrine that is "the secret fortalice of life" (A, 20).

In this imagined dialogue and dispute with Fallopius, the significance of Wharton's fascination with Vesalius becomes clear. Read in the context of the four dramatic monologues that begin *Artemis to Actaeon and Other Verse*, "Vesalius in Zante" seems the culmination of Wharton's preoccupation with the relationship between desire, the physical violation of the flesh (stabbing, cutting, rending, piercing, wounding), and the death that purchases immortality. Yet this poem provides the key that makes sense of the preoccupations of the other poems and carries their concerns a step beyond eroticism.

In this poem about the desire to know and see, the desire to tear the mysterious veil, we see that the site of inquiry is the female body: the secret of life hidden inside is the secret of fertility and reproduction. This is what is behind the "breached" wall (A, 18); it is "that buried labour underneath" that Vesalius calls the foundation of the "building" (A, 22). Vesalius describes himself as "the symbol of a man, / The sign-board creaking o'er an empty inn" (A, 18); but the structure of the human body in this case is not empty. When the page of the book of the woman is torn, when the living flower is cut to be placed lifeless in the book of life, it is the buried characters of fertility that are revealed. The juxtaposition of wounding and violation with the problem of penetrating the secrets of the female body culminates in these poems with an epistemologically and sexually charged concern with the female organs of reproduction.

On January 24, 1902, the day of her fortieth birthday, Wharton wrote to her friend Sara Norton, "I excessively hate to be forty. Not that I think it is a bad thing to be—only I'm not ready yet!" She continued: "Don't I know that feeling you describe, when one longs to go to a hospital & *have something cut out*, & come out minus an organ, but alive & active & like other people, instead of dragging with this bloodless existence!! Only I fear you & I will never find a surgeon who will do us that service" (L, 55–56). This fantasy about a surgeon of the soul who would cut out an organ suggests multiple interpretations. Wharton later defended herself against the accusation that she had "'stripped' New York society" in *The House of Mirth* by insisting that "the little corner of its garment that I lifted was meant to show only that little atrophied organ—the group of idle & dull people—that exists in any big & wealthy social body" (L, 96–97). Her fantasy of having an organ removed suggests a kind of birth that would release one from the responsibility of buried characters, or a hysterectomy that would remove the symbol of a woman, or a castration that would remove the symbol of a man. In any case, these images help to locate the poetic fictions of cutting, penetration, and surgery that Wharton would engage in during this year—and then recall and reactivate in returning to her poetry six years later. ("Vesalius in Zante," the poem that made Wharton "want to hide under the furniture ever since I've seen it in print" in 1902, was, of course, reprinted along with the old and new verse that share its concerns in *Artemis to Actaeon*.)

In May 1909, a month after the publication of *Artemis to Actaeon*, Wharton wrote to Morton Fullerton: "The tiresome woman is *buried*, once for all, I promise, & only the novelist survives!" (*L*, 179). Wharton's promise would be kept; following the period in which she had trouble writing fiction and "perversely" took to poetry instead, she would publish *Ethan Frome, The Reef, The Custom of the Country, Summer*, and *The Age of Innocence*. In *Ethan Frome*, however, the first longer work of fiction that Wharton published after she had compiled and published *Artemis to Actaeon*, one can see that she could not so easily bury her preoccupations with fertility, the interior of the woman, the desire to see behind the veil, and the wounding of the flesh. Nor is the woman, with or without the imaginary or atrophied organ that a surgeon might cut out, so easily buried.

Ethan Frome, the novel that Wharton wrote in 1910 and 1911, is with the poems in *Artemis to Actaeon* among the few fictions that she wrote using the first-person singular; it is the only one of her novels written from this point of view.[9] The narrator of *Ethan Frome* is an engineer who carries with him "a volume of popular science . . . on some recent discoveries in bio-chemistry";[10] like the scientists Vesalius and Fallopius, he literally and figuratively stands outside of walls and closed doors which contain the secret of a hidden life. Following the pattern of the classic story of regional discovery, the narrator is an outsider, a stranger who, while spending the winter in a remote mountain village, becomes obsessed with the "striking figure" (3) of Ethan Frome. The novel represents his attempt to know the story of the "ruin of a man" (3) who is marked with the scarred wound of a "red gash" (4).

In typical gothic fashion, the unknown interior of Frome's house comes to represent *The Structure of the Human Body*; and, as for Vesalius and Fallopius, the interior contains the story of the meaning of women and the secret of life and death. However, the story at the center of *Ethan Frome*, the vision in which the narrator imagines the events of the novel, is a story of female barrenness and relentless infertility. In revealing the lifeless blossom pressed inside the book of life, the narrative reveals that the interior is empty; and it reflects on the buried characters of fiction that lie at the center of the narrator's vision.

Both the narrative frame of the novel and the frame of the introduction that Wharton added in 1922 begin by raising the question of how and what the storyteller knows. "I had known something of New England village life long before I made my home in the same county as my imaginary Starkfield" (v), Wharton begins her preface, just as her narrator begins his account of the tale by saying, "I had the story, bit by bit, from various people, and as generally happens in such cases, each time it was a different story" (3). Wharton's claims for her knowledge of New England have the sound of the sociological observer as she speaks in her autobiography of coming to "know well the aspect, dialect, and mental and moral attitude of the hill-people"; indeed, she is somewhat defensive about her knowledge of the region.[11] In *A Backward Glance*, Wharton writes that her "two New England tales, 'Ethan Frome' and 'Summer,' were the result of explorations among villages still bedrowsed in a decaying rural existence, and sad slow-speaking people living in conditions hardly changed since their forbears held those villages against the Indians" (*BG*, 153-54).

Wharton explains that these explorations were made possible by the advent of the first motorcars: "The range of country-lovers like myself had hitherto been so limited, and our imagination so tantalized by the mystery beyond the next blue hills." With a motorcar, in which she often covered as many as sixty-five miles in a day, "there was inexhaustible delight in penetrating to the remoter parts of Massachusetts and New Hampshire, discovering derelict villages with Georgian churches and balustraded house-fronts" (*BG*, 153). Insisting that she "had wanted to draw life as it really was in the derelict mountain villages of New England" (a life "utterly unlike that seen through the rose-coloured spectacles" of Mary Wilkins and Sarah Orne Jewett) she describes how "insanity, incest and slow mental and moral starvation were hidden away behind the paintless wooden house-fronts of the long village street, or in the isolated farm-houses on the neighbouring hills" (*BG*, 293–94). In writing *Ethan Frome*, Wharton desires to penetrate beyond the hills to discover a hidden mystery, to follow her imagination behind the balustraded housefronts that block her view, to see what is hidden behind housefronts and inside farmhouses. As she tries to represent the silent characters of the novel in the "fullest relief, yet without an added ornament, or a trick of drapery" (vii), she is like the engineer who visits the "side-tracked" (21) village of Starkfield; and she is also like Vesalius.

This desire to penetrate to what is hidden behind exterior surfaces is related to the predicament of a narrator who is faced with characters who insist on remaining silent. The characters in the novel, like their paintless housefronts, suggest untold suffering, but these exterior features remain shut in silence against the inquiries of the narrator. It is worth noting in this context that despite *Ethan Frome*'s origins in Wharton's explorations in the hills of New England, the first version of the tale was actually begun in 1907 as a story written in French as part of a language exercise. Having engaged a French tutor to help her master the language of her adopted country, Wharton found that her tutor was too polite to correct her French as she spoke; so she began to write a story that turned out to be about characters who are unable to express themselves. Beginning a story to master her own sense of foreignness, to bridge the quaintly literary French that Bourget called "the purest Louis Quatorze" (*BG*, 295) to the language others spoke, she wrote a story about "the deep-rooted reticence and inarticulateness" (ix) of New Englanders. Four years later this remedial exercise would become *Ethan Frome*, Wharton's novel about the inaccessibility of what goes on inside others. The story centers around a storyteller who is provoked by silence into constructing a story about unspeaking people who keep him on the outside.

Ethan Frome is at once Wharton's most intimate and distanced story of estrangement; it is a personal meditation on what it means to write books as bridges across the abyss of her greatest fears. In these fears, as they are expressed in *Ethan Frome* and *Summer*, New England becomes the landscape of Wharton's psychic past. Among Wharton's deepest fears is what she represents as a prison of inarticulateness. As we will see in Chapter 5, her ghost stories dwell on the inability to express oneself and the social isolation that deprives one of anyone to speak to. Wharton ascribed her fear of animals to a fear of the otherness that she sensed in animals' inability to speak. "I am secretly afraid of animals," she wrote just two years after completing the introduction to *Ethan Frome*; "I think it is because of the *usness* in their eyes, with the underlying *not-usness* which belies it, and is so tragic a reminder of the lost age when we human beings branched off and left them: left them to eternal inarticulateness and slavery."[12]

Like Wharton, the narrator in *Ethan Frome* is compelled to tell a story about the depth of isolation: the inarticulateness, reticence, and silence of rural New Englanders who cannot or will not tell their story to outside observers. In the preface to the novel, she describes "these figures, my *granite outcroppings*" as "half emerged from the soil, and scarcely more articulate" (vi). The novel is about the vision that the narrator must project because he cannot know the story of the New England villagers.[13] Like Life in the poem "Life," he wants to evoke a voice from the "silent tribe" and make a piece of the "mute melancholy landscape" (14) speak.

If the story of Ethan Frome takes place within a narrative frame, in a fiction within a fiction, the novel is also concerned with the meaning of frames. For the engineer who finds himself on the outside, people are like houses: Mrs. Hale is said to have "a certain wan refinement not out of keeping with her pale old-fashioned house" (9–10). Frome's longest speech, his version of "his story," appears to the narrator to be evoked by the sight of his house. The lame "ruin of a man" explains that the "house was bigger in my father's time: I had to take down the 'L,' a while back" (the "L" is the structure housing the storeroom and toolhouse that links the domestic life of the house to the daily work of the barn), and the narrator sees "in the diminished dwelling the image of [Frome's] own shrunken body" (21). Trying to penetrate Frome's mysteries, he sees the structure of the human body in the house and the structure of the house in the body. As part of his architectural reading of life in Starkfield, the narrator sees the "L" as an "image" with a particular "symbolic sense" (21). The Frome house looks "forlorn and stunted" (20) because it has lost the limb which the narrator associates with "the image . . . of a life linked with the soil . . . enclosing in itself the chief sources of warmth and nourishment" (21).

Like *Absalom, Absalom!*, a novel that is subtly yet deeply informed by Wharton's novel, there is in *Ethan Frome* a narrative drive to fill a vacuum that is figured by a house that is not quite empty, a house occupied by the dead who are still living. Each work is profoundly concerned with the problem of an interior story that cannot be told, a story that lies in the gaps of a series of stories. The lush narrative of Faulkner gains an almost assaultive force as it feeds on "outraged recapitulation." The starker story of *Ethan Frome* is also about the narrative impulse to fill in the blanks, the gaps, the story of life hidden in a mysterious house. The plot of each novel is constructed before the eyes of the reader in the fictions that its characters make up. If Faulkner's novel is in some sense like Charles Bon's coffin, an illusory structure that only gradually leads one to question whether there is a body inside the box, the house, or behind the voice of the narrative, *Ethan Frome* is also a tale that is built on conjecture.[14]

From the outset, the narrator's vision is a response to the provoking silence of Mrs. Hale, his landlady and most perceptive local informant. Every evening she regales the narrator with "another and more delicately shaded version of the Starkfield chronicle" (10). The narrator explains this chronicler's relationship to the people of Starkfield in terms that anticipate Wharton's 1922 defense of the narrator's relationship to the characters he chronicles. There, she defends her decision to have a "sophisticated" "looker-on" interpret a "people" who are "simple." She writes: "If he is capable of seeing all around them, no violence is done to probability in allowing him to exercise this faculty." Just as the narrator is supposed to "act as the sympathizing intermediary between his rudimentary characters and the more complicated minds" (viii) of Wharton's readers, Mrs. Hale is the intermediary the narrator looks to in order to understand the minds of the villagers. "It was not that Mrs. Ned Hale felt, or affected, any social superiority to the people about her; it was only that the accident of a finer sensibility and a little more education had put just enough distance between herself and her neighbours to enable her to judge them with detachment."

Because Mrs. Hale was "not unwilling to exercise this faculty," the narrator forms "hopes of getting from her the missing facts of Ethan Frome's story, or rather such a key to his character as should co-ordinate the facts [he] knew." However, although Mrs. Hale's mind is said to be "a store-house of innocuous anecdote," and although inquiries about other people usually "brought forth a volume of detail," the narrator reports in his volume that on "the subject of Ethan Frome" Mrs. Hale was "unexpectedly reticent." He finds "no hint of disapproval in her reserve" but rather "an insurmountable reluctance to speak of him or his affairs." All she will say is, "Yes, I knew them both . . . it was awful . . ." (10–11; Wharton's ellipses).

Dissatisfied with "the story" he has "pieced together from these hints," the narrator is particularly moved by "the provocation of Mrs. Hale's silence." This provocation—this calling to voice—is compounded by what he describes as "personal contact with the man" who is "the most striking figure in Starkfield though he was but the ruin of a man" (3). Frome seems to be "marked" for the narrator because of "the careless powerful look he had in spite of a lameness checking each step like the jerk of a chain" (3). In Frome's face the narrator sees "something bleak and unapproachable"; there is a look "in his face" that, the narrator surmises, "neither poverty nor physical suffering could have put there" (11). He notes that Frome's "taciturnity was respected" in town and that even when "one of the older men detained him for a word" (5), the narrator is unable to hear what Frome says. The narrator hires Frome to drive him to the train that he takes to the power plant every day, yet despite their daily contact, there is no progression in their intimacy. The narrator notes: "He never turned his face to mine, or answered, except in monosyllables, the questions I put, or such slight pleasantries as I ventured" (14).

As Ethan Frome drives in silence, he becomes the focus of the narrator's imagination; he is said to be "like the bronze image of a hero" (14). To the talkative and inquisitive passenger, the unspeaking Frome "seemed a part of the mute melancholy landscape, an incarnation of its frozen woe, with all that was warm and sentient in him fast bound below the surface." The narrator adds: "There was nothing unfriendly in his silence. I simply felt that he lived in a depth of moral isolation too remote for casual access, and I had the sense that his loneliness was not merely the result of his personal plight . . . but had in it . . . the profound accumulated cold of many Starkfield winters" (14–15).

This "depth of moral isolation" divides Frome from the narrator's efforts to know him, to get beneath his surface of muteness and silence. "Only once or twice," he writes, "was the distance between us bridged for a moment; and the glimpses thus gained confirmed my desire to know more" (15). The moment of bridging that the engineer-narrator hopes will satisfy his desire to know the inner life of Frome centers on the exchange of a book: one day the narrator accidentally leaves a book on biochemistry in the sleigh. When Frome returns the book at the end of the day, they lapse into what the narrator calls their "usual silence"; but then Frome both looks at the narrator and speaks: "There are things in that book that I didn't know the first word about" (16). Hoping for speech from Frome and some entry into a knowledge of the man, the narrator loans the book to Frome; he hopes that "the incident might set up some more direct communication between" them. He is particularly intrigued by Frome's interest in the book: "Such tastes and acquirements in a man of his condition made the contrast more poignant between his outer situation and his inner needs" (17).

Provoked by Frome's silence, the narrator looks to the medium of a book with the hope that "the chance of giving expression" to these inner needs "might at least unseal his lips." However, the narrator is disappointed in his hope that the book will provide a bridge for conversation and communication, a key to Frome's character and history. The narrator concludes that "something in his past history, or in his present way of living, had apparently driven him too deeply into himself for any casual impulse to draw him back to his kind." Frome does not refer to the book, and the narrator concludes that their "intercourse seemed fated to remain as negative and one-sided as if there had been no break in his reserve" (17). Their intercourse is as one-sided as the intercourse between a book and a reader; frustrated in his attempts to become a reader of Frome's inner story, the narrator will have to become an author.

Frome is finally provoked into speech not by the book but by the sight of his house, which they come across one day while Frome is driving the narrator the entire distance to his power plant because of a storm. The narrator describes the house as "one of these lonely New England farm-houses that made the landscape lonelier." Frome says simply, "That's my place." To the narrator's eyes the house before him is "exposed in all its plaintive ugliness" (20–21). Frome speaks of how Starkfield was "side-tracked" by the railroads, how his mother's illness was worse because "nobody ever come by here to speak of" (21–22). When the falling snow blocks their view of the house, the narrator notices that "Frome's silence fell with it, letting down between us the old veil of reticence" (22). The narrator wonders at the evocative power of the scene that has called forth Frome's speech, "as if the mere sight of the house had let me too deeply into his confidence for any pretence of reserve" (21). As they face the house covered by what is earlier described as "a sheet of snow" (7), he hopes to "rent the veil" of the structure of Frome and his house and force a way into "the secret fortalice" (*A*, 20) of his life.

The entry that the narrator seeks does occur later that day when he is invited in from the blizzard to spend the night in the Frome house. "It was that night that I found the clue to Ethan Frome, and began to put together this vision of his story." In the moments before the engineer stands on the threshold of the kitchen and projects before the reader his extended vision of the story, he sees a sign of the house above him: "a square of light trembled through the screen of snow." He makes his way through this screen and the obstacles of snow drifts, just as he tries to penetrate and pass the barriers and obstacles that blind and block his desire to know the story of Ethan Frome; here he hopes to pass from his knowledge of Frome's "outer situation" to a knowledge of his "inner needs" (24–25).

The narrator follows Frome "into a low unlit passage" to a door "marked" by "a line of light" and hears "behind the door" a "woman's voice droning querulously." Frome "opened the door" and "as he spoke the droning voice grew still . . ." (25; Wharton's ellipses). It is this moment of revelation that is presented to the reader as the narrator's fiction of the story of Ethan Frome. This is the point at which the narrative frame yields to the fiction within the fiction, the nearly 150 pages of third-person retrospective narration (separated from the frame narrative on both sides by several lines of ellipses) that we are to imagine in the moment that the narrator stands on the threshold between the hallway and the kitchen of the Frome house.

Despite his penetration into the Frome house, when the narrator returns to Mrs. Hale's house, he still seems to feel on the outside as he faces Mrs. Hale and her elderly mother: "Beneath their wondering exclamations I felt a secret curiosity to know what impressions I had received from my night in the Frome household, and divined that the best way of breaking down their reserve was to let them try to penetrate mine" (176). Mrs. Hale tells him what bothers her about visiting the Frome household and why she chooses to visit when "Ethan's off somewheres. It's bad enough," she explains, "to see the two women sitting there—but *his* face, when he looks around that bare place just kills me . . ." (177; Wharton's ellipses). Repeatedly interrupted by her emotional response to the story that she herself tells, Mrs. Hale alludes to the sledding accident in which twenty years earlier Frome and Mattie Silver were injured, but she stops: "'Oh, I don't know why I am telling you all this,' Mrs. Hale broke off, crying." After she wipes off her "spectacles," she states: ". . . I never knew myself what Zeena thought—I don't to this day. Nobody knows Zeena's thoughts" (178; Wharton's ellipses).

At the beginning of the book the narrator's desire to know more and piece together a more complete story was spurred by "the provocation of Mrs. Hale's silence" (12). At the end of the book she speaks but does not entirely let him penetrate her reserve; and the interrupted and broken off story that she does tell is finally a story about words she cannot repeat and the silence of a woman whose thoughts cannot be known—a woman who is described by the narrator as having "opaque eyes which revealed nothing and reflected nothing" (173). Both the narrator and Mrs. Hale (the two chroniclers of Starkfield) have crossed the threshold into the Frome household and stood beside the cold hearth. The narrator tries to reinterpret Mrs. Hale's reticence and reserve as her decision to wait for someone who could share her vision. He concludes, "I guessed that if she had kept silence till now it was because she had been waiting through all the years, for someone to see what she alone had seen" (177). Yet in the final pages of the book, the narrator is struck silent, speaking only on two occasions. Like Mrs. Hale, the narrator has seen how the story of Frome, Zeena, and Mattie has ended; for Mrs. Hale, the ending has been going on for over twenty years as three crippled figures sit around the winter fire. As Mrs. Hale pauses in her reticent narrative, her silences seem to become fertile for the narrator. Near the conclusion of the book he writes, "I remained silent, plunged in the vision of what her words evoked" (179).

The narrator's vision—what is presented to the reader as the story of Ethan Frome—is the story that he has pieced together from his fantasies and a few statements of fact he has gathered from and about Ethan Frome. In the opening frame, the narrator realizes that his informant Harmon Gow has "developed the tale as far as his mental and moral reach permitted"; yet, he concludes, "there were perceptible gaps between his facts, and I had the sense that the deeper meaning of the story was in the gaps" (7). The statements of Mrs. Hale, even in the account she gives at the end of the book, described as coming from "an impulse of complete avowal" (180), are repeatedly broken by ellipses. Her broken statements, provocative silence, and evocative words, all add to the sense that "the deeper meaning of the story was in the gaps."

The deeper story is the story that lies in the gaps, the story that fills in the gaps, the story that the narrator is compelled to piece together because the blankness of silence cannot be borne. To the narrator the unspeaking landscape tells part of the "frozen woe"—the muteness of the unspeaking man. The elliptically marked spaces that separate the frame from the vision and at the conclusion of the narrator's projection separate the vision from the frame might be read as the gaps that are filled with the necessary fiction. These elliptical marks that both frame and punctuate the novel—the fifty-six ellipsis points that take up nearly three full lines of type on the page that precedes Chapter 1 and the thirty-three ellipsis points that again take up three lines of type at the end of Chapter 9—indicate silences: what remains unsaid, the moments and events that remain unknown or unrecorded. These extended ellipses divide the vision so emphatically from the narrative frame that they themselves mark the distance between the narrator's description of his own experiences and his vision of Frome's story. The story itself may be seen as provoked by and framed with the silences of these ellipses.[15]

This is also the moment that the book is opened. Crossing the threshold to Chapter 1, crossing the lines of ellipses and the blank spaces on the page that are as silent as the sheets of snow, the reader enters the frame of the doorway that also represents the structure of a book. This moment is repeated again and again within the narrative of the vision that is projected before the reader in the opening of a door. In the fiction within the fiction the reader repeatedly is placed before the closed door of a silent house listening for a sound, presented with the sight of a frame marked by a line of light shining from the other side. In the story projected by the narrator, Ethan Frome on two occasions stands before the door to his house wondering about the woman who waits for him on the other side, wondering whether there is life or death behind the door. In these passages, the door opens to reveal a woman holding a light standing in the frame.

As with Vesalius, the narrator's moment of vision comes in the turning of a page, the opening of a book; yet faced with a "blank past" (*A*, 15), he must author the characters he desires to see. As with Vesalius, the vision on the page of this book of life is a vision of the inmost characters of women; yet in the narrator's fantasy the interior is empty and silent. The female body is the site of barrenness rather than fertility. The recurring image of the frame of a house or door seen from the outside tells a story about the threat of the silent woman who waits behind the door, who represents the barrenness of the life within and the horror of both women's silence and women's speech.

At the end of the novel the narrator is "silent, plunged in the vision of what [Mrs. Hale's] words evoked" (179). Yet the vision that concludes the book, the vision that Mrs. Hale evokes in her "impulse of complete avowal," is a vision about silence, a story about a preference for death and final silence over the living death filled with the sound of unquiet women: "'. . . And I say, if she'd ha' died, Ethan might ha' lived; and the way they are now, I don't see's there's much difference between the Fromes up at the farm and the Fromes down in the graveyard; 'cept that down there they're all quiet, and the women have got to hold their tongues'" (181; Wharton's ellipses). Whereas Vesalius claims to find in the "pages of the Book" he opens a "blank past" that is "a scroll on which God wrote / His word of healing" (*A*, 15), the characters that the narrator unburies in his vision spell out words of wounding.

The image of a woman behind a door (which appears in the earliest version of *Ethan Frome*, the exercise Wharton wrote in French in 1907) emphasizes repetition and replacement. "Vesalius in Zante" is partly a story about replacement, as Vesalius enters into an imaginary dialogue with Fallopius, the man who took the chair of surgery he had vacated and continued his anatomical work. In the story the narrator imagines in *Ethan Frome*, Frome falls in love with his wife Zeena's young cousin, Mattie Silver. However, his fantasies of replacing the older wife with the young girl end with a sledding accident that leaves Frome and Mattie crippled and Frome as the caretaker of the two women. The repeated images of a woman framed in a door juxtapose the figures of the old woman, Zeena Frome, and the young woman, Mattie Silver, to represent a fertility ritual gone awry. In these scenes the young woman replaces the old woman but rather than renewal or regeneration this replacement prefigures a loss of youth and fertility.

From the beginning of the narrator's vision, Frome (like the narrator himself) is represented as being on the outside. He is pictured in the snow-covered village with its "white house-fronts" visible between the trees, seeing the lit basement windows of the church with their "shafts of yellow light" (26). Frome stands on the outside looking in at the scene of the church social where Mattie Silver dances and resists the attentions of an admirer. Described as a "hidden watcher," he is said to "follow the shadowy pantomime of their silhouettes" (42–43). Returning to the house with Mattie in the narrative of the vision, he twice has a fantasy about the death of his wife: "A dead cucumber-vine dangled from the porch like the crape streamer tied to the door for a death, and the thought flashed through Ethan's brain: 'If it was there for Zeena—.'" Moments later "another wild thought tore through him. What if tramps had been there— what if . . ." (51–52; Wharton's ellipses). He kneels "on a level with the lower panel of the door" and catches "a faint ray of light beneath it." Wondering, "Who could be stirring in that silent house?" he hears "a step on the stairs" and thinks again of the tramps he imagines might have killed Zeena. "Then the door opened and he saw his wife" (52).

The woman in the doorway, standing "against the dark background of the kitchen," holds a "light, on the level with her chin [which] drew out of the darkness her puckered throat . . . and deepened fantastically the hollows and prominences of her high-boned face under its ring of crimping-pins." The narrator continues, emphasizing the contrast between Zeena and the woman he has been watching: "To Ethan, still in the rosy haze of his hour with Mattie, the sight came with the intense precision of the last dream before waking. He felt as if he had never before known what his wife looked like" (52–53). Frome and Mattie walk past the unspeaking woman into the kitchen, "which had the deadly chill of a vault" (53). At the conclusion of the scene, Frome is said to go "up in his wife's wake," in which he "followed her across the threshold of their room" (55). They "had not exchanged a word after the door of their room had closed on them," and in the silence and darkness Frome is said to hear "Mattie moving about in her room, and her candle, sending its small ray across the landing, drew a scarcely perceptible line of light under his door" (56–57).

When Frome approaches his house on the next evening, knowing that Zeena will be away for the night, he sees a "light twinkling in the house above him" (79). He finds the door locked and rattles the handle "violently" waiting to hear Mattie's step. At this point the scene of the previous night is repeated, but with a difference. "Silence answered; but in a minute or two he caught a sound on the stairs and saw a line of light about the door-frame, as he had seen it the night before." Frome is conscious of the repetition: "So strange was the precision with which the incidents of the previous evening were repeating themselves that he half expected, when he heard the key turn, to see his wife before him on the threshold; but the door opened, and Mattie faced him." She is said to stand "just as Zeena had stood, a lifted lamp in her hand, against the black background of the kitchen. She held the light at the same level, and it drew out with the same distinctness her slim young throat" (81).

Although the narrative stresses the sameness of the two images, there is an obvious difference in the image of Mattie as a young, attractive woman. Yet as the evening progresses, a series of symbolic exchanges take place through which Mattie seems to replace Zeena. Mattie brings out the red glass pickle dish that is Zeena's most valued wedding gift. (Zeena hides it in a place that she tells the virginal Mattie, "you don't know about" [124].) The cat knocks the dish off the table and it breaks into pieces. Later, Frome asks Mattie to sit in "Zeena's empty rocking-chair," and he has a "momentary shock" as "her young brown head detached itself against the patch-work cushion that habitually framed his wife's gaunt countenance."

This fantasy of replacement is shocking, however, because Frome imagines that it is Zeena he sees in the chair, not Mattie: "It was almost as if the other face, the face of the superseded woman, had obliterated that of the intruder" (89). Vesalius sees the man who took his chair of surgery as "Successor, not usurper," since "My throne stood empty" (A, 17), yet (in a surprisingly Words-worthian passage) he describes how he heard

> That younger voice, an echo of my own,
> And, like a wanderer turning to his home,
> Who finds another on the hearth, and learns,
> Half-dazed, that other is his actual self
> In name and claim . . . stood dispossessed
> Of that same self. . . .
> [A, 20]

Zeena decides to replace Mattie with a servant before she finds herself replaced by Mattie.

Increasingly in the narrator's vision, Zeena's face seems to divide Mattie and Ethan. (Even Zeena's "name threw a chill between them" [82].) Ethan finally realizes that Zeena is the obstacle that has blocked all of his goals (for instance, becoming an engineer and moving to the city); she divides him from "his kind" (17)—that is, from men and engineers, from the narrator. To Ethan Frome "all the long misery of his baffled past, of his youth of failure, hardship and vain effort, rose up in his soul in bitterness and seemed to take shape before him in the woman who at every turn had barred his way" (118). Zeena's face appears one more time to block Frome from his final goal. In the narrator's vision Frome and Mattie decide to commit suicide because they cannot bear the idea of parting. As they speed down the hill in a sled aiming for a tree, Frome swerves momentarily because he suddenly imagines the barrier of his wife's image: "Suddenly his wife's face with its twisted monstrous lineaments thrust itself between him and his goal and he made an instinctive movement to brush it aside" (170). This apparition of Zeena thwarts the suicide, leaving Frome and Mattie crippled to live out a death in life.

Surrounded by images that recall and repeat the images that Frome has seen framed throughout the narrative vision, Frome and Mattie decide to kill themselves. After Zeena decides to send Mattie away, Mattie fears a future in which she will be replaced by a new servant girl, just as she had seemed to replace Zeena. She says to Frome: "And there'll be that strange girl in the house . . . and she'll sleep in my bed, where I used to lay nights and listen to hear you come up the stairs" (166). To Frome, these "words" are said to be "like fragments torn from his heart." From the fragments he puts together the story from his perspective and imagines the obstacle of Zeena: "the hated vision of the house he was going back to—of the stairs he would have to go up every night, of the woman who would wait for him there" (166).

Mattie and Ethan focus on different women, yet the characters of these fantasies once again seem to play on interchangeable or superimposed images. Mattie, the young woman who replaces Zeena in the narrator's version of Ethan's fantasies, fears being replaced herself by a young woman; yet by the end of the story, when the narrator crosses the threshold out of his vision into the Frome kitchen, Mattie herself has become the hated vision of the woman who waits for Frome. In the narrator's vision, which occurs in a moment that condenses twenty-four years in a flash (just as the narrator imagines Ethan in the graveyard imagining fifty years passing "in a flash" [80]), Mattie becomes the dreaded woman who waits at home. The accident that cripples Mattie and Ethan and prevents their escape leaves Mattie a broken and soured old woman, another version of Zeena. She becomes the woman with the querulous voice behind the door. *Ethan Frome* finally tells the story of the horror of sameness and repetition in an unchanging life. This is the meaning of the converging images of the women behind the door, the silent women framed by various perspectives. The repetition carried out between young women and old women does not mean regeneration. Replacement means barrenness as a young woman becomes an old woman.

In the narrator's vision, Frome finds Zeena's silence "disquieting" (36). He fears that Zeena's silence is the "inevitable result of life on the farm" (72), and he worries that she will become like his mother, who had become increasingly silent. "His mother had been a talker in her day, but after her 'trouble' the sound of her voice was seldom heard, though she had not lost the power of speech. Sometimes, in the long winter evenings, when in desperation her son asked her why she didn't 'say something,' she would lift a finger and answer: 'Because I'm listening'; and on stormy nights, when the loud wind was about the house, she would complain, if he spoke to her: 'They're talking so out there that I can't hear you'" (69). When Zeena "too fell silent," Frome recalls "his mother's growing taciturnity, and wondered if Zeena were also turning 'queer'" (72–73). Eventually they stop speaking: "When she spoke it was only to complain and to complain of things not in his power to remedy; and to check a tendency to impatient retort he had first formed the habit of not answering."

When he sees her standing in the kitchen door, he arrives at the more disturbing supposition that Zeena's "silence seemed deliberately assumed to conceal far-reaching intentions, mysterious conclusions drawn from suspicions and resentments impossible to guess" (72–73). After Zeena turns out Mattie he realizes that "there had never been anything in her that one could appeal to" (118). He interprets Zeena's silence at this point, the absence in her, as a poisonous presence: "She was no longer the listless creature who had lived at his side in a state of sullen self-absorption, but a mysterious alien presence, an evil energy secreted from the long years of silent brooding" (117–18).

Zeena replaces Ethan's mother but only by assuming her disquieting silence. Her silent brooding suggests that there is something more malignant in the cycle of repetition and replacement. The brooding silence reproduces itself in an infertile cycle of repetition as Mattie, too, becomes the silent woman framed in the door and then the woman "droning querulously" behind the door at the end of the opening narrative frame. At the end of the story the young woman has become the old woman; Zeena and Mattie are joined behind the door of the Frome kitchen, where both women's silence and women's speech are horrible. Each has become the vessel of inarticulateness, filled with what Wharton calls in another context "old, unsatisfied hates."[16] Ironically, Ethan initially asked Zeena (his mother's caretaker) to marry him after his mother's death because of his fear that he might have "'gone like his mother'" (70); but in the cycle of repetition and the repetition of sameness, Ethan, too, becomes "like his mother."

The accident that turns Mattie into Zeena leaves Ethan with a wound on his forehead that is described as a "red gash" (4). Inscribed with the mark and wound of womanhood, he also is left lame; the limpness of his crippled leg is compared by the narrator to the removal of the "L" from the farmhouse. Not surprisingly, the loss of these limbs has been seen as the cutting out of some organ: a sign of castration and the loss of masculine power. With none of the eroticism of the reed in "Life" or the lover in "Margaret of Cortona," Frome seems to bear the mark of a wound even before the accident: in the narrator's vision at one point Zeena's "retort was like a knife-cut across the sinews and he felt suddenly weak and powerless" (117). The loss of the "L" that the narrator thinks of as the nurturant center of the house marks Frome's wounded condition. It suggests, however, that he is not only a feminized or wounded man; he also is the figure of a barren woman, a crippled caretaker who is incapable of bearing progeny. He has removed the part of the structure of his house that the narrator believes is a symbol of "the chief sources of warmth and nourishment . . . the actual hearth-stone of the New England farm" (21).

Harmon Gow describes the Frome farm as "'bout as bare's a milk pan when the cat's been round.'" Frome feeds and provides for his family, but in Gow's words, "His folks ate up most everything"; in Gow's view, "When a man's been setting round like a hulk for twenty years or more . . . it eats inter him" (13). Frome is a caretaker whose milk has dried up; he has been consumed and left empty. The interior that the narrator tries to penetrate and imagine contains emptiness, the absence of a nurturant center. In the accident Frome seems to internalize the obstacle he crashes into; he becomes joined with what at first seems to be "a rock or some huge mass . . . lying on him." This "monstrous load on him" is described as "moving with him as he moved" (171). Frome is joined once again to the silent rock. One of the characters that Wharton calls "*granite outcroppings . . .* half-emerged from the soil, and scarcely more articulate" (vi), he once again seems "part of the mute melancholy landscape" (14). In becoming a mutilated and crippled man, he also seems to becomes the barren and infertile woman. Ethan Frome himself represents the failure of fertility and the insistent barrenness described throughout the novel.[17]

The vision of *Ethan Frome* is finally a vision of unrelenting infertility. The suicide attempt that cripples Mattie and Ethan is prefigured in the smashed pickle dish, "the bits of broken glass" that Zeena discovers and holds "as if she carried a dead body . . ." (128; Wharton's ellipses). The shattered pickle dish that is Zeena's most treasured wedding gift and the dead cucumber vine that makes Frome imagine Zeena's death are emblems of a lost or past fertility. The smashed glass under the foot of the bridegroom should symbolize the loss of virginity and the beginning of fertility; but the pickle dish, used or unused, can symbolize infertility only. The dead cucumber vine that "dangled from the porch like a crape streamer tied to the door for a death" (51) suggests the past fertility of an umbilical cord that now marks the barren interior of a house deprived of its "actual hearth-stone" (21). One critic has remarked that a "cucumber is no more than a pickle," yet without entering the ongoing critical debate about the vegetable symbols in the novel, it is essential to acknowledge that a pickle is a preserve that cannot reproduce itself.[18] In the magical supper that Frome and Mattie have during their evening alone, the pickle dish and pickles form a display, a kind of rehearsal, for the eroticized scene of the accident that finally breaks the vessel of the young woman's body and preserves her in infertility. Both the broken pickle dish and the breaking of the body of the young woman suggest the horror of fertility rituals gone awry.

In the narrator's vision, the fragments of the dish and Mattie Silver's body cannot be put back together again. Only the narrator's story projected onto the shards of the past (which he claims to have gathered "bit by bit") can form the mocking semblance of a whole and seamless narrative.[19] The narrative also has an ominous inevitability and circularity. *Ethan Frome* has its beginning in its ending: at the beginning of the story the narrator describes the crippled Frome, whose face "looks as if he was dead and in hell now!" (6). The vision of the narrator must end in this hell because the future of the story he tells will always be in the past. In the introduction Wharton remarks that her "tale was not one on which many variations could be played" (vi). The narrator's vision may contain variations, but the story must end in the same place, around the same barren hearth.

Frome's "bleak and unapproachable" face and the unspeaking presence that makes him seem "a part of the mute melancholy landscape" also suggest the impenetrable structures of the novel itself, structures that are repeatedly fig-ured in the image of the closed door. The closed door, like the unspeaking Frome and the "provocation of Mrs. Hale's silence," compels the narrator to piece together his fiction. However, the end of the vision suggests an impene-trable exteriority that extends to the narrative structure of the book itself. Intent on suicide, the characters of the narrator's vision encounter the existence of an impenetrable boundary; they drive "down on the black projecting mass" (170). We have seen that key points of the narrative are marked by the opening of the door. At one crucial moment the narrator says, "Then the door opened and he saw his wife" (52). The description of the sled ride down the hill ends with the broken phrase: "and then the elm . . ." (170; Wharton's ellipses). The elm that Frome and Mattie smash into is the door that does not open. Like the narrative structure of the novel, it frames and estranges the characters, sealing them in their heartless life: the living death that the narrator knows is behind the door of the Frome kitchen. The narrator projects his vision at the moment we are to see behind the closed door, and his fiction fills the elliptical center of the book, but what we see is an image of brooding silence.

In his desire to penetrate the mysteries of Ethan Frome, the narrator wants to act like "Life" in the "reed-bed," who (in the words of the reed) "rapt me from my silent tribe, / Pierced, fashioned, lipped me, sounding for a voice" (*A*, 7).

Yet even in his vision, even in the identification which might lead Wharton's authorial stand-in to feel that (in Vesalius's words) "that other" "on the hearth" "is his actual self," he finally imagines Ethan Frome not merely as taciturn but as a writer who cannot write. On the night before he decides to commit suicide with the woman who "seemed the embodied instrument of fate" (167), Frome reads a message from Mattie Silver and tries to write a letter.

The narrator, who has imagined that Frome took "a year's course at a technological college at Worcester, and dabbled in the laboratory with a friendly professor of physics" (27), pictures him in his "cold dark 'study'" with his books and "an engraving of Abraham Lincoln and a calendar with 'Thoughts from the Poets.'" Earlier in the empty kitchen Frome has found "a scrap of paper torn from the back of a seedsman's catalogue, on which three words were written: 'Don't trouble, Ethan.'" He reads "the message again and again." Although at first "the possession of the paper gave him a strange new sense of her nearness," he realizes that "henceforth they would have no other way of communicating with each other" besides "cold paper and dead words!" (129–30). (Later when Mattie says, "You must write to me sometimes," he responds, "Oh, what good'll writing do?" [158].) He starts to write a letter to his wife telling her that he has run off with Mattie, but after reading "the seductive words" of an advertisement for trips to the West, he has second thoughts: "The paper fell from his hand and he pushed aside his unfinished letter" (134).

Like Lily Bart, Frome tries to imagine an alternate plot for his unbearable story, but leaving his letter unfinished, he resigns himself to being a prisoner for life. Moments before Ethan and Mattie decide to attempt suicide, Mattie produces the unfinished letter: "She tore the letter in shreds and sent them fluttering off into the snow" (157). Soon her "words" of desperation are "like fragments torn from his heart" (166), and the failed suicide attempt leaves both of them torn and shattered. Mattie's elliptical message written on "the seedsman's catalogue" emphasizes Ethan's failure as a seedman. Later he strokes her hair so that the feeling of it "would sleep there like a seed in winter" (166), but these winter seeds bear no fruit. Like the woman whose "page" is torn by Vesalius, her life will be "ripened" only to a "bud of death"—in the words of Wharton's Margaret of Cortona, a "lifeless blossom in the Book of Life" (*A*, 14-15, 26). Writing under the calendar with 'Thoughts from the Poets,' Frome sees only "cold paper and dead words." Here the seeds of writing, despite the possibility of "seductive words," are not the seeds of the pomegranate—either the maternal fertility of Demeter or the transgressive eroticism of Persephone. The words on the seed catalogue cannot even lead to an alternate underworld of death. The cost of vision in this story is a failure of mortality as well as immortality as the characters are left imprisoned in a living death. The "symbol of a man, / The sign-board creaking o'er an empty inn," that pictures the barrenness of both women and rock-bound New England in the novel is also a sign for the failure of words to generate life.

In 1917, while living in Paris, Wharton published her second New England novel, *Summer*. *Summer* and *Ethan Frome* clearly were related for her: *Ethan Frome* in its original French version was entitled "Hiver" while Wharton playfully called *Summer* the "Hot Ethan."[20] The claims that Wharton made about the authenticity and realism of *Ethan Frome* were based in part on the evidence of *Summer*; this book about "the same class and type" (*BG*, 296) of the people of Starkfield, she claimed, demonstrated her knowledge of the taciturn New Englanders. Both novels depict mature men who are crippled by self-inflicted injuries (Ethan Frome and Lawyer Royall) and are attracted to young maidens (Mattie Silver and Charity Royall) who are at the threshold of sexual maturity. Both novels portray murderous crones (Zeena Frome—"the greatest hand at doctoring in the county" [13]—and the abortionist Dr. Merkle) who on some level threaten to rob the young women of their fertility. Both narratives, following the pattern of novels of regional discovery, begin with the arrival of strangers from the city (the engineer-narrator and the student of architecture, Lucius Harney) who are curious about the lives of the village folk. Both of these outsiders are distinguished by their obsession with the remnants of the past: both stories and unpainted, abandoned houses. In an allusion to the proximity of the novels, *Summer* includes the detail that Charity was almost sent to a boarding school in "Starkfield."[21]

However, despite the correspondences between Wharton's New England novels, *Summer* marks a change in Wharton's view of New England, as well as her view of America and the world. The two novels do not represent parts of the same seasonal life cycle; rather, they represent different readings of the significance of the old woman behind the door. In the impenetrable and infertile landscape of *Ethan Frome*, sexual passion offers a siren call to smash upon the rocks. The narrator constructs a vision of a cold hearth and a rocky landscape that offer the lure of death, a world barren of the fruit that would generate other fruit. *Summer* includes the possibility of cyclical passage that would escape dangerous repetition, a more fertile world that offers growth, flowering, fruit, and a reseeding that takes place after a period of necessary dormancy. Unlike the vision of *Ethan Frome*, *Summer* represents a cycle of growth in which repetition is welcomed as necessary renewal.

Both *Ethan Frome* and *Summer* present the problem of inarticulateness. However, whereas Wharton wrote in her autobiography, "It was not until I wrote 'Ethan Frome' that I suddenly felt the artisan's full control of his imple- ments" (*BG*, 209), in writing *Summer*, she asserts, she felt that she entered "the inner scene." In the Paris of 1916, surrounded by war, death, hunger, and disease, Wharton wrote a novel about a region that she described as "as remote as possible in setting and subject from the scenes about me." Elizabeth Am- mons observes that "the initial effect of the war was to make [Wharton] think even harder and more deeply about her native land, almost as an anthropolo- gist thinks about strange, distant cultures."[22] Wharton's memory of the compo- sition of *Summer* is a memory of a penetrating vision: "The tale was written at a high pitch of creative joy, but amid a thousand interruptions, and while the rest of my being was steeped in the tragic realities of the war; yet I do not remember ever visualizing with more intensity the inner scene, or the creatures peopling it" (*BG*, 356).

Ethan Frome represents a world of infertility and death in life in which the inarticulate landscape of New England and the family around the hearth are seen from the outside as constraining, crippling, and entrapping. *Summer* offers a revision of the story that Wharton tells in *Ethan Frome*. Unlike the narrator of *Ethan Frome*, who emphasizes his exteriority to the world of his story, the articulate Lucius Harney does not try to view the people of the village from a superior vantage point; Harney is not blocked by a closed door. He crosses both architectural and morphological thresholds. A student of the structure of houses, he plans to "open a round window in [the] wall" (*S*, 94) of the library where Charity works, and he causes Charity to experience "the wondrous unfolding of her new self, the reaching out to the light of all her contracted tendrils" after living "all her life among people whose sensibilities seemed to have withered for lack of use"; because of Harney, love becomes for Charity "bright and open" (*S*, 180).

Harney is literally the agent of fertility in the novel: he makes Charity pregnant, and he also causes her to imagine the mother who gave her away. From the moment he appears at the beginning of the novel, the idea of what he might see in her focuses Charity Royall's interest in her own identity. Although she "had never felt any curiosity" about herself and her past, "only a sullen reluctance to explore the corner of her memory where certain blurred images lingered," and although "she hated more than ever the fact of coming from the mountain," she finds that "even the hateful things had grown interesting because they were a part of herself" (*S*, 59).

Even before she is pregnant, when she sees a woodcutter from the mountain, her place of origin, Charity has a visceral image of her mother as being like herself. She felt "a tremor of surprise to think that some woman who was once young and slight, with quick motions of the blood like hers, had carried her in her breast and watched her sleeping." As in *Ethan Frome*, the images of Charity and her once young mother seem to merge with each other and with the image of an old woman in a doorway. "She had always thought of her mother as so long dead as to be no more than a nameless pinch of earth, but now it occured to her that the once-young woman might be alive, and wrinkled and elf-locked like the woman she had sometimes seen in the door of the brown house that Lucius Harney wanted to draw" (*S*, 59–60). This transformation from the dangerous repetition of the images of Zeena and Mattie framed in the doorway to the fertile repetition in which Charity is able to imagine a mother as well as herself as a mother is related to Wharton's experience of the war.

Wharton acknowledges that the war offered her insights into a world she wouldn't ordinarily have seen. At the opening of *French Ways and Their Meaning*, she writes: "The world since 1914 has been like a house on fire. All the lodgers are on the stairs in dishabille. Their doors are swinging wide open, and one gets glimpses of their furniture, revelations of their habits and whiffs of their cooking, that a life of ordinary intercourse would not offer."[23] During the war, Wharton made eight trips to the French countryside, including several trips to the front. In her book *Fighting France*, she records her impressions of villages where she saw "uprootings and rendings apart," the destruction of what she calls "the obscurest human communities." Here, the doors are open, but exposure is a violation of privacy and identity. Wharton writes of one village where "not one threshold is distinguishable from another." What appears at a distance to be a "living city" is "seen to be a disembowelled corpse." Wharton continues: "Every window-pane is smashed, nearly every building unroofed, and some house-fronts are sliced clean off, with the different stories exposed. . . . In these exposed interiors the poor little household gods shiver and blink like owls surprised in a hollow tree. A hundred signs of intimate and humble tastes, of humdrum pursuits, of family association, cling to the unmasked walls."[24] With "housefronts" torn away and walls "unmasked," Wharton may well have seen "different stories exposed" in both meanings of the phrase. Wharton transformed the "different stories" she saw exposed into stories. These stories represent the inner scene, the different story that Wharton both exposed and covered over in *Summer*.

In *A Backward Glance* Wharton defended the realism of her New England novels by arguing that *Ethan Frome* and *Summer* are depictions of life "as it really was in the derelict mountain villages," the "grim places" where "insanity, incest and slow moral and mental starvation were hidden away behind the paintless wooden house-fronts" (*BG*, 293–94). By 1916, Wharton literally had seen behind the housefronts. She not only had seen life exposed, she had been forced to reexamine the bases of human life—an examination that forced a reevaluation of her ideas of tradition as dangerous repetition and family as entrapment. In *Summer*, Wharton conceives a world beyond the New England village that is similar to the war-torn world she reports having seen in *Fighting France* where, of the "thousand and one bits of the past that give meaning and continuity to the present—of all that accumulated warmth nothing was left but a brick-heap and some twisted stove-pipes."[25] Indeed, the language that Wharton uses in *Summer* to describe this world very specifically recalls her descriptions of the devastation of war in *Fighting France*.

In her depiction of the outlaw colony on the mountain in *Summer*, Wharton seems to reflect on the heaps of rubble that in *Fighting France* represent the fragments of the past that once gave "meaning and continuity to the present." The mangled stove that represents all that is left of "the accumulated warmth" in *Fighting France* becomes a figure for the body of the mother in *Summer*. On the mountain, Charity arrives at her mother's house, the "most ruinous of the sheds" where she notices that a "stove-pipe reached its crooked arm out of one window and the broken panes of the other were stuffed with rags and paper" (*S*, 245). Moments later Charity sees the dead woman lying across "a squalid bed" in "ragged and disordered clothes." This mother in dishabille appears to be the bodily version of the stove that was her only possession; we read: "One arm was flung up above her head, one leg drawn up under a torn skirt that left the other bare to the knee: a swollen glistening leg with a ragged stocking rolled down about the ankle" (S, 248). Both the body of the mother and the body of the stove, emblems of potential warmth, are cold.

At this moment in *Summer*, Wharton, who describes her realism as a removal of drapes and cloaking language, depicts the desire to conceal the realm of animality, to cover the helplessly exposed body of the mother. Charity, Wharton writes, "tried to compose her mother's body. She drew the stocking over the dreadful glistening leg, and pulled the skirt down to the battered upturned boots. . . . She looked at her mother's face, thin yet swollen, with lips parted in a frozen gasp above the broken teeth. There was no sign in it of anything human: she lay there like a dead dog in a ditch" (S, 250). Charity tries to compose her mother's body in two ways: to draw the stocking over the dreadful leg and physically cover the body, and to rewrite by repetition, to compose her mother's body as she assumes the body of a mother. Having exposed a mother who is dead and like an animal, *Summer* seems to want to compose a mother: to compose a mother's body that is human because the child will be born of and into human tradition.

Wharton emphasizes her point by having Charity attribute the growth of her child to a series of remembered events rather than to a single physical act. The list of these moments in the narrative comprises a recapitulation of the events of the novel—what Charity calls "each separate stage of her poor romance." Wharton seems to insist almost literally that she is writing a life into existence. Charity's description of this child which will be born of human experience and feeling also suggests the hope of animation for the composed text. Wharton writes: "These things were hers; they had passed into her blood, and become a part of her, they were building the child in her womb; it was impossible to tear asunder strands of life so interwoven" (S, 231).

The memories that comprise tradition, the "bits of the past" that give "meaning and continuity to the present," are missing on the mountain. Charity initially is comforted by the thought that by going to the mountain she is repeating her mother's life. Charity imagines her mother's sympathy: "She herself had been born as her own baby was going to be born; and whatever her mother's subsequent life had been she could hardly help remembering the past, and receiving a daughter who was facing the trouble she had known" (S, 240). Yet, on the mountain, where she expected to find shared meaning Charity finds people without understandable relationships "herded together in a sort of passive promiscuity in which their common misery was the strongest link" (*S*, 259). The "savage misery of the Mountain farmers," an animal struggle for warmth and food, seems to divide the outlaw colony from any sense of relation—with each other or any other place or time. "Charity's bewildered brain laboured with the attempt to picture her mother's past, and to relate it in any way to the designs of a just but merciful God; but it was impossible to imagine any link between them" (*S*, 258–59). By the end of *Summer*, Wharton has replaced an animal mother with a human mother. As we shall see in the next chapter, this is in part accomplished through a new story about class and gender relations that insists on the benevolence of the father as the authority that shelters human civilization and the hierarchical relations that in Wharton's view redress the world and give it meaning.

At the closing of *Ethan Frome*, the last circle of hell is a house in which "the centre, the actual hearth-stone of the New England farm" (21) has been removed and the only fire is surrounded by the maimed and infertile voice of feminine complaint. In her depiction of the mountain colony in *Summer*, Wharton draws a world in dishabille, a world which offers no warmth or continuity—where there is no hearth with the stability and stasis that the hearth signifies. The place she fears, represented by "the Mountain" and its outlaw colony, is a place beyond the hearth—where cold, hunger, and deprivation interfere with any conception of tradition, human relationship, or memory beyond the struggle for animal survival. At the same time, however, Wharton imagines an alternative and readjusts her idea of the place of the New England village and farmhouse in the scheme of civilization. By 1916, Wharton has seen behind the door; she has seen the world in dishabille behind the "housefronts." In her revision of *Ethan Frome*, Wharton writes a story that reveals the horror of exposed stories, and in doing so she rehabilitates the figure of the woman behind the door.

THREE

Wharton and Wilkins

Rereading the Mother

(Summer)

But all its chief delight was still
On roses thus itself to fill,
And its pure virgin limbs to fold
In whitest sheets of lilies cold:
Had it lived long, it would have been
Lilies without, roses within.
—Andrew Marvell, "The Nymph
Complaining for the Death of Her Fawn"

Ethan Frome and *Summer* caused more controversy than any of Edith Wharton's books, and Wharton remained defensive and even embattled about them, particularly about *Ethan Frome*. In 1922, eleven years after the publication of *Ethan Frome*, Wharton added an introduction to the novel; in what she calls a "brief analysis—the first I have ever published of any of my books," Wharton seeks to explain why she chose her topic and why she "selected one form rather than another for its embodiment."[1] Four years later, after learning that Scribner's was planning to append a new introduction written by someone else, she wrote to inquire about the proposed author and to preempt her publisher's plan. "I am rather fond of 'Ethan Frome,'" she wrote, "and I should not care to have it spoken of by anyone who does not understand what I was trying to do."[2] Wharton's investment in her novel and in her own 1922 introduction is also suggested in yet another introduction that she wrote in 1936 to preface a dramatization of *Ethan Frome*. This introduction, in which, as Cynthia Griffin Wolff remarks, Wharton speaks of her characters with "a sense of insistent presence . . . that does not emerge when she refers to any other of her fictional creations,"[3] repeats the claim that Wharton makes in both the 1922 introduction and her 1934 autobiography, *A Backward Glance*, that she had "lived among" her characters "in fact and imagination [for] ten years."[4]

Wharton's investment in the characters and place of her fiction add to the sense that the 1922 introduction to *Ethan Frome*, which is concerned with negotiating questions of authorial distance and intimacy, stands before the text as both a personal and a literary defense. It is a defense that insists on the author's familiarity with the region that she is depicting. "I had known something of New England village life long before I made my home in the same county as my imaginary Starkfield," begins Wharton, "though during the years spent there, certain of its aspects became much more familiar to me." Wharton remarks that even before her actual experience with these folk, what she calls her "final initiation," she had been suspicious of the descriptions of the region she had found in "the New England of fiction" (*EF*, v). Wharton "justifies" her book by presenting it as a corrective to this New England of fiction. Insisting on both her own knowledge of the region and the greater realism of her fiction, Wharton presents *Ethan Frome* as a work that was polemical from the outset: an antidote for the regional view that she associates in particular with the female local colorists.

A Backward Glance reiterates and continues this explanation for Wharton's motivation in writing both *Ethan Frome* and *Summer*. "For years," she writes, "I had wanted to draw life as it really was in the derelict mountain villages of New

England, a life even in my time . . . utterly unlike that seen through the rose-colored spectacles of my predecessors, Mary Wilkins and Sarah Orne Jewett" (*BG*, 293). Wharton contrasts their rose-tinted view (and what she describes in the introduction as the sirens' "rainbow veils" [*EF*, vii]) with her own unfiltered view—a view which focuses on the unpainted housefronts that stand throughout the region. Yet even these housefronts, stripped of color and illusion, are for Wharton structures of concealment; behind their walls and doors are lives of inarticulate desperation: this is the repressed New England that Wharton claims to uncover in her own depiction of the region. She wants to reveal the New England of the villages that she saw in the first decade of the century: "still grim places, morally and physically" with "insanity, incest and slow mental and moral starvation . . . hidden away behind the paintless wooden house-fronts" (*BG*, 294).

In the introduction to *Ethan Frome*, Wharton describes her "uneasy sense" that the "New England of fiction bore little—except a vague botanical and dialectical [*sic*]—resemblance to the harsh and beautiful land as I had seen it." She continues: "Even the abundant enumeration of sweet-fern, asters and mountain-laurel and the conscientious reproduction of the vernacular left me with the feeling that the outcropping granite had in both cases been overlooked" (*EF*, v). The New England of fiction, according to Wharton, was a careful compendium of vegetation and spoken language that formed a deceptive covering which had only a "vague . . . resemblance" to reality, constituting a false or illusory realism. Despite its faithful rendering of plants and vernacular, this deceptive surface formed a sensual exterior that pleased the reader while obscuring less pleasant realities.

In a densely coded allusion, Wharton refers to the "insinuating wraiths of false 'good situations,' siren-subjects" that threaten to lure the novelist's "cockle-shell to the rocks." She writes: "I knew well enough what song those sirens sang, and had often tied myself to my dull job until they were out of hearing—perhaps carrying a lost masterpiece in their rainbow veils" (*EF*, vii). Wharton introduces these metaphors to assert that she was never once tempted by "false . . . siren-subjects" while writing *Ethan Frome*; the subject of her story is not the false subject that is veiled by the illusory colors of the rainbow but "the first subject I have ever approached with full confidence in its value" (*EF*, vii). The terms of the introduction imply that the accounts of benign vegetation and dialect are the alluring yet resisted stories carried in the "rainbow veils"; the sirens, the singing monsters who were once the flower-gathering handmaidens of Persephone, are by implication those writers who have constructed a fictional New England. These writers have stayed on the surface gathering flora and fauna rather than descending into the underworld with Persephone. As sirens, their seductive, female voices lure listeners to smash themselves on the rocks. Their songs of feminine illusion mask hard reality and threaten to wreck the unwary on the outcropping rocks.

As we have seen, for Wharton "the real" is a gender related, sexually charged category. She claims to have felt as a child that the truth was in opposition to what she called the feminine desire "to make things prettier and prettier."[5] In the world that Wharton describes, truth is associated with structure, which is realized in part by its opposition to decorative or concealing surfaces. *Ethan Frome* is itself a story of what to Wharton was a "truth"; it represented to her the hardness of life lived on the New England bedrock, in the shallowness of the American soil. She insists that "the theme" of her story of Starkfield "must be treated as starkly and summarily as life had always presented itself to [her] protagonists" (*EF*, vi). She describes herself as being "fascinated by the difficulty of presenting [the story of Ethan Frome] in the fullest relief, yet without an added ornament, or a trick of drapery or lighting" (*EF*, vii). In choosing what she saw as truth and realism, then, Wharton consciously opposed herself to what she saw as the theatrical setting of a feminine aesthetic—what she called in her essay "The Great American Novel" "the tottering stage-fictions of a lavender-scented New England."[6]

Both *Ethan Frome* and *Summer* provoked vociferous and personal responses. Although Wharton's first venture into the New England of fiction was generally well received, some readers found that Wharton's exposé of New England village life was too realistic and pessimistic. In *A Backward Glance*, Wharton notes that parts of *Summer* were "received with indignant denial" and *Ethan Frome* was "frequently criticized for being 'painful'" (*BG*, 294–95).[7] Wharton counterattacked by accusing her public of wounded narcissism: she blamed the outcry against these books on a feminized audience who liked their image as they saw it in the works of the female local colorists. Wharton attributes the anger of these readers to the disturbing power of her realism, arguing that "not the least vociferous [of her critics] were the New Englanders who had for years sought the reflection of local life in the rose-and-lavender pages of their favorite authoresses" (*BG*, 294). In self-defense, she admonishes these readers for neglecting to look into Hawthorne's pages (apparently forgetting, in her desire to ally herself with a more respectable popular tradition, her earlier criticism of Hawthorne for offering "the prismatic hues of a largely imaginary historic past").[8]

However, what seemed to have disturbed Wharton the most was not the charge that her novel was too grimly realistic but rather the accusation that it was not realistic enough—the accusation that its author could not have known either New England village life or a man such as Ethan Frome. In addition to "vociferous" remarks from dissatisfied readers, some of Wharton's friends expressed skepticism about her relation to her subject. Even Henry James, apparently identifying Wharton with the narrator of *Ethan Frome*, playfully questioned the plausibility of her presence at the scene of the fiction; the idea that Wharton, like the engineer-narrator at the beginning of the novel, might have been sent anywhere by *her* employers particularly strained his idea of verisimilitude.[9] Wharton did not seem to have been greatly concerned by the letters she received from textile workers following her publication in 1907 of *The Fruit of the Tree* correcting her mistakes with mill terminology and the work process of the factory, although she had actually visited textile mills and observed workers in order to research this novel. In the cases of *Ethan Frome* and *Summer*, Wharton is more defensive and she seems to find herself in a debate about what both she and the character of her narrator knew about the people and place depicted in her New England of fiction; she insists on her "ten years in the hill-region" and her knowledge of "the aspect, dialect, and mental and moral attitude of the hill people" (*BG*, 296), and on the privileged point of view of her narrator, the visiting male engineer who gets "the story, bit by bit" (*EF*, 3) from his limited informants.[10]

Yet I have been suggesting that this debate about the question of Wharton's relation to New England (whether she was an outsider or an insider, whether *Ethan Frome* and *Summer* were too realistic or not realistic enough, whether they were covered in rainbow veils or naked in their stark truth) was to some extent a debate that Wharton sought out in entering the New England of fiction. Wharton's polemic against "the rose-and-lavender pages" of the "favourite authoresses," her project of resisting "the rose-coloured spectacles of my predecessors, Mary Wilkins and Sarah Orne Jewett" (*BG*, 293–94), suggests Wharton's resistance to the sentimentalism of the local colorists, but it also conceals the degree to which she found herself in competition and dialogue with these predecessors even as she was writing her fictions of New England.

Critics have noted Wharton's intention to revise and correct the local color tradition. Blake Nevius finds her disparaging judgment of Wilkins and Jewett to be unjustified[11] while others have affirmed Wharton's criticisms of the local colorists, suggesting (as Wolff does) that the "venerable regionalists of New England" offered "a prettified spectacle of billboard art, a pastoral land seen through awestruck eyes."[12] Critics have accepted or disagreed with Wharton's condescending judgment of the local colorists, but finally few have considered the tradition of local color writing to be of more than minor importance to Wharton's work. The importance of the relation between Wharton and the female American authors she dismissed has not been fully acknowledged.[13]

Beyond the significance of *Ethan Frome* and *Summer* as highly charged psychic landscapes for their author, Wharton's defensiveness about her New England of fiction can be explained by her complex and ambivalent investment in the rose-and-lavender pages of the local colorists from whom she insisted on distinguishing herself. I will suggest that in reading Mary Wilkins, Wharton would have found resonances, even striking echoes, of her own fiction; and more important, that Wharton found in Wilkins's stories both provocation and inspiration for her second New England novel, *Summer*. In particular, I will argue that *Summer* is a revision and rewriting of Wilkins's important story, "Old Woman Magoun." We saw in Chapter 2 that Wharton is concerned in *Summer* with a daughter's efforts to compose her mother's body: both to bury the body of the mother and to compose a mother with her own body, a mother who could live in the orderly valley world of the father rather than the animal world of the mountain. In this chapter I will argue that the story Wharton tells in *Summer* of the burial of a mother named Mary is also written as a rejection of the women's stories represented by Mary Wilkins.[14] Wharton enters into a dialogue with Wilkins in order to bury a mother and to tell the story of a murderous mother. "Old Woman Magoun" plays a crucial role in both Wharton's and Wilkins's work because it is itself a story about the failure of mothers' stories and the failure of mothers to provide a place on earth for the potential female poet. In these terms, Wharton's literary struggle with the authoress she named as a "predecessor" is also a debate about the failure of realism.[15]

In comparing Wharton and Wilkins at the end of this century, one at first has the sense that a great distance separates them. This distance comes from the association of Wilkins with the New England of the nineteenth century and of Wharton with the New York of the twentieth century. Wharton, who was born in New York and who often wrote about the social relations of urban elites, is clearly influenced by her knowledge of what that world would become, even when she is writing about nineteenth-century America. In *The Custom of the Country*, Wharton explores the tensions in the birth of a twentieth-century America by dramatizing the destruction of the traditional culture of Washington Square by rootless invaders from the Midwest.

Yet even in her references to the denizens of Old New York as "survival[s]" destined to go down before a new order and "aborigines" who live in an embattled household called "the 'Reservation,'" Wharton presents an urban world that is separate from the rural and continuing "pasts" which are presented in *Ethan Frome* and *Summer*.[16] Starkfield and North Dormer, as the names of the towns of these novels suggest, are isolated and "side-tracked" (*EF*, 21). Each lies beyond the lines of the railroad, the artery to other worlds which will bring to each story an urban and educated visitor who in a sense journeys from the twentieth century into the nineteenth century. As we have seen, in both *Ethan Frome* and *Summer* the stranger arrives to discover the past, uncovering not only the social codes but also the hidden and intense passions of the taciturn and inarticulate New Englanders. These visits from the twentieth century mirror Wharton's own passage in writing *Ethan Frome* and *Summer*. Although, as I will argue, Wharton was more than aware of Mary Wilkins as a contemporary, she recognized Wilkins as a figure from an earlier literary and cultural tradition.

The publication in 1887 of her first volume of short stories, *A Humble Romance and Others*, established Mary Wilkins at the age of thirty-five as one of the most popular and respected authors in America. In her time Mary Wilkins was thought of as an "original," a writer who sprang from the New England villages she wrote about, uninfluenced by other writers. Despite the recognition that she received from her contemporaries as a founder of the nineteenth-century realist tradition, the story of her life remained obscure (romantically and in some ways intentionally obscure) even during her lifetime. Writing as early as 1899, Charles Miner Thompson told the readers of the *Atlantic* that little was known about the origins of Mary Wilkins: Thompson states that he has not even been able to find the date of her birth.[17] Thirty years later, in his article, "New England Stories," published a year after Wilkins's death in 1930, F. O. Matthiessen puts the year of Wilkins's birth as 1862 rather than 1852. (Coincidentally, 1862 was the year in which Wharton was born.)[18]

Despite any obscurity about the past, Wharton would have been aware of the presence of Mary Wilkins. Wharton referred to Wilkins as a "predecessor" (*BG*, 293), but Wilkins was in many ways Wharton's contemporary and even her rival on the national and international literary scene.[19] *A Humble Romance and Others* brought Wilkins an international reputation; her second volume, *A New England Nun and Others*, published four years later in 1891—the same year that Wharton published her first short story—drew the attention of Henry James, who expressed his enthusiasm for both collections to her English publisher.[20] Although Wharton, like readers today, might have associated Wilkins with a nineteenth-century tradition, she could not entirely relegate her to an archaic literary past. As prominent women writers, Edith Wharton and Mary Wilkins Freeman were linked together—and, as John Macy noted, even excluded together. In the 1912 preface to *The Spirit of American Literature*, commenting ironically on the list of twenty-eight men admitted to the National Institute of Arts and Letters, Macy remarked: "There is no other genius that one would nominate for a place in it, except Mrs. Wharton and Mrs. Freeman, who cannot be admitted because they are women." In 1926, both authors were among the first women to be admitted to the National Institute of Arts and Letters.[21]

The English critic W. L. Courtney provides some clues to the respective places of Wilkins and Wharton in the imagination of the public at the turn of the century. In 1904, in discussing Wilkins and Wharton as authors of "sub-genres" in the introduction to his book, *The Feminine Note in Fiction*, he states that the work of Mary Wilkins (to whom he devotes an entire chapter) is a "brilliant" example of the "miniature or genre novel." Courtney writes that while "no one could describe [Edith Wharton] as a great novelist," her work is both memorable and interesting: a female variety of the psychological novels associated with Henry James.[22] One year later, in 1905, with the publication of *The House of Mirth*, Wharton's place in the literary hierarchies would begin to change. Indeed, the praise she received for her work resembles the highest compliments paid to Mary Wilkins. *The House of Mirth* was praised by an eighty-two-year-old T. W. Higginson as a work which could be ranked with *The Scarlet Letter*.[23] A decade earlier in 1894, Arthur Conan Doyle had announced his approval of Mary Wilkins's novel *Pembroke* in almost identical terms, calling it "the greatest piece of fiction since *The Scarlet Letter*."[24]

As Wharton rose to prominence in the early twentieth century and Wilkins, although still prolific, began to lose her reputation as a fine artist, Wharton herself drew their names together. As we have seen, she defended her fiction of New England as depictions of the region that were meant to supplant the earlier "New England of fiction" which she condemned for displaying only a superficial realism: faithful descriptions of local language and plants. Four years after Wilkins's death, Wharton specifically named Wilkins (along with Jewett) as one of the "predecessors" with whom her view of New England was at odds. We have seen that Wharton's argument with the work of the local colorists is presented as an argument about realism and the proper realist view of New England. It also concerns the question of who can claim to be the originator of American realism, who can claim to be the first woman writer to confront a complacent New England with the harsh and unpleasant truth. Claiming that insanity, incest, and isolation are missing in the texts of Jewett and Wilkins, Wharton argued that her New England books revealed the hidden lives of misery that went on concealed behind the paintless house-fronts.

Wharton was to some extent recognized as a realist who was not afraid to deal with taboo themes, sometimes to the outrage of her readers. After the publication of Wharton's second collection of stories in 1901, an indignant reader wrote the author to demand, "Have you never known a respectable woman? If you have," she continued, "in the name of decency write about her!" (*BG*, 126). *The House of Mirth* charmed a large reading public, but like other of Wharton's novels, it also offended the sensibilities of some readers. William Dean Howells explained the failure of the dramatization of the novel by saying, "What the American public always wants is a tragedy with a happy ending" (*BG*, 147). Fearful of the direction her writing might be taking, Wharton's friend Charles Eliot Norton warned her as she was writing *The Custom of the Country* that "no great work of the imagination has ever been based on illicit passion" (*BG*, 127). (Apparently he forgot such works as *Phèdre*, *Madame Bovary*, and *Anna Karenina*).

However, Wharton's claim that the local color writings of Jewett and Wilkins covered over the grim realities of New England village life are not consistent with either the texts themselves or her contemporaries' reading of them. One could argue that torrid elements exist even in the relatively gentle coastal world of Sarah Orne Jewett's Dunnet Landing; they explicitly characterize the inland world depicted by Mary Wilkins. Within the reach of the imagination and memory of Jewett's Dunnet Landing are the "strange strayin' creatures," the "scatter-witted," the melancholy female hermits, and those that "hive" away from society.[25] Wilkins's works provide more frequent examples of New England gothic. Her first novel, *Pembroke*, published in 1894, is built around the focal image of an unfinished and unpainted house. Edward Arlington Robinson commented specifically on this aspect of *Pembroke*, which included (among other shocking scenes) depictions of a mother who beats her son—he dies shortly after—and rejects her unwed, pregnant daughter.[26]

Indeed, prior to the turn of the century, Wilkins's work was directly associated by critics with depictions of insanity, isolation, and even the taboo topic of incest. Writing in the *Atlantic* in 1899, Rollin Lynd Hartt quoted Wilkins's own statement about "the tropical intensity of the rural New Englander" and suggested that the snowcapped mountains of the natural world of New England might erupt with the force of volcanoes. Hartt's readers may have been offended or at least surprised by his frequent references to incest as the major problem in the region. In his article, "A New England Hill Town," he argued that incest could be blamed for the existence of the perverse and strange characters that could be found both in New England and in Mary Wilkins's fiction.[27]

Other critics, as well, respected Wilkins as an accomplished realist author. Charles Miner Thompson, for example, criticized *A Humble Romance* for favoring the bickering of families over the pleasant manners of the genteel classes. He complained that the stories were based on female gossip and favored female narrators, but he still praised Wilkins as a compelling realist: "This book came with the force of a new revelation of New England to itself. The literary merit was remarkable. The short terse sentences, written in the simplest, homeliest words, had a biting force. Its skillfully lavish use of homely detail, always accurate, always significant, gave it an astonishing reality." Thompson accepted Wilkins's stories as depictions of reality, but only of a narrow segment of the region—not New England in its entirety.[28] In "New England Stories," an article published one year after Wilkins's death, F. O. Matthiessen recalled that Wilkins may have been too realistic for some readers: "The readers of the eighties and nineties often found Miss Wilkins morbid and depressing. They asserted that her view of the New England nature was one-sided and distorted, that the people she drew were not typical but were mere exaggerations."[29]

It is ironic and perhaps revealing that the reception of Mary Wilkins's writing was not unlike the reception of Edith Wharton's New England fiction. In "New England Stories"—an article that Wharton read—Matthiessen describes Wilkins's rejection by her readers and praises her courage as a writer. The "biting force" and "astonishing reality" that Thompson remarked in Wilkins's work were also singled out by Matthiessen. "Her vision is uncompromising," he wrote; "her extraordinary power comes from the unflinching directness with which she sets down even the harshest facts."[30] These descriptions praised the early works of Wilkins in precisely the same terms that Wharton sought to describe her accomplishment in *Ethan Frome* and *Summer*. In the case of these texts, however, Wharton seems to have been compelled to praise the realism of her fictional world herself.

Wharton was complimented on the realism of her books about New York society; but to her dismay, she was considered by many to be an outsider when writing about the culture of New England. Matthiessen's comment that *Ethan Frome*—which he called "the outstanding story about New England written in the twentieth century"—was "the work of a woman whose life has been passed elsewhere"[31] evoked a defensive response in Wharton's autobiography. Writing of her attempts to disprove legends about herself and the writing of *Ethan Frome*, she notes that "in an article by an American literary critic, I saw 'Ethan Frome' cited as an interesting example of a successful New England story written by someone who knew nothing of New England!" (*BG*, 296). In "Regionalism in American Literature," Mary Austin rather subtly put Wharton in her place by naming *The House of Mirth* as Wharton's regional novel.[32] John Crowe Ransom, an advocate of regionalism, perhaps best represents the response of those who were offended by *Ethan Frome*. Writing about the novel in his 1936 article "Characters and Character," Ransom notes that since Wharton herself was an outsider to the region she could only tell the story through the voice of a character who was an educated visitor. In Ransom's description of what would have happened if Wharton had attempted to present the narrative from Ethan Frome's point of view, there is also an implicit criticism of the engineer-narrator; Ransom suggests that Wharton's "sophisticated sensibility" would have "falsified the whole."[33]

Wharton's expressions of confidence in the fictional narrator of *Ethan Frome* reflect some anxiety about the place of both the narrator and herself in relation to New England village life. She argues that her narrator, the visiting engineer, has a complex mind and is therefore capable of seeing further into the story than his simple informants (who are capable of telling only partial stories). When Ransom quotes from the narrator's statement in the prelude to the first chapter of *Ethan Frome* that he had found a clue to Frome and "began to put together this vision of the story," he actually misquotes Wharton's text and substitutes the word "version" for "vision."[34] However, Ransom's mistake is a politically astute misreading. Despite the increasing authority that Wharton claims for her realism, despite the superior access to the truth that she claims for her narrator in her later defense of the book, the "vision" in the end cannot be "truth"; it can only be a "version."

In the years following the publication of her New England novels, Wharton was increasingly insistent about the truth of these texts. To corroborate her "vision" or "version" of New England, she argued that her friend Walter Berry (an international lawyer and the head of the American Chamber of Commerce in Paris) "who was as familiar as [she] was with the lives led in those half-deserted villages" had "talked the tale over page by page" with her (*BG*, 296). She also defended the veracity of the story of the mountain colony in *Summer* (a story that provoked much public ire) by insisting that she had heard the story directly from the rector of the Episcopal church at Lenox (*BG*, 294). Both *Ethan Frome* and *Summer* were accepted as fine literary accomplishments, but Wharton seemed most concerned with arguing their harsh and biting realism. This realism was important to her because her view of New England had come to represent her view of history: both her own past and that of the human community.

Despite her stated distaste for the local colorists, then, and despite her wish to distance herself from them, Wharton would have been aware of Mary Wilkins as an important and respected literary figure. Indeed, I am suggesting that as she read critics who praised the realism of Wilkins's work and even contrasted that work to her own fiction, Wharton may have conceived of the older author as a rival. Wilkins was in any case a *predecessor*—to use Wharton's own description of Wilkins and Jewett in its strongest sense.[35] In the early years of her career Wharton would have seen Wilkins as a woman who had already achieved a wide reputation as an important American author. Even detractors of Wilkins found in her work an original use of language, an economy and exactness of speech, which was itself a contribution to a tradition of American realism. Wharton herself explains that Wilkins and "the New England of fiction" were on her mind when she wrote *Summer*. I am arguing that the very motivation for writing *Summer* came at least in part from Wharton's response to Wilkins's work. In writing *Summer*, Wharton was drawn into an overdetermined dialogue with a woman who stood as both literary mother and rival. This dialogue was mediated through a particular story entitled "Old Woman Magoun," the finest story in *The Winning Lady and Others*, a collection of Wilkins's late stories published in 1909.

Reading "Old Woman Magoun," Wharton would have found herself inscribed in a textual dialogue with her predecessor since the story appears to contain textual echoes of Wharton's own earlier work. The story of Lily Barry in "Old Woman Magoun" recalls the heroine of *The House of Mirth* in more than just the name of the central female characters. Lily Barry and Lily Bart each represent the flower of society, emblems of purity and beauty who will be destroyed by the society that created them; each, as her flower name suggests, is cut in full bloom, dying a virgin death.[36]

Despite their widely different social settings, the stories of Lily Barry and Lily Bart have much in common. Both are daughters of traditionally prominent families in the terms of their closed societies. Both are essentially orphans, gaining the "fatherly" interest of men only when their beauty is translated into a sexual commodity. These men (in the case of Lily Barry, the biological father who never previously noticed her existence) see the physical charms of the young women as objects for trade in order to discharge gambling debts. Lily Bart is expected by Gus Trenor to compromise her virtue for debts she has incurred unknowingly while allowing him to "speculate" for her in the stock market, whereas Lily Barry's biological father, Wilkins's story implies, has claimed his daughter to use in payment of his gambling debts. Both suffer at the hands of men who are predators rather than protectors. Lily Barry and Lily Bart end up poisoning themselves by their own hands. As they die, they are comforted by images of maternity: Lily Bart embraces herself, imagining she is holding Nettie Struther's baby, and Lily Barry is told that her mother has prepared a room for her in a heaven where her doll will become a living baby. Although both Lilys are thought by some to be tainted (Barry through her inheritance of her father's blood and Bart through implied sexual compromise), they die virgin deaths contemplating the pure and revered ideal of the mother with child in the absence of sexual defilement.

Whether or not Mary Wilkins read *The House of Mirth*, which attracted considerable attention when it was published in 1905,[37] the relation between the fictional Lily Barry and Lily Bart is not necessarily one of direct influence; there is a cultural and perhaps an archetypal level of associations that situates each of the stories as a version of a traditional story about female virtue. These early twentieth-century narratives, with their story of gambling, exposure by the male protector, threat of sexual violation, and subsequent suicide of the virgin woman, suggest a nineteenth-century version of the rape of Lucrece.[38] What gives the stories their specifically nineteenth-century character is that, unlike Lucrece, these women do not necessarily take their lives intentionally; both Lily Bart and Lily Barry are presented as powerless victims of society. The significance of drinking in "Old Woman Magoun" situates the story in the genre of popular stories about female virtue and the depravity of alcoholic male fathers who betray their paternal trust. Male instability, brought on by alcohol, was one of the mainstay themes of temperance melodrama. Both Wharton and Wilkins seem to suggest a more fundamental instability: marriage, as it affects the lives and deaths of Lily Bart and Lily Barry, is itself seen as a form of gambling for women.[39]

It is likely that Wharton would have recognized some connection between her own work and "Old Woman Magoun," which she probably read (perhaps for the first time) during World War I. *Summer*, which I will argue is intimately related to Wilkins's story, was published in 1917. Before we consider in detail the textual evidence from this period, however, it is worth noting that there is a trace of another connection between Wharton and Wilkins that might have caused Wharton to hear part of Wilkins's personal story during the war years. Among Wharton's closest friends in Paris during the war and afterward were Royall and Elesina Tyler. Wharton saw Elesina Tyler daily as they worked to organize a series of charity projects providing food, clothing, shelter, and work for the refugees Wharton called the "homeless." She also spent a great deal of time with Royall Tyler, the namesake and great grandson of the famous American playwright.

Less than forty years earlier in Brattleboro, Vermont, the Tyler family had hired an Eleanor Wilkins to care for the invalid Pickman Tyler, allowing the impoverished woman to join the household with her husband and only surviving daughter (who was then in her late twenties). When Eleanor Wilkins died two years later, her daughter Mary left the Tylers. Within only months Mary Wilkins began a meteoric literary career.[40] The reputation of this daughter of a servant in the Tyler household as the author of the first realist fiction about

Yankee village life placed her in a lineage of authors that began with the most famous of the Tylers: the first Royall Tyler, recognized as America's first playwright, was famous for his invention of the "stage Yankee." Wilkins might have been remembered for having fallen in love with one of the Tyler sons; at the least, she would have had a place in the Tyler family's literary genealogy. Given these associations, along with the many textual echoes which, I will show, link Wilkins's stories to *Summer*, it may not be a coincidence that Wharton's central characters in that novel are named "Charity Royall" and "Lawyer Royall" and that the first Royall Tyler was famous both as a playwright who made use of Yankee dialect *and* as a lawyer (indeed the first Chief Justice of the Vermont Supreme Court).[41]

Summer incorporates major themes and textual details from several stories in Wilkins's *The Winning Lady and Others*, yet it is most closely related to "The Joy of Youth" and "Old Woman Magoun." Both of these narratives, like *Summer*, tell the stories of girls who are at a dangerous threshold of sexual maturity. Like *Summer*, "The Joy of Youth" suggests a season of youth in which a boy and girl taste the "joy of the present."[42] Wilkins's central device in "The Joy of Youth" of calling her young male protagonist "the Boy" (even after he has been named) is repeated by Wharton in the opening pages of *Summer* where Charity Royall is referred to simply as "a girl" and Lucius Harney is called a "young man."[43] In both Wharton's and Wilkins's texts, these terms imply the universality of the experience of first love, a social threshold with a seasonal quality which Wilkins calls "The Joy of Youth" and Wharton calls *Summer*. The "Boy," Guy Russell, appears to be a prototype for Wharton's character, Lucius Harney. Both Harney and Russell are handsome strangers who have come to visit a female relative who happens to be the wealthiest woman in the village. Each imagines himself to be the protector of a young girl who tells him the story of a threatening father.

This plot seems particularly important to Wharton. She draws on the four pieces in *The Winning Lady and Others* that are concerned with class conflict and threats of violence by drunken and abusive men—in particular by predatory fathers. These stories reveal a middle-class fear of the poor, suggesting that among poor families there are unbridled and uncontrolled men who threaten their own daughters and are threats to the daughters of the comfortable classes as well. "Little-Girl-Afraid-of-A-Dog" and "Joy of Youth" tell stories about the character Emmeline Ames, first as a young girl and later at puberty, focusing on her fears of a poor and indolent family, the Ticknors.

In "Little-Girl-Afraid-of-A-Dog," Emmeline is sent to bring eggs to the needy family, which lives in a "very drunkard of a house, a habitation which had taken upon itself the character of its inmates. It was degenerate, miserable, and oblivious to its misery" (WL, 51). The young girl fears both their vicious dog and Mr. Ticknor. In this story Mr. Ticknor is absent, forced by the "temporary goad" of near starvation to plough for a neighbor; he is described as "plodding lazily along behind a heavy old horse" (WL, 53). In "The Joy of Youth," set some years later, this "plodding" man takes the place of the formerly threatening dog. Emmeline's early fears of dog and man seem justified when Mr. Ticknor mistakes her for his daughter Violetta and pursues her in a "staggering run" (WL, 88), threatening to beat her. Since Mr. Ticknor is known for his "brutal treatment of his family," Emmeline fears that he might "in his drunken rage be brutal to her." In Emmeline's flight from this father in pursuit of his daughter, Wilkins writes, "Her slim legs skimmed the ground as lightly as a bird's," and "she flashed through the ranks of the fodder-corn like a frightened bird." Stalked by the drunken and weaving Mr. Ticknor, "Emmeline heard the heavy padding footsteps nearer and nearer" (WL, 89).

Emmeline Ames's flight as a child-woman imaged as a frightened bird is a response to the violence of unwanted male desire; it echoes female acts of flight in classical texts, particularly the Muses' winged escape from the threat of sexual violation (as narrated in Minerva's song in Book 5 of Ovid's *Metamorphoses*).[44] In "Joy of Youth," however, Emmeline Ames fears the plodding figure of a brutal and brutelike father. What Mr. Ticknor intends besides beating Emmeline "within an inch of her life" is not known; Emmeline's fear might be explained in part by a scene of mistaken identity that occurs earlier in the story. Emmeline wears a love charm in her shoe, and when she meets an elderly man who has had three wives, she shudders to think that the herb might point to him as her intended husband. The old man, "fond of little girls," insists that she is his granddaughter, and he takes sticky candy from his pocket and "thrust[s] the sweet into Emmeline's mouth with a loud cackle of enjoyment" (WL, 78). The old man's unwanted candy, like the threat of Mr. Ticknor, is a physically odious intimacy that Emmeline wishes to escape. As Mr. Ticknor pursues her, threatening to beat her, Emmeline "heard the name of Violetta coupled with alarming threats" (*WL*, 89). His cries name Emmeline's fears of violence and violation.

Among the most important scenes in both Wilkins's and Wharton's texts, and also of central importance for linking "Joy of Youth" and "Old Woman Magoun" to *Summer*, are the threshold scenes. *Summer* begins with a girl's hesitation on a doorstep. In an almost ritualistic expression of fear, she withdraws into the house at the sight of a young man and pretends to "look for the key that she knew she had already put in her pocket" (*S*, 8). This scene, as Wolff notes, anticipates the actual moment of sexual initiation late in the novel.[45] In these narratives about female puberty, thresholds symbolize sexual and social boundaries that the young girl crosses as she becomes a mature woman; they are also emblematic of the female body which, after opening in the sexual act, becomes the door of birth. Wilkins's Emmeline Ames and Lily Barry and Wharton's Charity Royall share a particular threshold experience; they are each threatened at doorways by "fathers" who are drunk or smell of whiskey.

The climax of "The Joy of Youth" occurs when Emmeline escapes the stalking man: "There was a moment of breathless agony; the key turned very hard" (*WL*, 90). (Wilkins's scene reads as an uncanny transcription of one of Wharton's deepest fears: what Wharton herself described in her autobiography as the "choking agony of terror" that she felt at the doorway to her mother's house. To forestall this fear Wharton kept her latchkey at hand to shorten the moment of entry.)[46] In "Old Woman Magoun" the predatory father reappears when Nelson Barry arrives to claim his daughter Lily and faces Old Woman Magoun, who at first fills "the doorway with her firm bulk." Nelson Barry says ominously, "You know me of old. No human being can turn me from my way when I am once started in it. You may as well let me come in" (*WL*, 259). Wharton's Charity Royall in a similar scene blocks her guardian's entry. Charity assumes that Lawyer Royall has come for the key to the liquor cabinet which she had hidden, "but when she saw him in the doorway, a ray from the autumn moon falling on his discomposed face, she understood" (*S*, 28).

Wharton continues: "For a moment they looked at each other in silence; then as he put his foot across the threshold, she stretched out her arm and stopped him." To Lawyer Royall's plea that he is a lonesome man, Charity replies, "Well I guess you made a mistake, then. This ain't your wife's room any longer." Unlike Emmeline Ames and Old Woman Magoun, Charity is not "frightened"; she "simply felt a deep disgust" (S, 29). The threatening "fathers" in all of the stories are described in animal terms. Mr. Ticknor is known to be "brutal," and Nelson Barry is to Old Woman Magoun a "rebellious animal" and a "tiger" (WL, 259, 255). When Charity tells Harney of Lawyer Royall's sexual advances, Lucius Harney calls him "the damned hound! The villainous low hound!" (S, 168).

Another textual relation between these female characters is suggested in the similarity of their dress. Both Charity and Emmeline wear white, as if to symbolize their virginity, and both Charity and Lily wear muslin. This may have been the dressy fabric that was available to girls of their class, but the fact that all of the girls also wear white straw hats wreathed with roses suggests a level of resemblance that goes beyond fashion or conventional symbolism. Lily Barry's greater immaturity is suggested by the decoration of her hat with rosebuds, an indication that she will be picked before her bloom. Lily Barry never progresses to a romance or the stage of a romance that is marked for Emmeline and Charity by a white silk dress. Charity's dress, with its "virgin whiteness" (S, 187), signifies her passage from virginity and her difference from the North Dormer maidens who wear muslin. At this point in the narrative, in a characteristic sexual joke, Wharton already has recorded the loss of Charity's rose-trimmed hat; the loss of this hat, which has a distinctive "cherry lining," has exposed Charity to Lawyer Royall's charge that she is a "bare-headed whore" (S, 151).

Wilkins's "Little-Girl-Afraid-of-A-Dog," "The Joy of Youth," "Eliza Sam," and "Old Woman Magoun," and Wharton's *Summer* all depict female characters who feel threatened by animality or violence as they face vicious dogs, rats, or drunken men. In *Summer*, the inhabitants of "the Mountain" are compared to "nocturnal animals" (S, 248), "vermin in their lair" (S, 86), and a "miserable herd" (S, 261). These texts typically depict sharply divided worlds in which the lower classes are associated with animality. In "Little-Girl" and "Eliza Sam," there are successful efforts to domesticate the threat: the dog is trained and named by Emmeline Ames, and Eliza Sam reforms the drunken lawyer by destroying his liquor.

All of the stories move toward an ending that asserts the value of domesticity, and all (except for "Old Woman Magoun") conclude with the prospect of marriage; *Summer* ends with the marriage actually taking place. In *Summer*, marriage is the one ordering relationship that distinguishes the inhabitants of

North Dormer from the people on the mountain who "herd together like the heathen" (71). Yet for Wharton, marriage is part of the cold, hard reality that follows the heat of romance. At the end of *Summer*, "in the cold autumn moonlight," Charity and Lawyer Royall return to a familiar threshold: "the door of the red house" (*S*, 291). "Joy of Youth" ends with a proposal of marriage, but it is clear that the author leaves her characters in an illusory frame, outside of reality: "Happiness stood still in their heaven." The lovers are said to see "more than there really was because each saw with each other's eyes" (*WL*, 98). "Joy of Youth" does not include such a domestication; the presence of the brutal father yelling "Violetta" is not resolved, although Emmeline Ames does manage to escape the violence and possible violation that threatens her. Indeed all of Wilkins's female protagonists in these particular stories are "saved" either by themselves or by other women.

"Old Woman Magoun," however, does not succeed in domesticating the threat of male animality; it ends in death rather than in marriage. Indeed Old Woman Magoun, who tells Lily that she would not hurt her except to "save your life," allows Lily to inadvertently poison herself to save her from sexual violation—and perhaps even from sexual knowledge. "Old Woman Magoun" takes place in a backwoods world where marriage is in question, where (even in the civilized valley) it is the women who are tamed, trained to serve and obey their keepers like domesticated animals.

Among the best pieces that Wilkins wrote after the turn of the century, "Old Woman Magoun" lacks the smoothness and the finely tuned, controlled voice of the best of her earlier stories. The disjunctures of form, the stark juxtapositions that underline Wilkins's depiction of a world of divisions—particularly in the troubled relations between men and women—nonetheless make "Old Woman Magoun" the most disturbing and perhaps the most powerful story that Wilkins ever wrote. Although there are echoes of various stories from *The Winning Lady and Others* in Wharton's text, I will argue that it is this story that most engaged and preoccupied Wharton while she was writing *Summer*. I would like to read Wilkins's story of virgin death and child murder in order to suggest why and how Wharton rewrote "Old Woman Magoun" as if it were a troublesome nightmare, a disturbing dream of her own that had to be retold.

The major threat in the town of Barry's Ford seems to lie in the past and its power to foretell fatalistically the story of the future. Lily Barry replaces her mother (who dies after giving birth to her) by becoming the child of her mother's mother, Old Woman Magoun. Fearing that Lily will continue to follow the pattern of her mother's life, Old Woman Magoun tries to protect Lily by prolonging her childhood. She fears that Lily, like her mother, will become the prey of men, and she particularly fears Lily's father, the man who seduced Lily's mother. In the story, Old Woman Magoun sees her fears being realized in what seems to be an inevitable cycle of repetition. Nelson Barry comes for his daughter. The story suggests that he has promised Lily to the man who walked her to the store. Lily describes this man to her grandmother as a "handsome man," just as her father is described as a "middle-aged man" who is "still handsome" (WL, 246).

The grandmother's worst fear is realized. Lily has become the object of sexual exchange, a bargain between two men, probably even contracted in the store. The terms of what is to be Lily's sexual initiation are left unstated. What Old Woman Magoun foresees for her granddaughter is the fate of the child's dead mother—supposed sexual violation, early pregnancy (perhaps outside of marriage), and death. In order to save her from the sexual violation (or at least the early sexual experience) that seems inevitable, Lily's grandmother attempts to have her adopted by a childless couple in the valley town of Greenham. The potential father to whom she appeals refuses to adopt Lily because he believes that the child has inherited bad blood from her biological father.

In the opening description of "Old Woman Magoun," Wilkins emphasizes that the terrain of her story is a landscape of division.[47] Two worlds are described, as if divided and in opposition, but the landscape suggests that these worlds (which are also divided within) have dangerous similarities. The town of Barry's Ford is described as caught between two landscapes of deceptive waves: "Below it the hills lie in moveless curves like a petrified ocean; above it they rise in green-cresting waves which never break" (WL, 243). Between the static landscapes which give only the illusion of motion flows the "turbulent" Barry River which divides the backwoods community of Barry's Ford from the market town of Greenham.

The images with which Wilkins introduces her story suggest a dangerous similarity between the mountain and valley worlds, despite their division by the fast-flowing river which is itself a symbol of geographical and social division. The division of "Old Woman Magoun" initially seems to be between upland and lowland, mountain and valley, the backwoods and inaccessible hamlet of Barry's Ford and the civilized market town of Greenham. The essential division in the story, however, is between the power that men have to control women's lives and the powerlessness of women to help themselves and each other. The world of "Old Woman Magoun" is finally infertile: the division between the men's and women's culture is a deadly division which results in the sacrifice of the daughter. Lily is allowed to die, and thus both "couples" in the story, and therefore both communities, remain childless. This childlessness represents the cutting off of both tradition and the future.[48]

The story begins with a temporary victory by Old Woman Magoun; meant to overcome dangerous divisions, however, this accomplishment finally under-lines the division between the worlds of men and women. Old Woman Magoun attempts to get the men to build a bridge which will connect Barry's Ford to the civilized valley town of Greenham: "'If I were a *man*,' said she, 'I'd go out this very minute and lay the fust log. If I were a passel of lazy men layin' round, I'd start up for once in my life.'" Old Woman Magoun is a powerful figure; the men are said to cower visibly before her: "The weakness of the masculine element in Barry's Ford was laid low before such strenuous feminine assertion" (*WL*, 244).

There are, of course, powerful men in both the mountain hamlet and the valley town. Lily's earthly future appears to be in the hands of such men, her two potential fathers: Nelson Barry of Barry's Ford and Lawyer Mason of Greenham. "Lily's father, Nelson Barry" is described as "the fairly dangerous degenerate of a good old family." The description continues: "Nelson's father before him had been bad. He was now the last of the family, with the exception of a sister of feeble intellect, with whom he lived in the old Barry house. He was a middle-aged man still handsome. The shiftless population of Barry's Ford looked up to him as to an evil deity" (*WL*, 246). Barry is the biological and satanic father, pressing his paternal authority and claims only when his daugh-ter becomes nubile. As in Poe's "The Fall of the House of Usher," the "good old [Barry] family" (*WL*, 246) of Barry's Ford has become degenerate through stasis, a stasis which suggests a world weakened by too much sameness. Like Roderick and Madeline Usher, the Barrys have become so linked to a single location that their family name has come to identify the place. As with the inhabitants of the house of Usher, this stasis, fortified by Nelson Barry's half-witted sister, also seems to suggest incest and degeneration. The Barry house, like the house of Usher, is inhabited by a brother and sister, yet they are without the ethereal, feminized qualities of the spiritual Ushers. In contrast, Nelson and Isabel Barry are very much of the body.

Barry alternates in the story as a representative of Satan and as a predatory animal. From the outset, when Nelson Barry swears and walks away from Old Woman Magoun, who is insisting that the men build the bridge, there is a struggle between men and women—a conflict of both brute force and tradition. The battlelines are drawn throughout the story in a struggle that is played out in the fight over the fate of Lily. Domestication is a key issue: the struggle turns upon the question of who will train whom. Thinking of Barry, Old Woman Magoun imagines Lily "in the clutch of a tiger" (*WL*, 255), and when Barry appears at the door she looks at him "as she might have looked at a rebellious animal she was trying to tame" (*WL*, 259). Previously, when Lily entered the store with the stranger, Barry's chair fell "on all fours" (*WL*, 252) as if assuming the stance of an animal.

Nelson Barry, the leader of the "shiftless" (*WL*, 246) (that is, unmoving) whiskey-drinking and tobacco-chewing male populace of Barry's Ford, expects women to obey him. His female accomplice, the half-witted Isabel, is likened in the narrative to a trained animal. "She had learned with her feeble intellect some tricks, like a dog. One of them was the mixing of sundry drinks. She set the tray on a little stand near the two men, and watched them with her silly simper" (*WL*, 263). This is the sister that Nelson Barry claims will look out for Lily, insisting, "She knows more than you think." Isabel is depicted as an obedient animal who awaits and follows the orders of men. This can mean nothing to Old Woman Magoun but "wickedness," a characterization that Nelson Barry does not deny. He responds: "A knowledge of evil is a useful thing. How are you going to avoid evil if you don't know what it is like? My sister and I will take care of my daughter" (*WL*, 261–62).

Nelson Barry's first acknowledgement that Lily is his daughter is presented as a scene of seduction in which the father attempts to tame Lily as if she were a fearful animal: "Her father bent down and, for the first time in her life, kissed her, and the whiskey odor of his breath came into her face." When Lily shrinks from him, rubbing her mouth violently with her cotton handkerchief, Barry blames Lily's fear of him on "that damned old woman." Smiling again at Lily, he names her as his child: "I didn't know what a pretty little daughter I was blessed with." After saying this, he "softly stroked Lily's pink cheek under her hat." Lily no longer shrinks from his touch: "Hereditary instincts and nature itself were asserting themselves in the child's innocent, receptive breast." He then seductively offers her "sticks" of candy and suggests that to carry them she should "throw away" her doll: in other words, both her play child and her childhood. The narrator notes that there is "something mature" in Lily's expression of refusal: "the reproach of a woman" (WL, 253–54).

Old Woman Magoun, we are told, "poured the goodness of her own soul into this little receptive vase of another" (WL, 245). In conversation Lily also repeats her grandmother's contemptuous view of men: "Men ain't very nice, be they?" she asks. Old Woman Magoun answers: "No, they ain't, take them all together" (WL, 265). However, Lily's susceptibility is suggested by the fact that this is still a question to her. Just as Old Woman Magoun attempts to tame Barry and retain her influence over the child, Barry in the store begins his efforts to tame Lily so that she, like his half-witted sister Isabel, may learn the tricks of serving men. The warming response of Lily's "hereditary instincts and nature itself" suggests that despite her initial resistance she is vulnerable to seduction. When Nelson Barry offers to exchange her doll for the symbolic sugar sticks, he initiates a series of exchanges that would eventually result in a real baby.

The Barry brother and sister, both figures of evil for their sex, are the only couple mentioned in Wilkins's depiction of Barry's Ford. Although the brother and sister's relationship may remain unconsummated, the story suggests that Isabel is Nelson Barry's accomplice in wickedness; it is possible that Barry's sister, like his daughter, might have been used as an object for barter. Isabel's half-wittedness in itself suggests that she may be the product of an incestuous union. Wilkins suggests that Barry is not above taking advantage of their obedience to his authority and using both daughter and sister as sexual objects to trade. Nelson Barry is not a protector of women. He never acknowledged Lily's mother as his legal wife, and he does not claim Lily as his daughter until she is fourteen years old.

If Nelson Barry is the satanic and biological father—threatening seduction and the deadly entry into reproduction that was the fate of Lily's mother—then Lawyer Mason is the civilized father, chosen by Old Woman Magoun to overcome by law the hereditary claim of Nelson Barry. The marriage of Lawyer and Mrs. Mason represents an institution that protects women; by adopting Lily, the couple could be a father and mother who would shelter Lily from the abuses of a predatory father. Although they are the only married couple represented in "Old Woman Magoun," the Masons also represent a broken story: they have lost a daughter, their only child. While the grandmother tries unsuccessfully to persuade Lawyer Mason to adopt Lily, Mrs. Mason serves Lily "a plate of cake, a glass of milk, and an early apple" (WL, 267) in the garden.

She wants to adopt Lily, but Lawyer Mason refuses Old Woman Magoun's request without consulting his wife. Lawyer Mason's response to his wife's silent plea is definitive: "But the father! No, Maria, we can't take a child with Barry blood in her veins. The stock has run out; it is vitiated physically and morally" (*WL*, 269). In Greenham as well as in Barry's Ford, the final law is the unquestioned right of fatherly authority.

Old Woman Magoun, however, is also a powerful figure. She has "within her a mighty sense of reliance upon herself as being on the right track in the midst of a maze of evil, which gave her courage" (*WL*, 246). Old Woman Magoun stands against Nelson Barry as a "prophetess" (*WL*, 261): she stands as the voice of God and the power of nature. It is in her struggle with Barry that Old Woman Magoun discovers her power of voice. As a prophetess, she does not become a man, but she takes on the power of speaking for a higher authority, an authority who can overrule the dangerous and irresponsible father on earth. When Old Woman Magoun says, "the Lord will take care of her," it is Barry who names this higher power as male as he says derisively, "Very well, let Him" (*WL*, 261).

Although, as a prophetess, Old Woman Magoun affirms her reliance on "the Lord," in the course of the story she herself becomes godlike, assuming the role of a fate who oversees a deadly fatalism. Old Woman Magoun is an earthly deity and force of nature. She seems to be the prophetess of an older law of the mother that authorizes death over defilement. As grandmother and grand-daughter return from their expulsion from the garden in Greenham, Lily eats "the deadly nightshade" and Old Woman Magoun watches, knowing that the child is poisoning herself. Later, as Lily dies a painful death, Old Woman Magoun ushers her, as it were, into heaven, by telling her a story about the comforts she will find there.

In the end, in Old Woman Magoun's version of heaven, it is not the heavenly father who awaits Lily but rather Lily's mother, who has prepared a white room with white curtains and a white bed. There are no men mentioned in Old Woman Magoun's orderly village of heaven, other than Lily's allusion to the "Grampa" who gave her grandmother the gold wedding ring. Heaven, with gold streets, blue flowers and the shining things of everyday life, is a world entered through "a gate with all the colors of the rainbow" (*WL*, 275). The soothing colors and surfaces, images of flowers and asexual life, are contrasted with the horrible and explicit bodily death Lily is experiencing.

Old Woman Magoun's force of will suggests the power of the final fate, the third sister of the mythological Fates, a law of the mother's spiritual omnipotence that commands death as well as life. In Wilkins's story, women, as represented in the character of Old Woman Magoun, maintain the power of giving and taking life, but they are overruled by male authority on earth and prevented from providing a safe place for the character representing the potential female poet: Lily Barry, who is said to have "the making of an artist or a poet" (WL, 248). In the end, Old Woman Magoun assumes the role of the third Fate, clipping the string of life, serving as a midwife as she directs Lily's imagination into the traditional province of nineteenth-century female fiction: a vision of sentimental heaven.

Lily appears to be caught between the men's and women's cultures. She is crushed when she is threatened by sexual violation, yet Wilkins also presents a devastating critique of the place offered to Lily by the traditions and customs of the community of women. At the close of the story, Old Woman Magoun carries Lily's rag doll as if it were a baby. Her references to the breastpin of Maria Mason, the white room, the blue flowers, the gold (which Lily relates to the wedding ring that her grandfather gave Old Woman Magoun) are all signs of feminine order. Old Woman Magoun tells Lily about a heaven where picked flowers never die and dolls become babies. This heaven holds the promise of life after death—a place where a cut Lily will not die, where she will live and become a mother. There is also the implication that Lily, whose maturity has been denied and delayed and finally cut off by death, has been kept from life, just as she has been kept from her potential playmates, because she has been her grandmother's living doll. Lily repeats her mother's childhood before *her* defilement and desertion, her pregnancy and death.

When Maria Mason, wistful and misty-eyed, pleads with her husband, saying, "her grandmother had her dressed up as pretty as a little girl could be" (WL, 269), the clothes have spoken for the child. Lily has been carefully prepared to make such an impression: "Her grandmother had curled Lily's hair more punctiliously than usual. The little face peeped like a rose out of two rows of golden spirals. Lily wore her new muslin dress with a pink sash, and her best hat of a fine white straw trimmed with a wreath of rosebuds." Alive, Lily is a "pink fluttering figure" (WL, 264–65), but she is more connected to an ethereal world of color and flowers, a doll-like suspension of human growth, than to the animal world associated with men.

Lily, with the best of the old Barry line in her, is the "receptive vase" (WL,

245) into which all her grandmother's goodness has been poured; she represents the hope for a daughter for both Greenham and Barry's Ford. Both households, both families, have lost a daughter. The hope that Greenham represents in "Old Woman Magoun" remains less defined than the story of a heavenly village. Greenham suggests traditional order, paternal authority which is not degenerate. Yet the middle-class inhabitants are not capable of crossing class lines, and they retain their traditional prejudices. The law of blood and the male authority which enforces it is characteristic of Barry's Ford and Greenham: it does not protect or preserve the daughter. Neither the Masons nor Nelson and Isabel Barry represent a fertile couple; neither offers a place for the child to grow into a mature woman.

Mrs. Lawyer Mason recognizes Old Woman Magoun and Lily as "good" and "pretty" (WL, 269), but these feminine categories do not move a man such as Lawyer Mason. They have a different meaning to Barry and Mason, men who are entitled to exchange women. To Barry, Lily's purity and innocence add to her beauty and only increase her attraction. In a sense Lawyer Mason already has read Lily's "fate": her beauty and innocence to him have been translated into "tainted blood." Lawyer Mason is concerned with inheritance: the blood in Lily's veins. Lily's father is also concerned with inheritance: his paternal right to trade her flesh. As Lily dies, Old Woman Magoun directs her to her heavenly chamber just as she sent her upstairs to her room the day the bridge was built to protect her from the company of men. On that day, sitting in a tiny rocking chair, Lily listens as her grandmother explains the noise of the disorder below: "They've most all of 'em been drinkin'. They air a passel of hogs" (WL, 258).

Lily's story in "Old Woman Magoun" can be read as a version of the myth of Persephone and the pomegranate seeds. In Wilkins's story, however, the daughter's experience is reversed: by eating the berries, she escapes the sexual and animal world of her satanic father (an underworld on earth) and flees to the female world of heaven. There Lily's mother is said to await her in a life that resembles the asexual and pastoral world of Demeter—where young girls pick flowers and never become luring and dangerous sirens. Like Lily Bart, by poisoning herself Lily Barry escapes the blood rites of marriage and childbirth. Lily escapes from life to a world of reproduction without violence, a world that in "Old Woman Magoun" exists only in female story.

One can imagine that the story that Old Woman Magoun tells to the dying Lily—the sentimental fiction of a feminine heaven with flowers and "all the colors of the rainbow"—would have struck Wharton as horribly inadequate. However, in her effort to translate the "rose-and-lavender pages" of the sentimental "authoresses" into her own depiction of "life as it really was in the derelict mountain villages of New England," in her effort to avoid the "rainbow veils" of the "siren-subjects" that lure the writer's "cockle-shell to the rocks" (*EF*, vii), Wharton makes *Summer* a narrative about survival rather than death and resurrection. Lily Barry, as we have seen, dies in part because she is rejected as a potential daughter by the valley town inhabitant Lawyer Mason (the only man who is presented as being powerful enough to save her from her disreputable father). Charity Royall lives because (at the request of Charity's biological father, a convicted murderer) Lawyer Royall assumes responsibility for Charity by bringing her down from the mountain into his house, in effect adopting her. In "Old Woman Magoun," Lily Barry's father is presented as a predatory animal. Wharton's *Summer* goes to great lengths to rehabilitate the fallen father who for a moment only has predatory designs; he is transformed from the "damned hound," a "villainous low hound" (*S*, 168) into a representative of benevolent patriarchy.

In *Summer*, it is the mother whose body is compared to an animal—"a dead dog in a ditch" (*S*, 250); the young children on the mountain are said to nestle like puppies against the warm body of the old grandmother. In "Old Woman Magoun," the male culture of the backwoods is seen as the locus of animality: as we have seen, the animal-like father teaches his half-witted sister "some tricks like a dog." In the story that Old Woman Magoun tells to Lily, the female world of heaven is associated with Lily's mother; Wharton's *Summer* makes the point that it is difficult for Charity to imagine her mother in heaven, despite the minister's promise of life after death when the "vile body" will be changed into "His glorious body" (*S*, 255). (The mother's entry into *Summer's* Episcopal heaven requires the transformation of the woman's body into *His* body, the masculinized image of the son of God.) Charity tries to imagine God waiting for her mother, to see her mother as a part of "the designs of a just but merciful God, but it was impossible to see any link between them" (*S*, 259).

The daughter in "Old Woman Magoun" is fated to repeat her mother's past, although she is "saved" from sexual knowledge; like her mother, she dies an early death at the onset of sexual maturity. Charity Royall expects to repeat her mother's past. Near the end of the novel, she travels to Nettleton to see a doctor, who confirms her fear that she is pregnant. Charity realizes that the female doctor, who is described as having a "murderous smile," has mistaken her for a prostitute, a "miserable creature like Julia" (*S*, 225) (the only prostitute that Charity knows), and assumes that she has come for an abortion. In the original manuscript of *Summer*, Wharton writes that Charity realizes that this woman thinks she wants to "destroy [the word "murder" is crossed out here] Harney's child." This text states that Charity "felt the awe and reverence of motherhood";[49] the final version reads: "There came to her the grave surprise of motherhood" (*S*, 225). In the figure of the doctor, whose "murderous" smile alternates with a "motherly" smile (*S*, 225–26), Charity faces the figure of a murderous mother: a mother who in Charity's view would kill a child. She later claims to speak to Charity "as your own mother might" (*S*, 288). From the moment the doctor confirms that she is pregnant, saving her child becomes the most important goal of Charity's existence.

Identifying herself with and as a mother, she decides to find the unknown mother about whom she has only recently become curious. She decides to leave the New England village to have her child, just as her own mother, "a woman of the town of Nettleton" (208)—the draft has the word "streetwalker" crossed out[50]—had followed a man to the mountain and given birth to her there. Journeying to the mountain, Charity is initially comforted by the thought that she is repeating her mother's life. She imagines that her mother will accept her and understand her condition. Charity imagines her mother's sympathy: "She herself had been born as her own baby was going to be born; and whatever her mother's subsequent life had been she could hardly help remembering the past, and receiving a daughter who was facing the trouble she had known" (*S*, 240). The relationship Charity imagines with her mother is like her relationship with Harney; it seems to have a "past" that was "rich enough to have given them a private language" (*S*, 128).

When Charity arrives on the mountain, she confronts the body of her mother, which appears to her to be like a "dead dog in the ditch." Where she expected to find shared meaning she finds people without understandable relationships "herded together in a sort of passive promiscuity in which their common misery was the strongest link." The "savage misery of the Mountain farmers" (*S*, 259), an animal struggle for warmth and food, seems to divide the outlaw colony from any sense of relation—with each other or any other place or time. Not only is Charity's mother irrevocably divided from God: she is also a distant figure to Charity. We read: "She herself felt as remote from the poor creature she had seen lowered into her hastily dug grave as if the height of the heavens had divided them" (*S*, 259).

Charity had always thought of her mother as being "destitute of all human feeling" because she gave her daughter away. Having seen the way of life on the mountain, Charity asks herself: "What mother would not want to save her child from such a life?" In her single night on the mountain, staring at "the dirty floor" and a "clothes-line hung with decaying rags," Charity considers a future that would take her back to her mother's former life as a "streetwalker," a "woman of Nettleton." Although she imagines a life as a prostitute, Charity's fantasy is centered on her child: "She knew girls of that kind sometimes made enough to have their children nicely cared for; and every other consideration disappeared in the vision of her baby, cleaned and combed, and rosy, and hidden away somewhere where she could run in and kiss it, and bring it pretty things to wear" (*S*, 260–61). Imagining herself as a prostitute like her mother, Charity imagines herself as a mother.

It is Lawyer Royall, however, who saves Charity from reliving the life of her mother. Indeed, he saves her twice, since he brings her down from the mountain when she is a child and then returns for her after she flees as a woman with child. The second time he saves her not only from her mother's life on the mountain but also from her mother's life as a prostitute. Lawyer Royall's return to the mountain establishes a new pattern of repetition because it means that Charity's child will be raised in the same place where Charity has been raised; but there is a significant difference: in the second instance, the mother, embodied now by Charity, is accepted and brought back into civilization. Lawyer Royall is the protective "father" who insists on sheltering the "fatherless" children.

I am suggesting that *Summer* represents Wharton's compulsion to change the ending of "Old Woman Magoun." A mountain child with a life-threatening fever is saved when she is adopted by a valley lawyer. A girl who is about to become a mother escapes the fate of reliving her mother's story. Two generations of children are saved from death; the threat of male animality and brutality is domesticated. The ending of "Old Woman Magoun" serves as a point of departure for a novel in which the dangerous divisions exposed in Wilkins's text are revised and healed. The husband and the father are joined with the lawyer in an affirmation of the benevolence of paternal authority. Lawyer Royall, unlike Lawyer Mason, is the father who accepts the responsibilities of his class and, like Edith Wharton during World War I, provides charity in the form of food, warmth, and shelter for the homeless. In writing *Summer* and rewriting "Old Woman Magoun," Wharton rehabilitates the father and guarantees a protected place for the daughter and the child that will be born.

In discussing the "shadow" cast by the "grim realities" of World War I over the landscape of *Summer*, Blake Nevius suggests that Wharton's description of the dead body of the mother is written "in a manner appropriate to the combat diary."[51] As we have seen, Wharton herself remarks that her 1917 novel was written "at a high pitch of creative joy, but amid a thousand interruptions, and while the rest of my being was steeped in the tragic realities of the war" (*BG*, 356). Ironically, in this respect *Summer* resembles another fiction of New England written during a war: Harriet Beecher Stowe's *The Pearl of Orr's Island*. Stowe's 1862 novel—a pivotal work in the local color tradition—centers on the story of a "dark" orphan boy who is shipwrecked and washed ashore on the New England coast. The boy, who has southern origins, has a rebellious adolescence and is urged by some disreputable associates to betray his adoptive father. In a novel in which the storytellers "spin yarns" and cut tales "out of whole cloth," a sea captain changes the story by providing an alternate plot. Prompted by a sentimental heroine named Mara Lincoln, he saves the "son" (whose name is Moses) from dishonoring his "father."[52] Stowe, called by President Lincoln "the little lady who started the great war," was commonly pictured as an avenging angel at the Battle of Armageddon,[53] but in *The Pearl of Orr's Island* Stowe not only escapes from the realities of the Civil War, she rewrites the family romance of the war, averting tragedy and spinning a tale of reconciliation in which the storyteller preserves the authority of the father and the obedience of the son.

In the same manner, surrounded by death and disorder in Paris during the Great War, responding to Wilkins's depiction of a dangerous and divided world, Wharton wrote *Summer* not so much to escape as to rewrite both "tragic realities" and disconcerting stories. "Old Woman Magoun" is a critique of masculine power that emphasizes men's failure to protect children, as well as their denial of power to women, who are rendered unable to protect themselves or their children. Wharton revises that story, preventing the young girl's death by writing a story of benevolent class and gender relations. Lawyer Royall, representing the regal elites, serves as a representative of the paternal and social hierarchies that are designed to protect women and the young. *Summer* insists on the benevolence of this patriarch as the authority who shelters human civilization and maintains the hierarchical relations that in Wharton's view give it meaning.

In "Old Woman Magoun," Lily Barry is described as having eyes "as blue as blue light itself." Her "retrospective eyes" suggest her lost possibilities; they suggest that she had in her "the making of an artist or poet" (*WL*, 248). As Lily dies, her eyes lose their blue light; they become black and she moans, "It is dark." To comfort her, Old Woman Magoun describes the brightness of heaven: "There where you are going it is always light . . . and the commonest things shine like that breastpin Mrs. Lawyer Mason had on today" (*WL*, 274). Lily is offered an exchange. She loses her sight of the living world, but in the dark she is promised the light of the "breastpin" worn by the desired yet denied mother. Lily is promised a world in which she will become a mother and dolls will become live babies.

Wharton inscribes a similar figure at the center of *Summer*. Charity Royall (wishing for "the thousandth time that she had blue eyes" [*S*,8]) receives from Harney a blue pin: a "small round stone, blue as a mountain lake, with little sparks of light all round it" (*S*, 134). This "blue pin" with its blue light is kept by Charity in a secret place or worn "pinned . . . on her bosom" (*S*, 136). The breast pin is twice described as "talisman" (*S*, 159, 288); worn "on her bosom" (*S*, 159) and the object of a dangerous exchange, it seems inscribed with Charity's star-crossed fate, but it also is a symbol that tells its own story.

Although Charity learns to choose the blue brooch, it is not her first choice as she stands with Harney and looks at the jeweler's "glass counter, where, on a background of dark blue velvet, pins, rings and brooches glittered like the moon and stars." At first in her indecision she points to "a gold lily-of-the-valley with white flowers." Charity Royall, unlike Lily Barry, is now "of the valley," but she does not end up taking the lily; Harney shifts her desire by pointing out another jewel in this celestial display, thereby talismanically shifting her fate. When Harney asks, "Don't you think the blue pin's better?" she sees immediately that "the lily of the valley was mere trumpery compared to the small round stone, blue as a mountain lake, with little sparks of light all round it" (*S*, 134).

From among the stars and moon of the jewel case, Charity rejects the painted and gilded lily and chooses the pin that, in its evocation of a "mountain lake," points to her origins on the mountain. The mountain, "a bad place, and a shame to have come from" (*S*, 12), is also associated with the mother she thinks of as "no more than a nameless pinch of earth" (*S*, 60). Charity decides to journey to both her mother and the mountain when she becomes pregnant. The choice of the blue breast pin over the gilded lily also signals the beginning of Charity's erotic relationship with Harney, which will lead to her becoming a mother. Although she "would not have dared to wear it openly in North Dormer," when she first flees North Dormer for the mountain she "fastened it on her bosom as if it were a talisman" (*S*, 159). When Charity visits the abortionist, the "murderous" and "motherly" (*S*, 225–26) Dr. Merkle, and is forced to give up the brooch, it is as if the proffered and refused abortion had taken place: "It had been horrible to have to leave Harney's gift in the woman's hands" (227). Charity later includes "their choosing the blue brooch together" as one of the memories that is "building the child in her womb," one of the "strands of life so interwoven" in "her poor romance" (*S*, 231). Charity wants to get the pin back "for her baby: she meant it, in some mysterious way, to be a link between Harney's child and its unknown father." When she retrieves the brooch, it again lies "in her bosom like a talisman" (*S*, 288).

The blue pin that Charity wears on her bosom links her to mothers: to the mountain and mother she comes from and to the mother that she will become. As a talisman, then, the blue pin of *Summer* links Charity to Maria Mason, the bearer of the "breastpin" in "Old Woman Magoun"; in doing so, however, the blue pin of *Summer* marks the difference in Charity's story. Lily is denied the breast of Maria Mason and is supposedly poisoned by her milk. Maria Mason's breast pin is represented as one of the lures of the false heaven that Old Woman Magoun describes in her dangerous fictions. The blue pin in *Summer* that the murderous mother, Dr. Merkle, tries to take away, and that Charity buys back with "money from her breast" (*S*, 286) is finally a sign of protected mother-hood. In "Old Woman Magoun," it tells the story of the failure of mothers.

The breast pin also tells the story of the failure of female storytellers to protect the potential female poet, the daughter whose blue eyes suggest "the making of an artist of poet" (*WL*, 248). "Old Woman Magoun" tells the story of the failure of the breast and the failure of the pen: the failure of the weak-voiced mother to provide a safe place for the potential female poet. In Wilkins's story the female storytellers become the symbolic and actual murderers of the female artist. The blue light of the talismanic breast pin that Charity chooses instead of the gilded lily-of-the-valley, "blue as a mountain lake, with little sparks of light all round it" in its own heaven of stars and jewels, may evoke the eyes of Lily Barry, which are "as blue as blue light itself." In both texts the pin figures the place and the fate of the woman artist.

As a talisman, the breast pin is also a sign that points to a parent text. It is one of the marks of the exchange that takes place between "Old Woman Magoun" and *Summer*. A mystical sign which stands for the child and the link to its parent, the blue pin also suggests a literal signing which writes the link between the text and its author. As a talisman, the blue pin also stands for the text of *Summer* itself: an engraved sign of the great "wheeling fires" (*S*, 219) of the heavens, a permanent text that, like the constellations, goes beyond the "leafy arch of summer" (*S*, 273). As a talisman, as a text, as a sign that points to an author, like a blue pen, the blue pin tells a tale. The talismanic pin speaks of the teller of a tale, the narrator of a story, the author. The blue pin of *Summer*— "blue as a mountain lake, with little sparks of light all round it," like the eyes of Lily Barry, "blue, as the blue light itself," displaying "the making of an artist or poet"—rewrites the breast pin of "Old Woman Magoun." In this constellation of signs, Wharton replaces the story of failed storyteller mothers. This is the most threatening story told by "Old Woman Magoun"; it is the story of failed storytellers which ends in the death of the potential female poet that Wharton must replace with the story of a saved daughter who will write her story in the "strands of life."

We have seen that in writing *Summer* Wharton claimed to bring a harsher realism to the New England of fiction. *Summer* does in many ways contain harsh descriptions of what Wharton called "the derelict mountain villages of New England"—the "insanity, incest and slow mental and moral starvation" that she said were "hidden away behind the paintless wooden house-fronts." We have seen, however, that despite gruesome depictions of a corpse and the animal-like community of a "miserable herd," despite the grim details of the story of Charity Royall, *Summer* in many respects domesticates the horrors of the world Wilkins depicts in "Old Woman Magoun." Beginning Charity's story where Lily Barry's ends, Wharton rewrites Wilkins's plot to restore stable hierarchies and the benevolence of paternal authority. In the end, Wharton even domesticates the horror of incest by marrying Charity Royall to Lawyer Royall, the only father she has ever known.[54]

If Wharton's critique of the domestic realism of the local colorists seems to end in domestication, this is partly because it is not easy to critique a text that is itself a devastating critique of the sentimental story. I have been suggesting that "Old Woman Magoun" is a consciously subversive text. The sentimental story that Old Woman Magoun tells to the dying Lily is finally hopelessly inadequate—but Wilkins's story takes as its subject the inadequacy of this sentimental story. The text closes with the vision of a madwoman, a storyteller who has believed her own fiction that dolls can become real babies. She can save the potential female poet from the threats and failures of paternal power only by killing her; and she can spare her this death only by inventing the sort of fiction of sentimental heaven that children and madwomen might believe in. Like *Madame Bovary* (a novel to which *Summer* was compared),[55] "Old Woman Magoun" closes with an explicitly detailed death by poisoning which calls the sentimental story into question and thwarts both the characters' and the reader's desire for romantic conclusions.

As Old Woman Magoun narrates Lily's journey to heaven, the child dies a horribly painful death: "She suffered cruelly from the burning in her stomach, the vertigo, and the deadly nausea" (*WL*, 272–73). The passages recounting the grandmother's soothing story of the "beautiful place" alternate with the descriptions of Lily's cries of pain and delirium. "Old Woman Magoun talked as Lily had never heard her talk before, as nobody had ever heard her talk before. She spoke from the depths of her soul; her voice was as tender as the coo of a dove, and it was grand and exalted" (*WL*, 273). Lily's questions about her grandmother's description of heaven are a tribute to the power of the old woman's voice, but her responses are amidst her moans and her pitiful and persistent understatement, "I am so sick, grandma." She gradually becomes delirious: "Presently she sat straight up in bed and raved; but even then her grandmother's wonderful compelling voice had an influence over her." Even in her great pain "she seemed to understand through it all what her grandmother said" (*WL*, 274–75). Lily continues to moan and babble wildly, and "her grandmother's great voice of soothing never ceased, until the child fell into a deep sleep, or what resembled sleep; but she lay stiffly in that sleep, and a candle flashed before her eyes made no impression on them" (*WL*, 275–76).

The pain and severe bodily trauma Lily suffers is counterposed to the soothing and distracting, although finally inadequate, world of feminine story. Familiar sentimental formulas and motifs are transformed by the descriptions of suffering. The reader who is comfortably accepting or even condescendingly classifying the formulas is consistently confronted by alternating layers of "real" feeling and illusory images. It is as if Wilkins imagined a complacent female reader and then led her through reassuring passages of familiar language and formulas to a painful and almost wounding act of cultural criticism. One is faced with the measured and calculated anger of the story as a whole: the bitter realization of the inadequate stories of feminine comfort which soothe the pain while masking the ultimate powerlessness of the women's culture. Lily is crushed between the competing laws of men and women; neither side can provide a place in the world for Lily or the female poet she represents.

The most disturbing aspect of "Old Woman Magoun" is the soothing but otherwise impotent voice of the female storytellers; they have the power of love and soothing voices, but in the end they are the authors of the horrid death by poisoning. Neither Old Woman Magoun nor the misty-eyed and melancholy Maria can alter the social system that recognizes Nelson Barry, Lily's degenerate father, and stern Lawyer Mason as the final authorities: these men are the potential fathers who control the terms of Lily's life on earth. The very weakness of Maria Mason's responses to her husband, her inability to plead both Lily's case and her own desire to adopt the child, expose the pitiful resources of women in the story. Mrs. Mason says, "She is a beautiful little girl" and "the Grandmother seems a good woman." Her lawyer husband opposes taking "a child with Barry blood in her veins." Mrs. Mason can only comment weakly on Lily's surface appearance: "Her grandmother had her dressed up as pretty as a little girl could be" (WL, 268–69). The wistful, lavender-frocked Maria Mason is unable to change her husband's mind.

It is perhaps because of her weakness of voice, her inability to become Lily's mother, that Maria Mason becomes Lily's symbolic murderer. While Old Woman Magoun is in the lawyer's office, Maria Mason brings Lily a plate of cake, an "early" apple, and some milk. The old woman chastises Maria Mason severely for having given the child a sour apple and milk. Although the reader knows that Lily dies from eating what she calls "nice berries" (WL, 270)—the "lusty spread of the deadly nightshade" (WL, 266)—the reason given for Lily's death is the "sour apples and milk" she received from Maria Mason. Having eaten an "early apple" with "real nice milk" (WL, 267), Lily is driven from the lawgiver's garden by the worldly father who refuses to adopt her. The "early apple" may represent the bitterness of sexual knowledge, the threat of violation of the young girl, but it also can be read as the sour and forbidden fruit that curdles milk, a poisoning of the nurturant substance that suggests maternal love.[56]

As if deconstructing its own genre and fictions, "Old Woman Magoun" is a bitter act of self-criticism for Mary Wilkins and a commentary on the future of the female artist in America. Maria Mason, the symbolic murderer of the desired daughter who has in her "the making of an artist or poet," stands as a figure for Wilkins. Mary Wilkins gives the character a first name which is almost identical to her own; Maria's surname, while not literally the name of Mary Wilkins's father, names a trade that evokes her father's trade: mason. Maria Mason is a milk giver and the possessor of the breast pin, and the light of her breast pin is associated with the light of the would-be daughter-artist. However, through the weakness of her voice she fails to provide the nurturance and protection which could shelter the potential female artist. Her breast pin (like the pen of the artist) may be used to describe common things with a light which makes them shine in the domestically ordered world of female fiction, but its heaven must lie beyond life.

As author, Mary Wilkins has envisioned a world where the divisions between men and women are so dangerous that the young female child is destroyed. Maria Mason has been unable to prevent the death of her own daughter, and she is unable to adopt and thereby save the second daughter she desires. She has suffered two losses, just as Old Woman Magoun loses both her daughter and the granddaughter who took her daughter's place. On one level this is the dilemma of Mary Wilkins, who as artist writes as both mother and daughter to describe being caught between weak-voiced and strong-voiced traditions of women's writing. In "Old Woman Magoun," Wilkins also has written a story that might be seen as a critique of the other stories in her own collection, *The Winning Lady and Others* (which, in general, are less interesting than Wilkins's previous work). By portraying Maria Mason as the weak-voiced and melancholy mother, dressed in lavender and basing her ineffective "arguments" on surface appearance, Mary Wilkins has anticipated Wharton's dismissals of the female local color tradition.

In Maria Mason's participation in the murder of the potential poet, Wilkins may record her own failing hopes for both her own art and a potential artistic tradition. However, as a story about the limits of a genre and female voice, "Old Woman Magoun" itself transcends the stylized local color tradition it both belongs to and condemns. As a story it suggests that both Wilkins and Wharton were aware that rose and lavender authoresses were not entirely benign: Wilkins herself had deadly poisons in her botanica. Maria Mason in her lavender dress may represent the herbal metaphor of the "deadly night shade"; she may also be the "bella donna" (as the poison is more commonly known) who despite the external pleasantness of a "beautiful woman" must, like the "lusty spread of deadly night shade" (WL, 266), contain a deadly possibility. Maria Mason cannot be read as milk giver alone; standing in the lawyer's garden she is also the woman who offers the apple, and thus she stands for woman as both the first mother and as the source of death. The story depicts not only the division between men and women but also a divided view of woman herself.

With the figure of the lavender-frocked Maria Mason, then, the mother who murders through her powerlessness, Mary Wilkins has anticipated Wharton's critique of the local colorists. Wilkins's story about the failure of the breast pin and the inadequacy of a mother's milk and nurturance in the absence of the power to influence men also recalls Wharton's *The Custom of the Country*. In this novel, Ralph Marvell, like both Lily Barry and Lily Bart, is depicted as a potential poet who is caught between the decorative inadequacy of the world of feminine beauty and the economically defined social powers which favor the predatory male. Marvell kills himself, but the text implies that he, too, like Lily, has been destroyed by the surface illusions of beautiful and empty women. Feminine artifice is seen as a murderous deception for the would-be artist. Marvell is not only the victim of his attraction to a vacant female muse; he is finally, like Lily Barry, a victim of the division between men and women in society.

Wharton is not only revising Mary Wilkins in *Summer*; she is also revising her own work. In addition to reworking *The Custom of the Country*, as she rewrites the story of the dying Lily Barry, Wharton also revises her own stories of virgin death: not only the story of Lily Bart in *The House of Mirth* but also the story of Mattie Silver in *Ethan Frome*. Wharton brings Charity face to face with the murderous mother whom she must escape (the abortionist with the "motherly" smile) and the animal body of the mother Mary who must be buried. Charity is caught between the mother who would rob her of her child, who would take away the pin that stands for "Harney's gift," and the animal-like mother who gives birth to babies in an animal world where there is no past or future. Wharton is caught in the dilemma that Wilkins emblematizes in the breast pin: the double sign which joins woman to writer and the weak-voiced mother to the potential poet.

At this point we should recall that Charity Royall is the librarian in North Dormer. Twice a week in the afternoon she sits by a bust of Minerva "at her desk under a freckled steel engraving of the deceased author" that the library is named for, the man described as "the sole link between North Dormer and literature" (S, 44, 13). Although Charity insists to Harney, "I'm the librarian and I know the by-laws. This is my library" (S, 46), she "hated to be bothered about books" (S, 21). We learn that Charity insists that Lawyer Royall get her the job as librarian after he has crossed her threshold and threatened her virginity. Yet it is in the library (where, Charity says, people would "like to come . . . to meet the fellows they're going with" [S, 48]) that Charity first meets Harney, the student of architecture who comes looking for books about houses, the man who will introduce her to eroticism and make her a mother. His first display of interest in her almost causes her to lose her job and be replaced by a "trained librarian" (S, 42), and she becomes angry when Harney acquires his own key to the library.

Eventually, however, when she first decides to escape to the mountain, taking "the little packet of letters she had received from Harney" and fastening the talismanic "blue brooch . . . on her bosom," she takes "the library key" from under "the pincushion" where she habitually hides it and leaves it where it can be found (S, 158–59). She does not make it all the way up the mountain this time; losing the packet of letters on the way, she stops at the house halfway up the mountain where she and Harney will consummate their relationship. (She will carry out her plan to go up the mountain after she becomes pregnant.) Later she again has the library key "about her neck" (S, 178), but it becomes clear in the novel that the breast pin and child that are Harney's gifts will replace the library key. She will get the packet of letters back, but in the end she still seems to lose possession of letters. She gives up Harney and the key to the library and literature. To Charity, the library is a "vault," a "monument," a "mausoleum" (S, 44, 13, 50); in the end she chooses not to dwell in the underworld. She prefers the love that Harney makes "as bright and open as the summer air" (S, 180).[57]

In Charity Royall, Wharton conceives a young woman who "was blind and insensible to many things, and dimly knew it; but to all that was light and air, perfume and color, every drop of blood in her responded" (S, 21). Wharton gives Charity a "private language" (*S*, 128); indeed, her unspoken words and feelings constitute some of the most lyrical passages in the novel. However, Charity is inarticulate in spoken and written language. Her inability to express these feelings in spoken or written words, rather than the loss of her lover, is perhaps the most poignant aspect of the novel. Wharton describes Charity's truncated efforts to write letters to the distant Lucius Harney over what seems to be "an insurmountable barrier." In the early days of her separation from Harney, "she got out a sheet of paper, and sat looking at it, trying to think what to say; but she had the feeling that her letter would never reach its destination" (*S*, 213).

When she is unable to sleep, Charity plans to write to Harney, but "the letters were never put on paper, for she did not know how to express what she wanted to tell him" (220). After she learns that she is pregnant, Charity decides to write but she realizes that she has no paper: "She had a superstitious feeling that the letter must be written on the instant, that setting down her secret in words would bring reassurance and safety" (*S*, 232). She gets "some letter-paper" from Lawyer Royall but "when she got back to her room all the words that had been waiting had vanished. . . ." (Wharton's ellipses); we read: "For a long time she sat bent above the blank page; but she found nothing to say that really expressed what she was feeling. . . ." (*S*, 233–34; Wharton's ellipses). Charity feels that if she could go to Harney, "she would only have to show herself to let his memories speak for her." She realizes that there is a gulf that separates them, a gulf not only of class difference but of spoken language— characterized by the monologues that Harney fills with mysterious "allusions" about art and life; but she comes to see that the "bridge their passion had flung across" this gulf "was as insubstantial as a rainbow" (*S*, 212).

In the last pages of the novel, with the newly recovered brooch lying "in her bosom like a talisman," Charity is said to gain the strength she needs to buy a piece of paper and, "with the rusty post-office pen," write to Harney. Her letter reads: "I'm married to Mr. Royall. I'll always remember you. Charity." Wharton, who is approaching the end of the novel, adds: "The last words were not in the least what she had meant to write; they had flowed from her pen irresistibly. She had not had the strength to complete her sacrifice; but, after all, what did it matter? Now that there was no chance of ever seeing Harney again, why should she not tell him the truth?" (*S*, 288–89).

Charity's "last words"—what she looks upon as the expression of "the truth"—seem terribly inadequate to the intensity of experience that Wharton has captured in the novel; Charity's "I'll always remember" reads as an almost meaningless cliché. However, Charity has earlier conceived of memories in a different way: "The memories of her former journey, instead of flying before her like dead leaves, seemed to be ripening in her blood like sleeping grain." To Charity, these memories—among them the blue brooch—are the "things [that] were hers; they had passed into her blood, and become a part of her, they were building the child in her womb; it was impossible to tear asunder strands of life so interwoven" (*S*, 231).

Unlike Wharton, Charity does not compose the mother by writing about her; she overcomes the threats of the murderous mother, the animal mother, and the predatory father by embodying the mother. Although she performs the priestly acts of God by turning words into flesh, Charity is not able to compose writing: to turn flesh, feeling, and experience into words or letters. For this reason, in Wharton's view, the mother cannot finally cross the threshold of heaven. We saw that unlike Lily Barry, who is ready to picture her mother in the female heaven described by Old Woman Magoun, Charity cannot imagine her mother incorporated into "His glorious body" (*S*, 255). In her autobiography, "Life and I," Wharton writes of being oppressed by "two absolutely inscrutable beings": "God & my mother."[58] She associates her mother with politeness and pretty things; she associates God with truth and books and learning to read. In *Summer*, Wharton saves Lily Barry from sentimental heaven by providing her with a place on earth as a mother; but she does not make a place for her as a poet.

The Devouring Muse

(The Custom of the Country)

The pink grew then as double as his mind;
The nutriment did change the kind.
With strange perfumes he did the roses taint;
And flowers themselves were taught to paint.
—Andrew Marvell, "The Mower, against Gardens"

And I saw an angel standing in the sun; and he
cried with a loud voice, saying to all the fowls
that fly in the midst of heaven, Come and gather
yourselves together unto the supper of the great
God; That ye may eat the flesh of kings, and the
flesh of captains, and the flesh of mighty men.
—Revelation 19:17–18

Writing *The Custom of the Country* was difficult for Edith Wharton. Begun in the spring of 1908, the novel was still incomplete when Scribner's began its serial publication in 1913. These years, the longest period of time that Wharton was at work on a single novel, saw the publication of *Ethan Frome* (in 1911) and *The Reef* (in 1912). When Henry James read *The Reef*, Wharton's novel about Americans who live in France, he expressed concern that Wharton's accomplishment—which he called Racinean but which others called Jamesian—had stranded her in relation to her unfinished novel, leaving her "more in the desert (for everything else) that surrounds Apex City."[1] A decade later, in describing the composition of *Ethan Frome*, the novel that immediately preceded *The Reef*, Wharton used similar terms. She recalls her avoidance in writing *Ethan Frome* of "the insinuating wraiths of false 'good situations,' siren-subjects luring [the novelist's] cockle-shell to the rocks;" she continues: "Their voice is oftenest heard, and their mirage-sea beheld, as he traverses the waterless desert which awaits him half-way through whatever work is actually in hand. I knew well enough what song those sirens sang, and had often tied myself to my dull job until they were out of hearing."[2]

Both of these images of the desert, the waterless sea of the work at hand, allude to *The Custom of the Country*, Wharton's ambitious novel about the exploits of Undine Spragg, a young woman from Apex, Kansas, who advances a career in society through a series of marriages and divorces. It is the novel that remained in progress yet unfinished during the period that Wharton separated from her husband after twenty-six years of marriage and separated permanently from America by selling the house in New England that she refers to as her "first real home."[3] The completion of *The Custom of the Country* coincided with the year of Wharton's final divorce decree; and it was no doubt difficult, if perhaps also liberating, to write a book about this still-taboo subject as she herself was anticipating the response to her own divorce.

The problem of the unfinished book haunts *The Custom of the Country* and the story of the would-be writer Ralph Marvell. Marvell, who measures his life against his resilient yet diminishing hopes for literary accomplishment, is often pictured among scattered papers and the equally scattered fugitive sensations of beauty that he would like to turn into the stable form of a book. At a crucial point in the narrative, for example, just before he has the vision that prompts his decision to put aside his literary calling in order to follow the call of Undine Spragg, Marvell sits among books and the scattered pages of his own writing: "charming things, if only he had known how to finish them!—and, on his writing-table . . . scattered sheets of prose and verse, charming things also, but, like the sketches, unfinished."[4] On one level *The Custom of the Country* is about unfinished books—not only Ralph Marvell's but Wharton's as well.

Wharton certainly would have identified with the struggle of the writer she depicts in her long-unfinished novel, particularly with his predicament of trying to write while married to someone of limited literary interests. She also would have sympathized with the problem of having to write to make money; like her character Marvell, Wharton knew how difficult it was to support a highly decorative woman—known for her enjoyment of fancy houses, travel, and motorcars—on the fluctuating income of a novelist. However, Wharton's identification with Ralph Marvell is underlined more specifically by the titles of his unfinished works—titles which name or allude to Wharton's own unfinished works. Marvell's project for a critical piece called "The Rhythmical Structures of Walt Whitman" suggests the outline for a critical work on Whitman that Wharton began at approximately the same time as *The Custom of the Country*. In addition, a work with the same title as the dramatic poem that Ralph Marvell is said to have written and been dissatisfied with, "The Banished God," remains among Wharton's unpublished papers.[5]

The Custom of the Country is flanked by unfinished books in which Wharton attempts to tell the story of an American writer: the projected critical work on Whitman and the partly drafted novel called "Literature." Both texts attempt to imagine an American poet, and both reflect on the meaning of Whitman and his language. "Literature" tells the story of a young writer whose poetic awakening occurs while reading Whitman; many of the details of his literary development closely parallel the experiences Wharton records in her autobiographical writing. Wharton claimed that "Literature" remained uncompleted because it was interrupted by the First World War, although it may have been her realization that she might end up writing her autobiography in the novel as much as the demands of the war that caused her to put the manuscript aside. In *Hudson River Bracketed*, Wharton has a literary critic warn against the use of "raw autobiography" in writing fiction, claiming that "the 'me book' . . . however brilliant, was at best sporadic, with little reproductive power."[6] Wharton had to begin "Literature" for the same reason that she hesitated to complete or publish it. Writing in 1914, Wharton needed an affirmation of her own future as a writer; she needed to rewrite the devastating story that threatened to make *The Custom of the Country* autobiographical as well. After telling the story of an artist who is lured to destruction by the siren song of the dangerously shifting surface of language, Wharton turned to "Literature" in order to write a novel that would not demand the "poetic justice" (133) of the writer's suicide.

Unlike "Literature," *The Custom of the Country* tells the story of the failure of the American writer; as it chronicles the death of a writer who moves from Whitman and a poem about banished gods to a plan for a book that treats men as insects, from romantic ideals about chivalry and godlike men to a bleak determinism, it presents a powerful vision of the impossibility of art in America. In this chapter, I will argue that *The Custom of the Country* is about the destruction of the writer who is seduced by the siren song of a false muse. Undine Spragg represents this artificial muse. As the embodiment of a superficial beauty and a dangerous artifice that conceals an interior emptiness, Undine represents a fatally alluring surface language; she is a devouring muse who feeds on the language of description. I will claim that Undine is Wharton's emblem for American culture; but more specifically, I will argue that in her attraction to and embodiment of a language and aesthetic based on ornamentation, decorative color, and deceptive surface, she represents the aesthetic that Wharton identified with the feminine. Ralph Marvell is destroyed because of his susceptibility to feminine artifice, which he confuses with the elemental forces of nature. He is destroyed by a fatal attraction to the rainbow veils of passion and the language of lyric poetry and description.

The struggle between art and artifice, the struggle between the susceptible artist and the sirenlike muse, is also figured in *The Custom of the Country* as a struggle between culture and what Wharton calls a "phantom 'society'" (273). In "Literature" Dickie Thaxter's tutor defines culture by citing a passage from the *Phaedrus*. The passage (which opens with an appeal to the deity who was Wharton's "Banished God") reads: "Beloved Pan, give me beauty of the inward soul; and may the outward and the inward be one." At this point the tutor exclaims, "That's important, that's eternal, that's culture."[7] In *The Custom of the Country* Wharton contrasts a culture where "the outward and the inward" are one with an aesthetic of the factitious: where (in the opinion of one character) "the most satisfying proof of human permanence" is found in "human nature's passion for the factitious, its incorrigible habit of imitating the imitation" (273). The "seemingly solid scene" of this society is formed of "layers on layers of unsubstantialness" (272) that mask the absence of coherence and interiority. *The Custom of the Country* is about dangerous divisions between men and women and between interiority and exteriority; it is also about the monstrous union of the decorative language of Fifth Avenue and the devouring capitalism of Wall Street, a union that results in the most significant divorce in the novel: the separation of language and meaning.

The critical work on Whitman that Wharton planned around the time she began *The Custom of the Country* focuses on aesthetic issues that are central to her novel. The four paragraphs of prose, supplemented by extensive lists of references to Whitman's poems, are concerned almost entirely with discussions of Whitman's adjectives and the power of description that, according to Wharton, enabled him to cut through ornamental language. Paraphrasing Whitman, she writes: "Of some of his adjectives it might be said who touches this touches a man." The language of Whitman, according to Wharton, reveals rather than conceals: "His epithets, his images, go straight to the intimate quality of the thing described—to 'the inherences of things.'" Whitman, she writes, "has the direct vision; his characterization of natural objects is extraordinarily suggestive; he sees through the layers of the conventional point of view & of the conventional adjective, straight to the thing itself . . . to the endless thread connecting it with the universe." To Wharton, this "sense of the absolute behind the relative gives to [Whitman's] adjectives their startling, penetrating quality, their ultimateness."

Wharton's analysis implies a belief in a hidden reality—"the inherences of things"—a reality that is occluded by language, particularly by the "layer of conventional adjective" that must be penetrated or seen through. "The best adjective," she advises, "is that which while most vividly embodying the salient quality of the thing described or its external appearance throws light upon the greatest number of these indirect associations with which the simplest object has become gradually encrusted by the slow accretions of thought." It is as if Wharton wanted to surprise language, to startle a sleeping word, to make the reader conscious of both the encrustations and the series of associations; she wants to throw the reader into renewed contact and intimacy with the "simplest object."[8]

Wharton's concern with ornament as language and language as ornament also appears in the first book she published, *The Decoration of Houses*. The epigraph (which could serve as an epigraph for *The Custom of the Country*) is taken from *La Composition décorative* by Henri Mayeux: "Une forme doit être belle en elle-même et on ne doit jamais compter sur le décor appliqué pour en sauver les imperfections."[9] Working in collaboration with the architect Ogden Codman, Wharton's stated intention in *The Decoration of Houses* was to rescue house decoration from the province of dressmaking and to return it to its former place in the realm of architecture. The "standpoint" of the book, writes Wharton, is "that of *architectural proportion*—in contradistinction to the modern view of house-decoration as *superficial application of ornament*."[10] She warns against "decorative schemes concocted by the writers who supply our newspapers with hints for 'artistic interiors.'" She continues: "The use of such poetic adjectives as jonquil-yellow, willow-green, shell-pink, or ashes-of-roses, gives to these descriptions of the 'unique boudoir' or 'ideal summer room' a charm which the reality would probably not possess. The arrangements suggested are usually cheap devices based upon the mistaken idea that defects in structure or design may be remedied by an overlaying of color or ornament."[11] As this passage suggests, Wharton's antipathy to conventional adjectives and decorative color is closely related to her preference for structural clarity in architecture and interior design.

Indeed, Wharton's belief that any changes made in interior decorating should lie "in the direction of alteration" rather than "adornment" is reflected in the writing of *The Decoration of Houses* as well as the theories it promotes. Near the conclusion of the book, Wharton offers a proverb about revision as removal and presents the necessity of revision as a general aesthetic principle: "*Tout ce qui n'est pas nécessaire est nuisible.* There is a sense in which works of art may be said to endure by virtue of that which is left out of them, and it is this 'tact of omission' that characterizes the master hand."[12] In *A Backward Glance*, Wharton recalls the experience she had rewriting *The Decoration of Houses*, changing it under the direction of Walter Berry from an unshapely "lump" into a book, and remarks that this taught her what she knew "about writing clear and concise English" (*BG*, 108). The molding of the lump into a book, language into art, required the master hand of exclusion, and Walter Berry at this crucial moment in Wharton's career became her imaginary (and often her actual) first reader. She credited Berry with exacting from her with each successive book a purer and more concise English prose. Consistent with her belief that the removal of gewgaws could improve even a bad room, Wharton went over the drafts of her writing to clear away the excess ornaments.

In *A Backward Glance*, Wharton describes herself and Berry setting out on "adjective hunts" over her manuscripts and coming back with "such heavy bags" (*BG*, 116). Ralph Marvell and Undine Spragg share a similar fantasy in *The Custom of the Country*. After Undine's father expresses astonishment that his son-in-law intends to maintain "a household on the earnings of his Muse," we are told of Ralph and Undine, "One of the humours of their first weeks together had consisted in picturing themselves as a primeval couple setting forth across a virgin continent and subsisting on the adjectives which Ralph was to trap for his epic" (146). When Ralph suggests on their honeymoon that they could find a place in Switzerland where they could avoid the crowds and "sit and look at a green water-fall while I lie in wait for adjectives" (146), the joke is no longer amusing to Undine. Indeed, the joke is ominously prophetic. Whereas Wharton hunts for adjectives in order to remove them, or searches for the Whitmanesque adjective that will cut through to the inherences of things, Marvell imagines his literary project in terms of the acquisition of adjectives and descriptive words.[13] As the novel progresses, we become aware that Undine feeds on adjectives, particularly descriptions of herself—although it will turn out that she requires more than ornamental language to sustain her.

These adjective hunts take place in the context of a society that Ralph elsewhere calls "a muddle of misapplied ornament" (73). The world that Ralph Marvell comes from refuses to acknowledge change as it enters an era in which everything appears altered, but this aristocratic nineteenth-century world seems to represent culture for Wharton. However circumscribed, the Marvell house on Washington Square, with its "quiet 'Dutch interior'" (73), seems to have a "beauty of the inward soul" in which the "outward and the inward" are one. Ralph Marvell looks at the "frugal marble ornament, as he might have looked into a familiar human face"; his mother and grandfather are "so closely identified with the old house in Washington Square that they might have passed for its inner consciousness as it might have stood for their outward form" (72–73). However, the "familiar human face" and the matching interior of home and family provide a marked contrast to the "architectural physiognomies" of the houses "at the other end of Fifth Avenue" (73). As he tries to understand his changing world, Marvell reads these physiognomies as facades that mask disintegration. He links them to the fabricated constructions of the portrait painter Claude Walsingham Popple, concluding that "what Popple called society was really just like the houses it lived in: a muddle of misapplied ornament over a thin shell of utility."

According to Marvell, the "steel shell was built up in Wall Street, the social trimmings were hastily added in Fifth Avenue; and the union between them was as monstrous and factitious, as unlike the gradual homogenous growth which flowers into what other countries know as society, as that between the Blois gargoyles on Peter Van Degen's roof and the skeleton walls supporting them" (73). Marvell's vision of the gargoyles that have become the monstrous ornament of a skeletal (that is, culturally vacuous) structure anticipates the indictment offered by Charles Bowen later in the novel of the "phantom 'society,' with all the rules, smirks, gestures of its model" that is "evoked out of promiscuity and incoherence." The society that Wharton does not frame with quotation marks is said to be "the product of continuity and choice" (273); in this world there appears to be a correspondence between the inner and the outer, a coherence that comes from the continuity of tradition and powerful associations with the past.

The "passion for the factitious" (273), the threatening preference for the artificial over the natural, is a central concern in the novel. While the Marvells represent an older, organic form of society with a traditional culture, Undine is the representative of a ravaging and imitative society. The world she prefers and advances is made up of "layers and layers of insubstantialness." Wharton introduces what might be called an undinal aesthetic in the scene in which Undine first visits a home of the Marvells at a dinner party given by Ralph's sister, Mrs. Fairford. Here we first see her antipathy toward the simple, the natural, and the real. She is alarmed by the absence of artifice, which she interprets as a lack of style, and she suspects that she is not at a "real 'dinner party'" (32). Only the attention given to the other guests by Clare Van Degen, whom Undine recognizes as "one of the choicest ornaments of the Society Column," convinces her that her dinner companions "must be more important than they looked" (33).

Undine's preference for display and artifice causes her to be disillusioned by the dinner party; she is particularly annoyed by that which seems natural and undisguised: "Undine was too young to take note of culinary details, but she had expected to view the company through a bower of orchids and eat pretty-colored *entrées* in ruffled papers. Instead, there was only a low centre-dish of ferns, and plain roasted and broiled meat that one could recognize—as if they'd been dyspeptics on a diet!" She is especially disappointed that "instead of a gas-log, or a polished grate with electric bulbs behind ruby glass, there was

an old-fashioned wood-fire, like pictures of 'Back to the farm for Christmas'"
(32). Wharton's description of Undine's preference for hothouse flowers, colors, paper ruffles, dressed and unrecognizable meat, and the artificial light of
ruby glass, seems to associate Undine with the "rose and lavender pages" of the
"authoresses" who (in Wharton's view) transformed the world through the
pink light of "rose-coloured spectacles" (*BG*, 293–94). However, in her distaste
for the rooted ferns and the untidy wood fire, Undine seems to offer her own
critique of the "old fashioned" and nostalgic view of the rural past. To Undine
"Back to the farm" is only a picture. Despite her preference for "rainbow veils,"
she is not connected with the rural past of the New England (or even the
Midwest) of fiction. By definition, Undine is in constant metamorphosis, unat-
tached to any past at all.

Like the water spirits who share her name, Undine has a formless quality. An
archetypal figure of the protean woman, Undine has a relational identity;
always conscious of herself as spectacle, even when she is alone, her self-
conscious theatricality turns all places into settings for her and all people (even
her young son, Paul) into accessories. I have suggested that an affinity for
description, color, and adjectives adds to the ornamental and layered surface
which conceals the absence of stable content in Undine. In *The Writing of
Fiction*, Wharton insists that description, whether of "the impression pro-
duced by a landscape, a street or a house" had to be "an event in the history of a
soul."[14] In *The Custom of the Country*, the events in Undine's soul are found in
the descriptions of her soullessness. Like the mythic undines, she does not
have a soul, and her affinity with the language of description underlines that
lack. As it describes her shifting figure and her posed exterior, the novel insists
that her devotion to an aesthetic of surface and ornament is linked to her
absence of interiority.

Undine is not in her element in the established society of the Marvells. She
finds the house of Ralph's sister to be "small and rather shabby" (31). The
shaded lamps and the walls of books that remind her of "the old circulating
library at Apex" form part of Undine's general impression: it was "dull" of Mrs.
Fairford, she feels, "not to have picked up something newer" from "the hints in
the Sunday papers" (32). She later feels that by marrying into the Marvell
family she is throwing in her lot with the "exclusive and the dowdy when the
future belonged to the showy and the promiscuous" (193). This creature of
light notes critically that "there was no gilding, no lavish diffusion of light" (31–

32). To her eyes subtlety and simplicity are dullness, although she finds herself provoked by the muted tones of the Marvells: "All was blurred and puzzling to the girl in this world of half-lights, half-tones, eliminations and abbreviations; and she felt a violent longing to brush away the cobwebs and assert herself as the dominant figure of the scene" (37).

In contrast, Undine is in her element when she appears (in a scene that takes place a week after the dinner party) at the opera. Seated in her box, she finds herself on stage, elevated to "the sacred semicircle whose privilege it is, between the acts, to make the mere public forget that the curtain has fallen." Aware that she is being seen, Undine absorbs into her conscious experience "the whole bright curve of the auditorium, from the unbroken lines of spectators below her to the culminating blaze of the central chandelier." At once Undine becomes the conduit for both the artificial light and the gaze of the audience: "She herself was the core of that vast illumination, the sentient throbbing surface which gathered all the shafts of light into a centre."[15] She feels "almost a relief when . . . the focus of illumination" was shifted to the stage below. The "mist" of the theatrical accoutrements is said to temper "the radiance that shot on her from every side." Undine seems to be aware that she might be seen through; in the intervening darkness, she attempts to "adjust herself to this new clear medium which made her feel so oddly brittle and transparent" (60). Her conception of enjoyment is "publicity, promiscuity . . . the crowd, the close contact of covetous impulses" (223–24). She feeds on the light of public attention.

Even on the night of the opera, Undine is aware that between the boxes at the theater, as between the guests at Mrs. Fairford's dinner party, there is an unspoken form of communication, a "mute telegraphy" that makes explicit gestures unnecessary. Yet Undine has a talent for imitating even what she cannot understand. She is said to be capable of suggesting the natural by using the "glare of the wall-lights" to make herself appear to bloom "out like a flower from the mirror" (300). Seeing her own reflection, she stands still, knowing that her image will arrest her departing lover. She learns how to attract the attention of men of refinement such as the aristocratic Raymond de Chelles, the Frenchman who will become her second husband. Charles Bowen admires her "adaptability" (278–79); he finds Undine's beauty "too obvious, too bathed in the bright publicity of the American air," but he admits on one occasion that "she seemed brushed by the wing of poetry, and its shadow lingered in her eyes" (277). Just as she learns to "soften her bright free stare with dusky pencilings" (285), Undine learns to strike a pose that will give her the illusion of interiority, the surface suggestion of some inner and unspoken quality. Her deep command of artifice allows her to draw a seemingly natural radiance from artificial light. This artificial light, like the artificial fire she wishes for at the Marvells' dinner party, is light without heat, the false fire that symbolizes her own cool passions. Although she is filled with a burning desire for many things, her response to physical affection is said to be "remote and Ariel-like, suggesting . . . the coolness of the element from which she took her name" (152). This coolness allows Undine to be both self-conscious and calculating: "A cool spirit within her seemed to watch over and regulate her sensations, and leave her capable of measuring the intensity of those she provoked" (294).

Nowhere is this undinal aesthetic more apparent than in the letters that Undine sends to represent herself in her absence to the husband and son she leaves behind when she goes to Paris. The letters she sends to Ralph Marvell are said to be distinguishable by their size and color: Ralph searches the letter-box for a "big tinted envelope with a straggling blotted superscription" (308). Ralph is said to look forward to their arrival more as "a pretext for replies than for their actual contents" (306). Ironically, Ralph finds the content of the letters to be "colourless" (306); a "desert of perfunctory phrases" (308), they repeat the same mundane facts of existence—who she had been "'round' with" or that the weather had been "too lovely or too awful." The "most eloquent passage of the letter" in one case is due to Undine's genuine interest as she tells her mother about "a new way of doing hair or cutting a skirt" (307).[16]

When the weekly letters cease to arrive from Paris and finally no letters come at all, Marvell's "illusions" are said to shrivel "down to their weak roots" (309). Devoid of content and empty of affection, the letters have been occasions for his fantasies about Undine. He imagines her "with him" "in the moment of writing." He sees her "palpably before him" sitting "at her writing-table, frowning and a little flushed, her bent nape showing the light on her hair, her short lip pulled up by the effort of composition; and this picture had the violent reality of dream-images on the verge of waking." Such dream images are disrupted by Undine's own description of herself at the moment of composition. In a letter that Marvell destroys immediately after reading it, she writes: "Everybody's talking to me at once, and I don't know what I'm writing." With an appropriateness that will become apparent only later, the narrative continues: "That letter he had thrown into the fire . . ." (308; Wharton's ellipses).

Despite the empty words and the straggling and blotted script of her hand-writing, Marvell responds to Undine's letters as if they were her physical presence: "Sometimes the mere act of holding the blue or mauve sheet and breathing its scent was like holding his wife's hand and being enveloped in her fresh young fragrance: the sentimental disappointment vanished in the pene-trating physical sensation." Tracing the first and last lines, Marvell overleaps the emptiness of the phrases in between them, replacing the sentimental "desert" of only "perfunctory phrases" with "the vision of their interlaced names, as of a mystic bond which her own hand had tied" (307–8). Although he is left with only blue or mauve sheets of paper, Undine's "youth and physical radiance" are said to cling to Marvell's "disenchanted memories as the scent she used clung to her letters" (309). With her power to create illusions, to evoke her image through letters that are no more than surface color and smell, Undine has the power of an "enveloping" presence which Marvell experiences as "penetrating."

In a sense, the most important letter Ralph receives from Undine is her final "letter"—which is in fact only a "mauve envelope." Marvell's "hands trembled as he tore open the envelope"; inside is another envelope addressed to him which "looked like a business communication and had apparently been sent to Undine's hotel in Paris and forwarded to him by her hand." Marvell assumes that his wife has simply forwarded another bill but as he "felt in the outer envelope for her letter" he discovers: "There was nothing there, and after a first sharp pang of disappointment he picked up the enclosure and opened it" (325). In his discovery that there is "nothing there," only an envelope within an envelope, Marvell is forced to observe the fact of Undine's emptiness. The colored envelope sent by Undine's "hand" does not in this instance become his wife's hand; devoid of personal content, there is nothing to sustain his illusions of sentimental presence, nothing to make him feel "enveloped in her fresh young fragrance." Undine is figured by the envelope, all color and smell, which conceals her absence of interiority. This is the language of her letters.

However, although to Ralph Marvell there is "nothing there," the envelope within Undine's colored envelope is not entirely empty. It contains a litho-graphed circular, a mass-produced advertisement, offering the services of a Parisian firm of detectives. The advertisement reads as a message to Marvell, as well as one of the series of warnings that Wharton sends to her readers. The detective agency offers "in conditions of attested and inviolable discretion, to investigate 'delicate' situations, look up doubtful antecedents, and furnish reliable evidence of misconduct—all on the most reasonable terms" (325). The question of "doubtful antecedents" leads back to two earlier moments in *The Custom of the Country* in which Wharton warns the reader to read carefully: the two visions which figure so importantly in Ralph Marvell's experience. It is in these visions that Marvell creates Undine and—in what I will argue are crucial moments of misreading—construes her as the source of his art. At these moments he decides that the purpose of his creative calling will be "to save her" (82). These central segments of the novel call into question the traditional story of the poet-hero and his female muse.

In its parable about the American artist, *The Custom of the Country* shows how the would-be poet Ralph Marvell destroys himself because he is too susceptible to surface beauty. Taking Undine as a figure for nature and art, he mistakes artifice for natural beauty. In the course of the novel, Ralph Marvell has two visions; each is prophetic and appears to Marvell in the night, and each follows a significant discussion about the meaning of Undine's name. Undine's name becomes an equivocal symbol, a sign that deceives Marvell because he interprets its emptiness, its absence of stable content, as innocence. Her beauty becomes the blank sheet on which Marvell inscribes his lyrical excess. The visions center on Marvell's interpretation and misinterpretation of Undine, as well as his reading and misreading of his own insights. His culminating visions and the discussions of Undine's name which precede them provide the governing metaphors of the novel. Once the signs are set, these visions provide the substance of Marvell's recollections, the moments of rereading that provide structural coherence for the novel.

In La Motte Fouqué's tale, *Undine*, one of the sources of *The Custom of the Country*, the protagonist has dreams that are both visionary and monitory.[17] The narrative tells the story of a knight who marries the soulless water nymph, Undine; she is able to gain a soul by marrying him. Like Wharton's Undine, Fouqué's soulless water spirits are "nothing but an elemental mirror of the outer world, which cannot flash back the inner one." Fouqué's novel warns against seduction and the siren song of things which are not what they seem: "The malignant power, which lies in wait to deceive us, loves to lull its chosen victim to sleep with sweet songs and golden stories."[18] In *The Custom of the Country*, however, Ralph Marvell is the author of his own siren song; although the woman he chooses as his wife lacks a soul, he himself is the source of the "sweet songs and golden stories" that lure him to his destruction. As in *Undine*, Marvell has visions, but he realizes too late that they are also warnings.

Marvell's first vision takes place after a discussion he has one afternoon with Undine's mother about the origins of her daughter's name and the Spragg family fortune. Seated in his room in the old Washington Square house, Marvell sees himself as a heroic figure who, like Perseus, will protect the "virgin innocence" (82) of the Spraggs.

> He seemed to see her—as he sat there, pressing his fists into his temples—he seemed to see her like a lovely rock-bound Andromeda, with the devouring monster Society careering up to make a mouthful of her; and himself whirling down on his winged horse—just Pegasus turned Rosin-ante for the nonce—to cut her bonds, snatch her up and whirl her back into the blue. . . . [83–84; Wharton's ellipses]

The second vision takes place on Marvell's honeymoon. Like the first vision, it follows a reverie about Undine's name and the meaning of Undine. In an extravagant scene which he later relates to the "transfiguring hopes" (217) of his denial, Marvell focuses on Undine's hand as the symbol of his muse. When he attempts to tell Undine about his "vision," the soulless Undine responds with deadly honesty that she "never cared much about spirits." Marvell explains to Undine that he is not thinking of the evocative efforts of a seance:

> I don't mean a dead spirit but a living one! I saw the vision of a book I mean to do. It came to me suddenly, magnificently, swooped down on me as that big white moon swooped down on the black landscape, tore at me like a great white eagle—like the bird of Jove! After all imagination *was* the eagle that devoured Prometheus. [152]

Marvell's two visions are related in obvious ways. Both are based on stories from Greek mythology that center on bound figures who are threatened with devourment. Both imagine heroes in conflict with the gods. Initially, Marvell seems to represent himself (as Undine elsewhere describes Popple) "like the hero of a novel" (190). His role in the first vision is not unlike Popple's representation of himself, in which being "the artist" is said to imply that "'passion' . . . would have been the dominant note of his life, had it not been held in check by a sentiment of exalted chivalry" (191). Marvell's casting of himself as the hero is related to his sense of himself as the author of *Undine*; his attraction to her is amplified by a Pygmalion impulse, a desire to create her from the images of his imagination: to animate her soul, her absent spirit, through the powers of poetic description. However, there is an ominous shift in the second vision, which turns out to contain a warning. Whereas in the first vision Marvell sees himself as Perseus rescuing the rock-bound Andromeda from the devouring monster in the wave, in the second vision he seems to become Prometheus, the rock-bound figure whose punishment is to have his insides devoured every day by the bird of Jove. Marvell himself has become the figure threatened with being devoured by "imagination," the devouring words of his own images and propensity for lyrical description.

Immediately prior to the first vision, Marvell is aware that he is giving up his "self" and his art in order to play a quixotic role on his "Pegasus turned Rosinante for the nonce." He asks whether saving Undine from the threats of despoiling men who would add her to "the ranks of the cheaply fashionable" was "really to be his mission—the 'call' for which his life had obscurely waited? It was not in the least what he had meant to do with the fugitive flash of consciousness he called self; but all that he had purposed for that transitory being sank into insignificance under the pressure of Undine's claims" (82). On the night of his second vision, Marvell is still trying to balance Undine's pressing material claims with his response to the beauty which calls him to write: "For the first time, as his senses thrilled to the deep touch of beauty, he asked himself if out of these floating and fugitive vibrations he might not build something concrete and stable." As he tries to convince himself that the "dull common cares" which oppress him might "become the motive power of creation," he imagines that he could earn money as a writer, that he could do "something that should both put money in his pocket and harmony into the rich confusion of his spirit" (150). Here Wharton alludes to the conflict between "figures" and "figures" that she makes explicit elsewhere in the novel. In a joke about art and financial survival, similar to the joke about subsisting on adjectives, Wharton has Undine repeat a conversation she heard at a dinner party about "the figures" that are "within reach of the successful novelist" (284). These are the only figures that this muse demands.

Before Marvell goes to tell Undine about his vision of himself as Prometheus, the vision of his book, he tries to convince himself that this vision really does tell of his literary calling: "'I'll write—I'll write: that must be what the whole thing means,' he said to himself with a vague clutch at some solution which should keep him a little longer hanging half-way down the steep of disenchantment" (150). Part of Marvell's "vague clutch" at a solution is his shift from his earlier acknowledgement that Undine's demands were replacing his literary calling to his conflation of her demands with his literary calling. However, as he chooses Undine for his muse, the vision of the eagle as the devouring imagination casts an ominous light on the possibilities of language and lyric poetry.

As he sits in the natural beauty of a summer afternoon in a grove near Siena in a scene which he will reread again and again, Marvell glimpses "the releasing power of language." Lying on his back in the shifting light, he is thrilled by the lyrically ecstatic effluviance of his own descriptive powers: "As he lay there, fragments of past states of emotion, fugitive felicities of thought and sensation, rose and floated on the surface of his thoughts. It was one of those moments when the accumulated impressions of life converge on heart and brain, elucidating, enlacing each other, in a mysterious confusion of beauty" (140). As he experiences "a sharper sense of individuality than can be known within the mere bounds of the actual," he experiences what is described as "the releasing power of language. Words were flashing like brilliant birds through the boughs overhead; he had but to wave his magic wand to have them flutter down to him" (141). The birds that are like words in the Italian grove become in the subsequent vision of the night the predatory imagination that tears at him like an eagle.

Marvell's choice of Undine as his muse in this scene confirms his susceptibility to female artifice, a fatal preference for a surface aesthetic to which he consciously subjugates the beauty of the natural world. In the passage which precedes Marvell's awareness of "the mysterious confusion of beauty" in which "fragments of past" feeling "rose to the surface and floated there"—the passage which precedes his realization of the "releasing power of language"—Marvell is pictured as being drunk with the color and scent of the landscape. As he lies "enclosed in a ring of fire" (139), the intense light and heat of the July sun, Ralph beholds a landscape the description of which is perhaps the most intense example of local color writing in Wharton's novel. This is not a vision of decorative color, however, but rather of "the secret treasures" of more subtle gradations between light and dark, the colors of shadows.[19]

> The sun, treading the earth like a vintager, drew from it heady fragrances, crushed out of it new colours. All the values of the temperate landscape

were reversed: the noon high-lights were white, but the shadows had
unimagined colour. On the blackness of cork and ilex and cypress lay the
green and purple lustres, the coppery iridescences, of old bronze; and
night after night the skies were wine-blue and bubbling with stars. [140]

Marvell finds the air not only breathable but "intoxicating" as he imagines that
"new" and "unimagined" color may be "crushed out of it" (140). The passage
suggests the drunken pleasure of giving oneself over to descriptive writing and
the mysteries of color, but it also suggests the dangerous seduction of descriptive writing. Almost immediately, Marvell moves from his "fugitive felicities of
thought and sensation" (140) to the woman at his side. In a moment which
explains the tragedy of the man who will hold a colored and perfumed sheet of
paper and be penetrated with the physical sensation that he is holding his
wife's hand, Marvell takes the hand of Undine and decides that this hand will
be the sign of his own power to write. However, even as he places himself and
the future of his art in the hands of Undine, he seems aware of the aesthetic
inadequacy of that hand, which he examines as if it were a decorative object, "a
bit of precious porcelain or ivory." This decorative hand is also demanding; in
what will become a recurrent image of Undine's grasping attitude toward
money and things, Marvell remarks that the hand was "one to be fondled and
dressed in rings, and to leave a rosy blur in the brain" (141). Undine's hand has
become the fatal emblem to which he consigns his response to beauty; he
relegates the natural world of "unimagined" color to the pastel limits of his
wife's hand: the hand with "nails as smooth as rose-leaves" that "leave[s] a rosy
blur in the brain" (141–42).

   Marvell, as we have seen, makes "a vague clutch at a solution" that still
includes the possibility of his literary calling within his marriage to Undine.
Despite his premonitions, he delivers himself into the hands of Undine Spragg,
clutches at her hand, as if it will serve as a sprag—a twig or limb that will hold
him "a little longer hanging half-way down the steep of disenchantment"
(150).[20] The hand seems to eclipse everything else:

The upper world had vanished: his universe had shrunk to the palm of a
hand. But there was no sense of diminution. In the mystic depths whence
his passion sprang, earthly dimensions were ignored and the curve of
beauty was boundless enough to hold whatever the imagination could

pour into it. Ralph had never felt more convinced of his power to write a great poem; but now it was Undine's hand which held the magic wand of expression. [142]

Focusing on the description of the exterior world, Marvell adds to the "layers and layers of unsubstantialness" (272); with his figurative language he attempts to describe "the spirit of shifting magic" of his wife, the "radiant creature." By using figurative language he creates a shape for Undine and conceals from himself the formlessness and the devouring emptiness of the woman he has taken for both wife and muse.

In classical myth, Undine, the beautiful water nymph or water spirit, can gain a soul only by having a child. Wharton's Undine becomes a mother but (as Elizabeth Ammons points out) she still does not gain a soul.[21] A scene which emphasizes Undine's lack of interiority in spite of her motherhood precipitates Marvell's first rereading of his visions. Absorbed at a tea given by Popple in which she and her portrait are the center of attention, Undine forgets that it is her son Paul's birthday. (She forgets the day of his birth, as if his birth had never taken place.) The birthday cake remains uncut because Undine forgets to bring her son to the Marvell house in Washington Square. In this evening of revelatory disappointment, Marvell goes to his own childhood room and recalling "the night when he had heard the 'call,'" realizes that his "transfiguring hopes and illusions" are gone: "Fool as he had been not to recognize its meaning then, he knew himself triply mocked in being, even now, at its mercy" (217). Marvell admits to himself that his life has become a long struggle to win attentions from Undine in which his "concession[s]" include "the sacrifice of his literary projects, the exchange of his profession for an incongenial business, and the incessant struggle to make enough money to satisfy her increasing exactions." He summarizes bitterly: "That was where the 'call' had lead him . . ." (218; Wharton's ellipses). Undine conceals the reason for her lateness with half-truths but admits that she got a ride home from Peter Van Degen: the man who will be her lover, the man whom Marvell had imagined in his first vision as the ominous force threatening the virgin innocence of the "lovely rock-bound Andromeda" who figured Undine.

In the light of these revelatory disappointments, Marvell moves on with critical accuracy to reread the ecstatic afternoon when he took Undine as his muse:

The turnings of life seldom show a sign-post, or rather, though the sign is always there, it is usually placed some distance back, like the notices that give warning of a bad hill or a level railway-crossing.

   Ralph Marvell, pondering upon this, reflected that for him the sign had been set, more than three years earlier, in an Italian ilex-grove. That day his life had brimmed over—so he had put it at the time. He saw now that it had brimmed over indeed: brimmed to the extent of leaving the cup empty, or at least of uncovering the dregs beneath the nectar. [221]

Marvell sees through his illusions to discover the "empty cup," the absence of substance, the emptiness of the "curve of beauty"—which in his previous figure "was boundless enough to hold whatever the imagination could pour into it" (142).

   Increasingly, Marvell acknowledges that the signs were always there but that he had deluded himself with the "transfiguring hopes" of denial. Having glimpsed the emptiness, the uncovered dregs, he discovers that these are signs that he already has read: "He knew now that he should never hereafter look at his wife's hand without remembering something he had read in it that day. Its surface-language had been sweet enough, but under the rosy lines he had seen the warning letters" (221). Marvell realizes that he has misread the surface language of Undine's hand. He has let physical or surface beauty blind him to the meaning of his wife's language, even to the actual words that she speaks. For example, in celebrating the protean nature of the woman who seems to mirror the changing shapes of the landscape, he has claimed to be seeing Italy through Undine's eyes: "Four months of beauty, changeful, inexhaustible, weaving itself about him in shapes of softness and strength; and beside him, hand in hand with him, embodying that spirit of shifting magic, the radiant creature through whose eyes he saw it" (139). However, when the radiant creature speaks for herself she complains about the heat and the bad food; her only interest appears to be a supposedly aristocratic, "extremely good-looking cavalry-officer" (143).

   Undine, whose physical presence pervades Marvell's lyrical response to the landscape, tells her husband that she does not like Europe. Surprised "that such unguessed thoughts should have been stirring in the heart pressed to his," Marvell learns that their honeymoon has not been "amusing" Undine. She tells him: "It's dirty and ugly—all the towns we've been to are disgustingly dirty. I loathe the smells and the beggars. I'm sick and tired of the stuffy rooms in the hotels" (153–54). Even before this outburst the "warning letters" that Marvell has refused to read are suggested in the discrepancy between the truncated dialogue and the lyrical rhapsodies of Marvell's interior monologues. Marvell tells Undine, "You look as cool as a wave"; it is at this point that we read his extended interior monologue about her hand and "the boundless curve of beauty." Undine's response is jarring: "I don't *feel* cool. You said there'd be a breeze up here" (141–42).

Although he hears his wife's complaints, Marvell does not understand them or take them as a measure of his muse. Instead he prefers to be overwhelmed by the imagined wave in which he pictures Undine as an undine: "His eyes softened as they absorbed in a last glance the glimmering submarine light of the ancient grove, through which Undine's figure wavered nereid-like above him" (144). The wavering figure of Undine, who smiles "vaguely" when Marvell tells her, "You never looked your name more than you do now," suggests that Undine does not understand Marvell's interpretation of her or her name. Wharton plays on the French word for wave, *vague*, as well as the multiple meanings of "figure," as she underlines the distance between Undine's limited world and the complicated system of reference and allusion in which Marvell has placed her. Ralph realizes that Undine does not understand, but "her smile was no less lovely for its vagueness, and indeed, to Ralph, the loveliness was enhanced by the latent doubt" (144). He ignores the discrepancy between the Undine who is elsewhere said to be a "creature of skin-deep reactions" (224) and the nymph of his illusions that inhabits the figurative world of imagination. Part of his hubris is to believe in his creation of Undine and to be charmed by the idea that his musings are beyond her understanding.

From the very beginning of his acquaintance with the Spraggs, Ralph Marvell has misread the story of Undine—the significance of both her origins and the source of her name. In the discussion with Undine's mother that precedes Marvell's first vision of Undine as "the lovely rock-bound Andromeda," the narrator warns the reader that "Ralph Marvell was too little versed in affairs to read between the lines of Mrs. Spragg's untutored narrative." In her narrative Mrs. Spragg tells of the death of two of her three children who caught typhoid from drinking bad water, the ruin of her father in land speculation, and the fortune that her husband made in a deal called "the Pure Water move." Mr. Spragg, she recounts, "had taken over some of poor father's land for a bad debt, and when he got up the Pure Water move the company voted to buy the land and build the new reservoir up there: and after that we began to be better off, and it *did* seem as if it had come to comfort us some about the children." Neither Ralph nor Mrs. Spragg are said to understand "the occult connection between Mr. Spragg's domestic misfortunes and his business triumph." Although Mr. Spragg, in his wife's terms, is said to have "helped out" (81) his father-in-law by buying his land and then turning a great profit for himself, the "Pure Water move" (like Undine and the Spraggs, who are imagined by Marvell to have a "virgin innocence" [82]) is neither pure nor innocent.

The source of Undine's name, which is related in the text along with a series of italicized words which describe her father's business deals in Apex, suggests a type of naming in which labels are meant to mask content, to conceal rather than convey meaning. In Ralph's conversation with Mrs. Spragg, the discussion of the "Pure Water move" follows the story of Undine's unusual name. Undine's mother explains: "Why, we called her after a hair-waver father put on the market the week she was born. . . . It's from *undoolay*, you know, the French for crimping; father always thought the name made it take." Despite this explanation, which is said to leave Ralph "struck and silent" (80), he insists on interpreting Undine as a water nymph, a goddess of the waves; he seems to ignore the nature of the element for which she is named. The chemical hair waver links her to feminine artifice and divides her from Marvell's world of deeper meaning, where nereids cavort in pure water and natural waves.

In hearing the story about Undine's grandfather, who is said to be "quite a scholar" with "the greatest knack for finding names" (80) for commercial products, and the brief history of family ruin and rise from land speculation and a "Pure Water move," Marvell becomes fixated on the "virgin innocence" of the Spraggs and the vulnerability of the Undine he imagines as the pure maiden threatened by the monster in the wave. In his translation of her name he hears Montaigne's words *"divers et ondoyant"* (79) echo in his mind.[22] Undine, however, is not named for a water nymph or a spirit of nature; she is named for a chemical substance meant to imitate the effects of nature, a commercial product designed to transform natural hair into an artificial wave. These are the "doubtful antecedents" of Undine's origins.

In the final scenes of his life, Marvell is forced to reread his memories of Undine as he saw her in the afternoon light of the grove near Siena. Under unbearable pressure to obtain a large sum of money with which he can pay off Undine (by this point his ex-wife) so that she will not take their son away from him, Marvell enters into a business deal with Moffatt (the ruthless entrepreneur who turns out to be Undine's former as well as future husband). In a discussion about Undine's expected refusal to go down in her price, Marvell becomes angry when Moffatt speaks so familiarly about Undine and warns him with proprietary zeal that "the fact that I've been divorced from Mrs. Marvell doesn't authorize any one to take that tone to me in speaking of her" (465). Moffatt, with his inclination for "poetic justice" (133), replies: "That so? Well, if that's the case I presume I ought to feel the same way: I've been divorced from her myself." He then tells Marvell "the whole story," adding, "It's mighty wholesome for a man to have a round now and then with a few facts" (466).

Although he is faced with Moffatt's unavoidable physical presence, Ralph Marvell still is unable to focus on what Moffatt is telling him. As his mind races with "unimportant and irrelevant things" (466), Marvell focuses on "the crystal toy that stood on the desk beside Moffatt's hand" and thinks: "That such a hand should have touched it" (468). The "crystal toy" at this moment becomes a figure for Undine. When he entered Moffatt's office, Marvell immediately recalled the similarity of this "little crystal vase" to one that Moffatt had shown him on a previous visit. Moffatt holds the vase "against the light, revealing on its dewy sides an incised design as frail as the shadow of grass-blades on water." His question to the entering Marvell—"Ain't she a peach?" (460–61)—recalls Moffatt's conversational opening to Marvell on the previous visit: "Fond of these pink crystals?" On that occasion, as he held "the oriental toy against the light," Moffatt added, "Oh I ain't a judge—but now and then I like to pick up a pretty thing" (451). Marvell is unable to face Moffatt's assertion that "Undine Spragg and I were made one at Opake, Nebraska"; yet unable to avoid the immense "bodily presence" of "*this* man" (467–68) blocking every perspective, he looks at the vase, one of the pretty things that make up Moffatt's collection of crystal vases, pink crystals, and toys that personify the feminine. At the moment of his disillusionment, perhaps focusing on the crystal toy, Marvell can finally see beneath the rosy lines, the "incised design" that looks like a reflection of nature; he can finally see that the beautifully lit vase is pink and empty.

Undine, the pink and empty container, gains a monstrous opacity when seen through her union with Moffatt. In this new light, Moffatt, whose "bodily presence" Ralph had dismissed as "the mere average garment of vulgarity," looms before him "huge and portentous as some monster released from a magician's bottle" (467–68). Moffatt, as the monster in the bottle, and Undine, as the "monstrously perfect result of the system" (208), are the ingredients of the monstrous union that destroys Ralph Marvell. When he returns to his room Marvell hears in his mind a version of Moffatt's statement, "We were made one in Opake, Nebraska," and he sees Undine "before him" as she was in Siena "leaning against the tree-trunk in her white dress, limpid and inscrutable" (471). Marvell realizes that Undine has been inscrutable, that he has been unable to read her, to see through her opaqueness to her Opake past.

In the room where he had his first vision, Marvell realizes that Undine has "lied to him, deliberately, ingeniously and inventively." "For the first time in months," he becomes prey to the "overwhelming sense of her physical nearness which had once so haunted and tortured him. Her freshness, her fragrance, the luminous haze of her youth, filled the room with a mocking glory." As Marvell attempts to "shut it out" by dropping "his head on his hands," the "vision" is said to be "swept away by another wave of hurrying thoughts" (471–72). Just as he presses "his fists into his temples" when he has his first vision of Undine as the "lovely rock-bound Andromeda" (84), Marvell uses his hands to force his eyes shut to block out the "things to be said or done," the things that had become "as unreal and meaningless as the red specks dancing behind the lids against which he had pressed his clenched fists" (472).

In the "silence of the empty house," Marvell does not want to see light again, and he cannot bear the idea that an inquiring maid will cross the threshold of his room. He takes a last look at the room, the site of his failed literary efforts and his vision of an innocent Undine: "For a moment he was conscious of seeing it in every detail with a distinctness he had never known before; then everything in it vanished." All that remains is "a drawer under one of the bookcases" that Marvell opens as he prepares to take his life with his own hand. He takes a revolver and positions it by passing "his left hand over the side of his head, and down the curve of the skull behind the ear" (474). Having glimpsed the emptiness of the boundless curve of beauty, Marvell traces the curve of his skull before he empties his mind of the haunting images of Undine.

The Marvell family story attributes Ralph's death to "the sudden rise of temperature—one of the fierce 'heat-waves' that devastate New York in the summer" (487). Ironically, what appears to be a delicately concealing euphemism—Marvell is killed by a "'heat-wave' "—becomes in the metaphoric scheme of the novel a literal naming of the "turnings of life," the "sign-post set some distance back." Marvell is devastated by the meaning of Undine's name that he refuses to acknowledge: a heat wave, a permanent wave, a bad permanent. Like Ajax on his rock, Marvell has lived in his illusions about man as a heroic creature who performs exploits among the Gods; and he is destroyed when he is swept away by the new and restless wave of the impermanent.

Wharton (who speaks in A Backward Glance of "the white heat of the creative fires" [BG, 212]) states in The Writing of Fiction that dialogue should be "regarded as the spray into which the great wave of narrative breaks in curving toward the watcher on the shore"; she adds that the "lifting and scattering of the wave, the coruscation of the spray" should "reinforce the contrast between such climaxes and the smooth effaced gliding of the narrative intervals."[23] In The Custom of the Country, Ralph Marvell is destroyed by a heat wave that represents the artificial wave of the language of description, the ornamental language of feminine artifice embodied by Undine. Undine, who aims at "glittering equivocation" (536), is the heat wave, the artificial wave that emits a deceptive and equivocal light: a light without heat.

To understand the image of Undine as artificial and monstrously devouring language, we need to recall Marvell's first vision of her as "a lovely rock-bound Andromeda, with the devouring monster Society careering up to make a mouthfull of her." Undine is the "monstrously perfect result of the system" (208) which Charles Bowen calls "the custom of the country" (206). This is a system in which the men are concerned with business and the women are compensated for their exclusion from men's lives with material objects. Near the end of the novel, when Moffatt comes to the de Chelles chateau in an attempt to buy the family's historic tapestries, Undine does not understand the "epic recital of plot and counterplot" of Moffatt's exploits in business; but she listens like "a new Desdemona" because she does know that the "meaningless syllables stood for success" (537). Together Undine and Moffatt form the "monstrous and factitious" "union" that Marvell thinks of as "what Popple called society . . . a muddle of misapplied ornament over a thin shell of utility. The steel shell was built up in Wall Street, the social trimmings were hastily added in Fifth Avenue" (73). Together they are fluent in the language of this society: "Every Wall Street term had its equivalent in the language of Fifth Avenue, and while he talked of building up railways she was building up palaces" (537). It is no coincidence that when he proposes marriage to Undine for the second time Moffatt says, "No, don't cry—it ain't that kind of a story . . . but I'll have a deck suite for you on the *Semantic* if you'll sail with me the day after to-morrow" (576).

The cannibalistic ethics of business are obvious in the novel as Mr. Spragg profits from his father-in-law's ruin, and Elmer Moffatt enjoys the "poetic justice" of precipitating *his* father-in-law's (that is, Mr. Spragg's) demise. Mr. Spragg tries to explain to his then son-in-law Ralph Marvell that it is up to men "to take care of their own skins" (261) and more ominously, that "shipwrecked fellows'll make a meal of a friend as quick as they would of a total stranger" (260). Moffatt is part of this cannibalistic business world that Marvell never understands: "Ralph had never seen his way clearly in that dim underworld of affairs where men of the Moffatt . . . type moved like shadowy destructive monsters beneath the darting small fry of the surface" (258). Moffatt and Undine, then, in their monstrous union, are "the devouring monster Society" threatening to destroy Andromeda.

In the classical story, Andromeda is bound to the rocks because her mother's boasting about her beauty has offended the nereids—the undines.[24] We have seen that in *The Custom of the Country* Undine represents an artificial wave that in Wharton's private literary mythology itself represents an artificial language. We can see that Andromeda represents a kind of language which offends Undine by its beauty if we recognize in Wharton's evocation of this mythological figure an allusion to the creative mythology Henry James drew upon in "The Question of Our Speech," a lecture that James gave to the 1905 graduating class of Bryn Mawr College.[25] In his lecture, James exhorts the young women of Bryn Mawr to become missionaries of speech, to go forth to improve the tonal quality, form, and pronunciation of American speech. James mixes his mythology in his speech: he figures the English language as an "unrescued Andromeda," an "Andromeda awaiting her Perseus" to rescue her from the many-headed monster of American speech. Andromeda, who is "dishevelled, despoiled, divested of that beautiful and becoming drapery of native atmosphere and circumstance," is threatened by (what James calls a few pages later) "some myriad-faced monster."[26] James's images gain power from their various explicit and implicit associations. The "myriad-faced monster" recalls the many heads of Scylla, herself a water nymph turned into a devouring monster; and of course the head that Perseus is supposed to sever is the head of Medusa, whose waving hair of snakes itself suggests many heads. The tonguelike snakes of the Medusa suggest the threat of many languages, as well as the dangerous and perpetual wagging of many tongues.

Early in the novel, immediately before Ralph Marvell hears the story of Undine's family and her name, he thinks that the Spraggs are different from the "invading race" who are condemning "those vanishing denizens of the American continent" like his mother and grandfather to "rapid extinction" (73–74). Most of the "Invaders," he thinks, "had already been modified by contact with the indigenous: they spoke the same language as his, though on their lips it had often so different a meaning." The Spraggs seem not to have "acquired the speech of the conquered race"; Mrs. Spragg "still used the dialect of her people" (79). This is what makes the Spraggs seem so "innocent" to Marvell, what makes Undine seem in need of being rescued.

However, Undine becomes expert in the speech of "'society' "; and toward the end of the novel, the husband who replaces Marvell has a similar revelation about the language of Undine. After Undine insists that de Chelles sell the Boucher tapestries, de Chelles, looking at her "as though she were some alien apparition," says, "You come among us from a country we don't know, and can't imagine. . . . You come among us speaking our language and not knowing what we mean; wanting the things we want, and not knowing why we want them . . . and we're fools enough to imagine that because you copy our ways and pick up our slang you understand anything about the things that make life decent and honourable for us!" (545). Undine may literally be an alien and speak a foreign language in France, but de Chelles realizes what Ralph Marvell tries to ignore: Undine only seems to speak the same language; the same words have different meanings. The invaders have not only conquered a race; through their imitation of "the speech of the conquered race," they have robbed language of meaning.

In his initial vision, Ralph Marvell wants to save Andromeda (James's figure for the English language), but he dedicates himself to championing the "surface-language" represented by the beauty of Undine. This surface language with the "warning letters" written under "rosy lines" is the siren song that lures the poet to destruction, the call that threatens to devour his authentic language. In the hand of Undine, language is a social garment, a kind of "glittering equivocation" in which words are divorced from meaning. In the second vision, Marvell anticipates being devoured by his own imagination; but he does not understand that the imagination that devours him will itself be devoured by the need to describe the shifting image of Undine, that he himself will be engulfed in the artificial wave of her sparkling surface presentation. Again, Wharton may be joking with James, who at the time she was writing *The Custom of the Country*, called her "the golden eagle, the Fire Bird, the Shining One, the angel of desolation or of devastation, [and] the historic ravager," and expressed his fear that her visits and her insatiable need for amusement would threaten his quiet life and literary labors.[27] Whether or not she recalled this image of herself as the golden eagle, however, Wharton depicts Undine as the representative of the predatory bird that is, of course, the symbol of the United States.

When we see Undine writing a letter at the beginning of the novel, we are told that she had read in the Sunday papers "that the smartest women were using the new pigeon-blood notepaper with white ink; and rather against her mother's advice she had ordered a large supply, with her monogram in silver" (18). The image we are asked to imagine of Undine Spragg's initials—U.S.—in silver on pigeon-blood paper figures nicely her national and predatory associations. Driven by a need for public notice, Undine begins her career of notoriety in her hometown newspaper, "The Apex Eagle"—a name that suggests a totem for Undine herself. The devouring muse, Undine is also the predatory eagle, the Apex eagle who consumes and destroys with words the "words that fly like birds overhead." As the representative of a surface language and a decorative aesthetic, Undine is characterized by a devouring emptiness.

Like her commercially inspired name, Undine represents the language of consumption; but joined with Moffatt as the devouring monster "Society" she also represents a consuming type of language that threatens to devour the rock-bound Andromeda who stands for both culture and pure English. This consuming language of consumption, designed to promote desire, provides the vocabulary of a surface aesthetic that is concerned with exterior forms. Misnomers, like the "Pure Water move," suggest the distance between words and the meanings they are intended to conceal. The world of the novel is one in which "reasonable terms" has come to mean the cost of a detective agency. In *The Custom of the Country*, the language of consumption is seen as a serious attack on tradition. Surface language feeds on culture, making "social trimmings" of deeper structures of association and meaning.

This process of removing language from its meaning seems to result in a loss of interiority, a soullessness that signals the death of culture. Commenting in her article "The Great American Novel" on the standardized banality of modern America as described in *Main Street*, Wharton writes that Sinclair Lewis's novel "with a swing of the pen hacked away the sentimental vegetation from the American small town, and revealed Main Street as it is, with all its bareness in the midst of plenty."[28] If Sinclair Lewis with his hacking pen cleared away the sentimental undergrowth to reveal that there was nothing there, Wharton created Undine as her symbol of that "bareness," that emptiness. In *The Custom of the Country*, Wharton warns that this emptiness is not benign: the consuming emptiness is devouring.

We have seen that *The Custom of the Country* is about the meaning of the name of Undine, as well as the problem of naming in a society symbolized by Undine. Wharton also sets a warning sign in her novel in the name of Ralph Marvell. Early in the novel, when Undine receives a letter from "Mr. Marvell's sister," the socially conscious masseuse Mrs. Heeny asks, "Marvell—what Marvell is that?" (5). With this gesture Wharton elegantly if ironically signals the presence in her novel of another Marvell—indeed, another poet named Marvell: Andrew Marvell. Wharton was a careful reader of Andrew Marvell. She includes his name in the small group of writers (along with Coleridge, Marlowe, and Goethe) who first inspire Vance Weston's literary awakening in *Hudson River Bracketed*. She also includes "To His Coy Mistress" in the anthology of English love poems that she edited with Robert Norton.[29]

Among the details that lead to Andrew Marvell in the text of *The Custom of the Country* is the presence of another unusual name, the last name of the portrait painter Claude Walsingham Popple. One page after Mrs. Heeny asks, "What Marvell is that?" she hears another name and asks, "What Popple?" (5–6). The odd name of Popple is linked to the name of Marvell; it appears in introductions to Andrew Marvell's poems because it is the married name of Marvell's sister and the name of the nephew, William Popple, who is credited with having prepared the manuscripts of some of his uncle's poems.[30] It is also possible that Ralph Marvell's criticism of Popple's paintings for their conspicuous display of wealth has some relation to Andrew Marvell's pamphlets and poems (particularly his "Advice to a Painter") about the threat of "popery."[31] However, the evidence of an intimate relationship between *The Custom of the*

Country and the poems of Andrew Marvell goes beyond this web of specific and speculative details, beyond hints that there might be more than one Marvell or Popple. The relation is most evident in the intricate dialogue that links Andrew Marvell's poems (especially "The Garden," "The Unfortunate Lover," and "The Gallery") to the lyrical passages associated with Ralph Marvell. I will suggest that Wharton draws upon Andrew Marvell in constructing her critique of American culture, her warning about the siren song of a dangerous feminine aesthetic that threatens to lure the writer to destruction.

Critics have noted in passing the remarkable poetic quality of the passages in *The Custom of the Country* that concern Ralph Marvell.[32] I will suggest that the densely coded and lyrical prose that Wharton allows herself to write to describe the experience of her would-be poet Marvell often contains both general and specific echoes of Andrew Marvell's poems. For example, the description of Ralph Marvell's passage through the fever that completes his transformation from what he calls a "lyric idiot" to a "plodding citizen" (456) evokes Andrew Marvell's "The Unfortunate Lover." The poem begins with a recollection of a more fortunate past:

> Alas! how pleasant are their days,
> With whom the infant love yet plays!
> Sorted by pairs, they still are seen
> By fountains cool and shadows green.
> [M, 58]

From this idyllic scene, the second stanza enters immediately into a description of the birth of the unfortunate lover from a shipwreck that places him among a "masque of quarrelling elements" and makes him the "orphan of the hurricane" (M, 59). Thrown against the elements, the "poor lover floating lay, / And, ere brought forth, was cast away" (M, 58). The lover in the poem is also, like Prometheus, threatened by predatory birds—not the eagle that Ralph Marvell imagines but a "numerous fleet of cormorants black":

> They fed him up with hopes and air,
> Which soon digested to despair,
> And as one cormorant fed him, still
> Another on his heart did bill;
> Thus, while they famish him and feast,
> He both consumèd, and increased,
> And languishèd with doubtful breath,

The amphibium of life and death.
[*M*, 59]

The unfortunate lover who once played with the "infant love" is "called to play" with weapons "at sharp" against Fortune and the "tyrant Love":

And tyrant Love his breast does ply
With all his winged artillery,
Whilst he, betwixt the flames and waves,
Like Ajax, the mad tempest braves.
[*M*, 59–60]

Described as "nak'd and fierce," the unfortunate lover struggles with his hand to "grapple, with the stubborn rock, / From which he with each wave rebounds, / Torn into flames, and ragg'd with wounds" (*M*, 60).

In *The Custom of the Country*, the unfortunate lover, Ralph Marvell, lies in a fever that is like "a silent blackness far below light and sound." He is said to have risen, to have "floated to the surface with the buoyancy of a dead body" (327). At this point we can see Wharton's prose entering into a close dialogue with Andrew Marvell's poetry:

But his body had never been more alive. Jagged strokes of pain tore through it, hands dragged at it with nails that bit like teeth. They wound thongs about him, bound him, tied weights to him, tried to pull him down with them; but still he floated, floated, danced on the fiery waves of pain, with barbed light pouring down on him from an arrowy sky. [327]

Wharton's images of "barbed light" and "an arrowy sky" recall the arrows of Marvell's "tyrant Love" who with weapons "at sharp," with his "winged artillery," plies the breast of the unfortunate lover. The lover of Marvell's poem, who is caught "betwixt the flames and waves" and "torn into flames, and ragg'd with wounds" becomes in Wharton's description of Marvell's raging fever subject to "jagged strokes of pain" and "fiery waves of pain." Wharton's word "jagged" echoes Andrew Marvell's word "ragg'd" in both sound and meaning. The tearing motion in the Marvell poems that is described as the unfortunate lover tries to "grapple, with the stubborn rock," in Wharton's version is cast as an attack in which Ralph Marvell feels himself torn by "the hands [that] dragged . . . with nails that bit like teeth." The rhyming of sound and meaning of "ragg'd" and "jagged" is echoed once again in Wharton's word "dragged." The "hands [that] dragged at [the body] with nails that bit like teeth" recalls

Andrew Marvell's use of the word "grapple" to describe the hand of the unfortunate lover as he attempts to grasp the rocks and becomes "ragg'd with wounds."

Wharton enters her closest textual dialogue with "The Unfortunate Lover" in what may be the most lyrical sentence of the novel: "They wound thongs about him, bound him, tied weights to him, tried to pull him down with them; but still he floated, floated, danced on the fiery waves of pain, with barbed light pouring down on him from an arrowy sky" (327). Andrew Marvell's "floating" lover who "with each wave rebounds / Torn into flames and ragg'd with wounds" in Wharton's language becomes the restrained lover who has thongs "wound . . . about him" and is "bound" and tied. Wharton repeats specific words from the poem, but in her passage the words "wound" and "bound" (Marvell's "rebound") change meaning as they describe the physical constraints and ties that have ensnared her poet and pulled him under the fiery waves. As Charles Bowen predicts elsewhere in the novel, Ralph Marvell is destined to "go down in any conflict with the rising forces" (280).

I am suggesting that in describing Ralph Marvell, Wharton often seems to experience a "releasing power of language" that is directly informed by Andrew Marvell's poems. Her description of her poet's experience of language and lyric possibility in the scene in which he feels the "confusion of beauty" in the ilex grove outside of Siena seems to borrow images from Andrew Marvell's "The Garden." In this scene, Ralph Marvell is said to feel himself "a mere wave on the wild stream of being, yet thrilled with a sharper sense of individuality than can be known within the mere bounds of the actual" (140–41). Wharton describes her poet as he experiences "the releasing power of language":

> Words were flashing like brilliant birds through the boughs overhead; he had but to wave his magic wand to have them flutter down to him. Only they were so beautiful up there, weaving their fantastic flights against the blue, that it was pleasanter, for the moment, to watch them and let the wand lie. [141]

As Ralph Marvell rests under an ilex tree imagining a waterfall where he might "lie in wait for adjectives" (146), he appears to enter into the lyrical world described in the seventh stanza of "The Garden," Andrew Marvell's poem about the pleasure of pastoral solitude:

> Here at the fountain's sliding foot,
> Or at some fruit-tree's mossy root,

Casting the body's vest aside,
My soul into the boughs does glide:
There, like a bird, it sits and sings,
Then whets and combs its silver wings,
And, till prepared for longer flight,
Waves in its plumes the various light.
[M, 100]

There is a general resemblance here, as well as an echoing of certain details. For Ralph Marvell, words are like birds; for the speaker in "The Garden," the soul is like a bird that glides into the bough. Both texts employ images of birds, flight, and boughs, while representing a metaphysical experience of "being" and the "soul." Each describes a moment of potential lyrical expression: the "fountain's sliding foot" and the soul that "like a bird . . . sits, and sings / Then whets and combs its silver wings" in "The Garden" and the image of Ralph Marvell with "words . . . flashing like brilliant birds through the bough overhead" in *The Custom of the Country*.

The birdlike soul of the speaker in "The Garden," which "whets and combs its silver wings / And, till prepared for longer flight, / Waves in its plumes the various light," closely parallels the moment in Wharton's novel in which Ralph Marvell realizes the possibility of his own soul's flight through writing. The soul of the speaker in "The Garden" "waves in its plumes the various light," a motion that suggests the passage of time and the motion of writing poetry in and about the diaphanous and temporal medium of light as the soul prepares for its separation from the body. The lyrical passage that describes Ralph Marvell's own vision of poetic possibility might be seen to rework these stanzas from "The Garden." In *The Custom of the Country*, however, the winged flight of Ralph Marvell's Pegasus symbolizes his hopes for his literary calling as well as its demise. During the afternoon in the grove Ralph Marvell senses himself to be on a wave amidst "the mysterious confusion of beauty." Although he imagines that he "had but to wave his magic wand" in order to have the words that are like birds "flutter down to him," his wand, unlike the "plume" of the speaker's soul in "The Garden," does not wave. Ralph Marvell senses the "releasing power of language"; as "words were flashing like brilliant birds," he sees them "weaving their fantastic flights against the blue," but he decides to "watch them and let the wand lie" (141).

"The Garden" celebrates the poet's solitude among the innocent scenes of nature. In the stanza that follows the description of the soul's flight into the boughs, the speaker suggests the early days in the first garden ("Such was that happy garden-state, / While man there walked without a mate") and concludes with the thought, "Two paradises 'twere in one, / To live in paradise alone" (*M*, 100). Ralph Marvell is not alone in the Italian grove; as we have seen, he makes the mistake of shifting his vision from the words which seem to fly overhead to the woman beside him who leans "against a gnarled tree with the slightly constrained air of a person unused to sylvan abandonments" (141). It is at this point in the novel that Ralph Marvell shifts his glance from the "weaving . . . flight" of the words overhead to take the hand of Undine, the hand that becomes his plume, his "magic wand":

> The upper world had vanished: his universe had shrunk to the palm of a hand. But there was no sense of diminution. In the mystic depths whence his passion sprang, earthly dimensions were ignored and the curve of beauty was boundless enough to hold whatever the imagination could pour into it. Ralph had never felt more convinced of his power to write a great poem; but now it was Undine's hand which held the magic wand of expression. [142]

Not only does Wharton seem to refer extensively to Andrew Marvell's texts in these scenes; the scene in which the absorbed poet consigns himself to the hands of a devouring muse is uncannily similar to the gold intaglio that appeared on the cover of the "Muses' Library" edition of *The Poems of Andrew Marvell* published by Wharton's publisher, Scribner's.[33]

On the cover of the "Muses' Library" edition of Marvell's poems, the figure of the muse holds a crown of leaves over the head of a seated man. The man appears to be a poet holding a "plume" or quill pen in the posture of writing; the shape of this feather is repeated again and again in the leaves of the trees. One hand of the muse reaches wandlike into the pennate world of the leaves, holding a banner that reads, "The Muses' Library," while the other arm in a continuous curve stretches downward to place a crown of bay leaves on the head of the poet. Although the muse's arms are outstretched in a sweeping curve which suggests winged flight, the poet absorbed in his writing does not seem to notice either her extravagant gesture or the crown of leaves that, held at its center, curves into the feathery shape of gold wings—like the "silver wings" of the soul in "The Garden." While the poet holds his plume, looking downward at the book on his lap, another book with lines representing print lies open, placed on an unusually shaped plaque that is suspended above the crown of leaves and the poet's head in the limbs of the tree.

I am suggesting that this image from the book that may have been on Wharton's writing table as she worked on these passages of *The Custom of the Country* could serve as an illustration for the vision the poet Marvell has in the grove of words, his book, and his muse. However, the vision of Ralph Marvell offers a disturbing interpretation of the book from the Muses' Library. The figure of the book suspended on the plaque seems to be on a different visual plane from the figures—perhaps, like the images of Ralph Marvell, beyond "the mere bounds of the actual." The elegant posture of the muse who bends her back as she stands before the tree is translated into the image of Undine, "a person unused to sylvan pleasures," whose "beautiful back could not adapt itself to the irregularities of the tree-trunk" (141) she leans against. More disturbing, perhaps, is the transfiguration of the suspended book, which suggests the "words flashing like brilliant birds," into the ominous shape that appears to Marvell in the night of his vision. In this vision, he sees the spirit of a book that he links to imagination—the eagle that devoured Prometheus. In the illustration, the book is placed spread-eagled, so to speak, on the outstretched wings of the oddly shaped plaque that draws the eyes downward to a sharp point suspended over the poet's head. In the context of *The Custom of the Country*, this suspended plaque might be read as the stylized shape of a predatory bird seen at the moment of descent, diving beak first to devour the seated poet.

We have seen that both the language and the themes of Andrew Marvell's poetry are echoed in *The Custom of the Country* in the language of the dreams and literary longings of Ralph Marvell. Yet the closest relation between Wharton and Andrew Marvell can be seen in the relation of the novel to Marvell's poem "The Gallery." Wharton's use of "The Gallery" goes beyond a mere borrowing of details or the cross-fertilization of allusions; she constructs a subtle textual dialogue between the poet and the would-be poet, both named Marvell, that finally provides an interpretive key for the entire novel. Placed in relation to *The Custom of the Country*, "The Gallery" reads as if it were an autobiographical poem written by Ralph Marvell from the impossible standpoint of his death; in this context, Andrew Marvell's poem also reads as if it were written about Undine.

Like *The Custom of the Country*, "The Gallery" represents a woman with a protean aspect; her shifting surface as it appears in alternating stanzas suggests the form of a goddess of light and of love, but she also is like a murderess and an enchantress. These images recall the visions and the revised visions of Ralph Marvell as he rereads his muse throughout the scenes of the novel. Marvell's poem opens with an appeal to the goddess of flowers: "Chlora, come view my soul, and tell / Whether I have contrived it well." In "The Gallery," the speaker is haunted by a series of images of a woman that have become his soul, a soul which is "contrived" and "composed into one gallery." Tapestries are removed to empty the interior which is given over to multiple images of Chlora:

> the great arras-hangings, made
> Of various facings, by are laid,
> That, for all furniture, you'll find
> Only your picture in my mind.
> [M, 61]

The shifting images alternate in the four stanzas at the center of the poem in which the female figure is variously described as "an inhuman murderess," an idyllic, waking "Aurora in the dawn," a "vexing" "enchantress," and the "Venus" of a quiet sea (M, 61–62). In the sixth stanza, the narrator speaks of being tormented by the shifting illusions that the protean female figure invents:

> These pictures, and a thousand more,
> Of thee, my gallery doth store,
> In all the forms thou canst invent,
> Either to please me, or torment.
> [M, 62]

The visible soul, "composed into one gallery," that Chlora is invited to view is composed of images that alternate between the peacefulness of goddesses of nature and the destructiveness of feminine artifice.

In its opposition of the woman who is like the goddess of dawn and the "inhuman murderess," "The Gallery" evokes the contrast of Clare Van Degen (with her shadowy drawing room) and Undine Spragg (with her voracious appetite for artificial light). The painter Popple sees these women in terms of their potential portraits and thinks that a portrait of Undine could be exhibited "splendidly as a *pendant* to my Mrs. Van Degen—Blonde and Brunette . . . Night and Morning" (72). Wharton builds on the opposition of the light and the dark maiden, between the paradoxical opacity and emptiness of Undine and the cool and dark—but clear—shadow world of Clare. In Popple's characterization, Undine is the blond figure representing night, and Clare is the brunette who symbolizes morning.

The final picture of "The Gallery" recalls the opening address of the speaker to Chlora, the female figure with the name of the goddess of flowers. Described as having "the same posture and the look" that first "took" the speaker, it displays "A tender shepherdess, whose hair / Hangs loosely playing in the air." The portrait shows a woman in nature who decorates herself with flowers, "Transplanting flowers from the green hill / To crown her head and bosom fill" (M, 63). This closing image, which the speaker finds most agreeable, is the entrancing image of female beauty joined with nature; flowers are not cut from life but rather transplanted onto the woman. The stanzas that picture the figure as being like the goddesses of nature (Aurora and Venus) picture woman and nature as nurturant landscapes. In particular, the figure who is like Aurora, who "stretches out her milky thighs" in a world where "manna falls and roses spring" (M, 61–62), suggests a feminine landscape that offers sustenance and sensual comfort.

The birds of the idyllic landscapes, however, the "wooing doves" who "Sit perfecting their harmless loves" and "The halcyons, calming all that's nigh" (M, 62), suggest that there might be harmful loves and stormy seas. This suggestion is underlined by the first "picture" of the poem, the figure "painted in the dress / Of an inhuman murdress" whose "fertile shop of cruel arts" contains the weapons of female artifice: "Black eyes, red lips, and curlèd hair" (M, 61). Artifice and innocent nature may exist side by side in these shifting images, but the poem suggests that nature in the hands of woman may be a decorative but dangerous disguise. The weapons of artifice, tested on the "hearts" of admirers, anticipate the portrait of the figure who, "like an enchantress," divines the story of her disembowelled lover. This stanza of "The Gallery" could be read as an account of Ralph Marvell's spiritual death:

Like an enchantress here thou shows't,
Vexing thy restless lover's ghost;
And, by a light obscure, dost rave
Over his entrails, in the cave,
Divining thence, with horrid care,

How long thou shalt continue fair;
And (when informed) them throws't away
To be the greedy vulture's prey.
[M, 62]

This picture, with its details of the devourment of the lover's entrails by vultures, recalls the feeding cormorants of "The Unfortunate Lover," as well as Ralph Marvell's vision of himself as a Promethean figure devoured by the eagle of imagination. The entrails of the lover have become the source of prophecy. However, in reading the entrails, the female figure of artifice finds only the fate of her own beauty: "how long" she shall "continue fair."

In *The Custom of the Country*, Ralph Marvell's hopes for his literary calling and indeed his interiority are represented by a cave that he finds along the shore. The cave is described as a "secret inaccessible place with glaucous lights, mysterious murmurs, and a single shaft of communication with the sky." Like the obscurely lit cave of "The Gallery," it is threatened by an enchanting female figure. We read of Marvell's "inner world" that "if the light in the cave was less supernaturally blue, the chant of its tides less laden with unimaginable music, it was still a thronged and echoing place when Undine Spragg appeared on its threshold . . ." (76–77; Wharton's ellipses). Like the speaker in "The Gallery," Ralph Marvell is consumed by the images of the soulless woman who has replaced his soul. His interior, like the entrails of the lover in "The Gallery," has become the text the female figure disposes of after being assured of her fairness. Ralph Marvell's words like brilliant birds become the vultures that are figured in Andrew Marvell's poem: the devouring bird that preys upon the poet's interior.

In *The Custom of the Country*, when Ralph Marvell becomes aware of Undine's plans for a divorce, "an outer skin of indifference" is said to form "over his lacerated soul" (339). Ralph Marvell feels mocked by the room where he had his original vision of Undine as "the lovely rock-bound Andromeda," and he reflects bitterly on where his Pegasus has landed him. His old room in the Washington Square house has become a version of the gallery in Andrew Marvell's poem: "The walls and tables were covered with photographs of Undine: effigies of all shapes and sizes, expressing every possible sentiment dear to the photographic tradition." These pictures "throned over his other possessions as her image had throned over his future the night he had sat in that very room and dreamed of soaring up with her into the blue . . ." (339;

Wharton's ellipses). Marvell tries to put away these images of Undine but each drawer and every corner "was packed with the vain impedimenta of living" (339). Ralph Marvell then reverses and repeats the process of the speaker of "The Gallery": he removes Undine's pictures, but finding no other place to put them, he puts them back "one by one." On the next day he discovers that Undine's images have been removed: "The photograph of his wife's picture by Popple no longer faced him from the mantel-piece"; all of the photographs of Undine "had been stripped" from the wall, and perhaps most significantly, "her image had vanished" from his "writing-table" (340).

However, Ralph Marvell's mind is still taken over by images of Undine, images that comprise the gallery of his soul. He understands that "what had been done to his room he must do to his memory and imagination: he must so readjust his mind that, whichever way he turned his thoughts, her face should no longer confront him" (340–41). Eventually, finding that the "face of life was changed for him," Marvell attempts to "readjust" and "take an inventory" of his values, to "reclassify them, so that one at least might be made to appear as important as those he had lost; otherwise there could be no reason why he should go on living" (423). His "two objects in life were his boy and his book," and he realizes "the boy was incomparably the stronger argument, yet the less serviceable in filling the void" (423–24). At this point he turns with "cold fervour, to his abandoned literary dream," finding that with "the day's work over, he was possessed of a leisure as bare and as blank as an unfurnished house" (424).

Later, Marvell loses his last illusions when Moffatt gives him a "round . . . with a few facts" (466). Returning home, he suffers from an acute sensual awareness "as though he were some vivisected animal" (470). Knowing he will be robbed of his boy by the grabbing Undine, Marvell feels robbed of his interior, of the dreams that have "filled the void" and furnished the "bare" and "blank" house of his leisure. Just prior to his suicide, he is once again haunted by the image of Undine, by the "overwhelming sense of her physical nearness": "her freshness, her fragrance, the luminous haze of her youth" are said to fill "the room with a mocking glory" (471–72). Undine mounts her attack on meaning by removing deeply valued and symbolic objects. The objects that represent cultural tradition are decontextualized to become a decorative setting for Undine, part of the layered surface of her "phantom 'society.' " Amidst "the blurred half-light and half-tones, deletions and abbreviations" of the Marvell family customs, Undine has asserted herself as "the dominant figure." Just as she removes the tapestries from the de Chelles' gallery, she robs the Marvells of their "quiet Dutch interior"—replacing the soul of her husband with a gallery of Undines. The speaker in Andrew Marvell's "Gallery" might be speaking for Undine's unfortunate lovers when he says,

> the great arras-hangings, made
> Of various facings, by are laid,
> That, for all furniture, you'll find
> Only your picture in my mind.
> [M, 61]

On the opening page of *The Custom of the Country*, Wharton introduces Mrs. Heeny's "shabby alligator bag" (3). Mrs. Heeny, "'society' manicure and masseuse" and "manipulator and friend" (4) of Undine and Mrs. Spragg, appears with this bag on several occasions, including the beginning and the end of the novel. The bag is "stuffed with strips of newspaper"—the newspaper "clippings," the "piles and piles of lovely new clippings" (581) that she pulls out by the handful to instruct Undine on the social importance of the Marvells. After Undine's marriage to Ralph Marvell, the clippings increasingly report the exploits of Undine Spragg. Undine's ambition from the outset of the novel is to live the life of the women described in the articles she reads in magazines and newspapers, such as "A Society Woman's Day" in *Boudoir Chat* (41). She thinks of herself as living the life of the "'society novels' " (228) that she read in Apex, and eventually she senses herself to be "breathing the very air of French fiction" (404). Early in the novel Mrs. Heeny asks Undine if she has "read the description" of herself in the morning paper, adding, "I guess I'll have to start a separate bag for *your* clippings soon" (86).

At the end of *The Custom of the Country*, Mrs. Heeny reappears with the young Paul Marvell; both the son and the masseuse are strangers to the new Parisian mansion of Undine and Moffatt. To Paul Marvell, the only familiar objects are the tapestries that he remembers from the home of his "French father." When Mrs. Heeny offers to let him look at her clippings, "the word woke a train of dormant associations"; he can remember rummaging "in the depths of a bag stuffed with strips of newspaper" (581). Paul (like the reader of the novel at this point) reads the clippings with the hope that they "might furnish him the clue to many things he didn't understand. . . . His mother's marriages, for instance" (582). Mrs. Heeny produces (and in effect enters into the record of the novel) the sensationalistic account of Undine's divorce from de Chelles and her marriage to Moffatt. This particular "long discoloured strip" is torn because "so many's wanted to read it" (584).

Even before Mrs. Heeny suggests to Undine's son that he could "make a beauty" of a "scrap-book" about his "Ma with her picture pasted in the front" (582), Mrs. Heeny's black bag has become a figure for both Undine and Wharton's own scrapbook, her "beauty" about Undine. Despite the novel's references to the "bareness of the small half-lit place" where Undine's "spirit fluttered" and the "mind" which is "as destitute of beauty and mystery as the prairie school house in which she had been educated" (147), the soulless Undine is not entirely empty. With her penchant for imitation, she incorporates an assortment of texts which, like Moffatt's collections, might be said to form an "assemblage of unmatched specimens" (538): magazine articles, Sunday supplements, sentimental novels, and finally the clippings that make up her life story. (In a sense *The Custom of the Country* itself, with its multiple allusions and literary references, could be seen as a scrapbook or as an "assemblage of unmatched specimens" like the "collection" [538] that Moffatt strives to put together.)

This image of Undine as a bag stuffed with sentimental texts could be read as an allusion to Goethe's play, *Der Triumph der Empfindsamkeit*—which might be translated, *The Triumph of Sentimentality*. Wharton, who claimed to have read all of Goethe's plays by the time she was fifteen years old, wrote to Robert Grant while she was writing *The Custom of the Country* that she was "capable of reading only Goethe and Schopenhauer." The play contains a masque that would have attracted Wharton's attention: a long monologue is delivered by a character named Proserpina.[34] Like *The Custom of the Country*, Goethe's play was written to satirize (in George Henry Lewes's description) "every fashion-able folly, in dress, literature, or morals."[35] It tells the story of a prince who has built a "mechanical imitation of nature" that utilizes blown glass waterfalls and tapestries depicting various natural scenes.[36] In Lewes's description, the prince "adores Nature; but not the rude, rough imperfect nature whose gigantic image would alarm the sentimental mind; but the beautiful rose-pink Nature of books. He likes Nature as one sees it at the Opera."[37]

The prince also has a life-size doll that he prefers to the woman of which it is an exact replica. At the end of the play, a trapdoor in the doll springs open to reveal a hollow interior filled with various sentimental books. The books scatter onto the stage, revealing the stuff that makes up the sentimental doll worshiped by this prince of artifice. Among the books that fall out of the doll and are then disparaged is *The Sorrows of Young Werther*; Undine, also an artificial creature composed of sentimental texts, is more likely to include books such as *When the Kissing Had to Stop* (37) than *Werther*, but she also knows a tragic story about a young lovesick poet who commits suicide by shooting himself.

The Custom of the Country, like *Der Triumph der Empfindsamkeit*, tells the story of an artificial doll made up of sentimental texts, a doll whose natural element is the opera stage set that imitates the natural. Both works, like Andrew Marvell's "The Gallery," tell a story about a woman of artifice who is in part created by the illusions of her lover; Ralph Marvell is said to have "vivified, coloured and substantiated" Undine, who was only "the miserable ghost of his illusion" (221–22). Each of these three stories of feminine artifice also contains tapestries: the "great arras-hangings" in "The Gallery," the theatrical backdrops that replicate nature for the prince in Goethe's play, and the "Boucher tapestries" (543) in *The Custom of the Country*. In Wharton's novel, these tapestries—"the great Boucher series" (498)—that hang in "the Boucher gallery" (517) of the de Chelles chateau, more than any other objects, represent the link between the aristocratic family and its prestigious past. Undine's desire to remove the tapestries from the de Chelles family home represents both her assault on culture and her deep affinity with the tapestries themselves.

Just as the pictures of Chlora replace the "arras-hangings" in the mind of the speaker of Andrew Marvell's "The Gallery," Undine's campaign to remove the tapestries from the de Chelles family chateau is at least partly motivated by a desire to "assert herself as the dominant figure of the scene" (37). Because of their importance as symbols of the de Chelles family line and tradition—"They were given by Louis the Fifteenth to the Marquis de Chelles" (530)—the tapestries become the object of Undine's attack on the cultural traditions that she is unable to understand. She is driven to rend the tapestries from the de Chelles family, and she cannot understand why they seem smaller when they are finally transferred to the Moffatt mansion. She does not understand why they seem to have been reduced to a mere decorative surface, a new backdrop for the costly things that Undine feels should surround a woman like herself.

As the wife of Raymond de Chelles, Undine ostensibly wants to sell the tapestries to get the money that she needs to pursue her pleasures in Paris; the great house (as she tells Moffatt, who appears on the scene to look at the tapestries) "eats it all up" (536). Yet when Undine has divorced de Chelles and married Moffatt, she accomplishes what she had always desired in relation to the tapestries: removing them from the family chateau. Moffatt, who says that acquiring the tapestries was "like drawing teeth" (589), accomplishes Undine's goal of robbing the "mouth" of the Boucher gallery, leaving behind an empty *bouche* and a toothless maw where there were once "smiling scenes" (517). Formerly in competition with the house that "eats it all up," Undine succeeds in devouring the interior of her rival. When she first proposes selling the tapestries, de Chelles is said to look at her "as though the place where she stood was empty" (527). Like the shifting feminine figure in all the "images thou cans't invent, to please or torment," Undine has replaced the "storied hangings" (527) of the soul of the house with haunting images of her consuming presence. In doing so she robs de Chelles of a past.

This attack on tradition is analogous to Undine's destruction of the identity of the wedding ring and necklace that are the Marvell family heirlooms. Just as she removes the tapestries from the context that gives them meaning, Undine removes the jewels from their settings. The destruction of these Marvell family jewels is said to inflict a "wound" (214) on Ralph Marvell. The sexual implication is obvious: the tapestries that are removed like teeth and the wound that results from the destruction of family jewels represent a loss of both power and patrimony. Moreover, in destroying the links to the past and the power of tradition, Undine seems to attack deeper structures of meaning, to rob interiors, to rob both the Marvells and the de Chelles of their future. Ralph Marvell commits suicide when he knows that his son will be taken from him, and Raymond de Chelles is deprived of an heir because the Catholicism that forbade his marriage to Undine before Ralph Marvell's suicide will not recognize his divorce from Undine.

There is also "poetic justice" in Moffatt's acquisition of the Boucher tapestries for his collections after his marriage to Undine. In a novel about visions, deceptive surfaces, and the potential dangers of an attraction to light, the fact that the tapestries are said to be by Boucher (the only painter besides Popple who plays a role in the plot of the novel) must have specific significance. The reader is more than once asked to imagine what the Boucher tapestries look like. The Boucher gallery is said to be Undine's favorite room in the de Chelles chateau: "The smiling scenes on its walls and the tall screens which broke its length made it more habitable than the drawing rooms beyond" (517). From the outset, there is an affinity between Undine and the tapestries, which are described as, like Undine, "fading too, on the walls of the room in which Undine stood" (490).

At one point, as Undine walks in the gallery, "her glance" is said to rest "on the great tapestries, with their ineffable minglings of blue and rose, as complacently as though they had been mirrors reflecting her own image" (529). With their "fabulous blues and pinks," the tapestries are said to look "as livid as withered roses" (498). Their colors recall the feminine aesthetic that Wharton associates with "the rose and lavender pages" of the local color "authoresses," the interior decorators Wharton attacks in *The Decoration of Houses*, and especially the pastel preferences of Undine—who leaves a "rosy blur in the brain." The painter Popple (who is "an authority on decoration") seems to be thinking of this undinal aesthetic when he suggests for Undine's drawing room "a French 'period' room, all curves and cupids: just the setting for a pretty woman and his portrait of her" (229).

Contrasting Boucher's work to that of Greuze, Robert Rosenblum writes of Boucher's "powdered, pastel tints," "impulsive, errant contours," and human figures that are "diminutive, pampered dolls capable only of pleasure."[38] In the eighteenth century Boucher was attacked for displaying all of the excesses of the rococo. Michael Fried notes that Boucher was criticized by his contemporaries for being "artificial in color, mannered in drawing, and uncertain in expression."[39] Many of Boucher's paintings suggest the world and concerns of Wharton's novel. The *Pastorale*, one of a series of six paintings by Boucher called *Pastorales et Paysages*, is described by Rosenblum as an "unreal, erotic Arcadia in which the amourous shepherd and shepherdess are freed from all responsibilities but the fulfillment of their own desire."[40] Wharton's reference to "the great Boucher series" (498), however, whose "history has been published" (530), suggests that she may have particular works by Boucher in mind. Two paintings that are particularly relevant to *The Custom of the Country* are *Le Lever de Soleil* and *Le Coucher du Soleil*, both of which were made into renowned tapestries.[41]

These paintings depict an allegorical rising and setting of the sun. In each painting there is a circular light, meant to represent the sun, which emphasizes the central figures of Apollo and Thetis. Apollo, the god of light, lyric, and prophecy, stands with Thetis—the protean water nymph who transformed herself into a fish, a wave, and a flame in order to avoid marriage to a mortal. Standing above the water in the soft light of the sun, Apollo and Thetis in their scenes of parting and welcome are unnoticed by the many nereids and dolphins who frolic among the waves below. These self-absorbed figures, fleshy and full-bodied undines, appear to emerge from the darkness along with cherubs and sea creatures. In *Le Coucher de Soleil*, there is an odalisque-like undine "whose vast undinal belly moonward bends" (to borrow a line from Hart Crane) as she stretches out on a wave beneath the gentle light. One could easily imagine that these are the tapestries that Undine Spragg sees as "mirrors reflecting her own image" (529).

There is yet one more image of an Undine that seems to stand with the Undine of *The Custom of the Country*, an image that may illuminate Wharton's cultural critique of the undinal aesthetic represented by both Undine Spragg and Boucher: Turner's painting *Undine Giving the Ring to Massaniella, Fisherman of Naples*. Turner, of course, is famous for his paintings of light, paintings described at great length by Ruskin in his *Modern Painters* (which Wharton lists as one of the books she read in her father's library [BG, 70]). His painting of Undine, along with its companion painting, *Angel Standing in the Sun*, might allow us to see the Boucher paintings in a different light. Although the Angel appears to be emerging from the intense light of the sun, the Undine is a vague figure who appears in the center of the light in a sea of fire. Guy Whelen, who refers to fire and water as "the *primum mobile* of Turner's imagination," the "union of water and sparkling light," describes the light of *Undine* as "phosphorescent mists."[42]

Unlike Boucher's images of the rising and the setting of the sun, Turner's *Undine* and *Angel Standing in the Sun* suggest an apocalypse: the destruction of all the creatures that inhabit the liminal world where light merges into shadowy darkness. Lawrence Gowing's description of the light in Turner's painting evokes this apocalyptic world in terms that recall the element of Wharton's Undine: "Light is not only glorious and sacred, it is voracious, carnivorous, unsparing. It devours impartially, without distinction, the whole living world."[43] The "Angel Standing in the Sun," who carries a sword upright, has been seen as the angel of death described in Revelation 19:17–18: "And I saw an angel standing in the sun; and he cried with a loud voice, saying to all the fowls that fly in the midst of heaven, Come and gather yourselves together unto the supper of the great God; that ye may eat the flesh of kings . . . and the flesh of mighty men." Seen by some critics as a female figure representing Judith or Delilah,[44] this angel might also recall the figures James used to describe Wharton: the "Angel of Destruction," the "Angel of Devastation," the "shining one," the "historic ravager."[45] In the *Angel Standing in the Sun*, the angel appears to be emerging from the brilliant center of light. In *Undine*, the light itself seems to threaten annihilation. It is as if the figure of Undine were disappearing rather than emerging, as she is melded into the bright blindness of the devouring light.

The dialectic of light in *The Custom of the Country* is illumined by the contrast between Boucher's and Turner's paintings of light—their paintings of Undines. Wharton's Undine may be the pastel and decorative nereid of Boucher's art, but like Turner's Undine, she also represents a dangerous and apocalyptic light. She is "the core" of a "vast illumination, the sentient throbbing surface which gathered all the shafts of light into a centre" (60). Described against the "brilliant background" of "blazing" electric light as she poses before a mirror, Undine's "black brows, her reddish-tawny hair and the pure red and white of her complexion" are said to defy "the searching decomposing radiance: she might have been some fabled creature whose home was in a beam of light" (21). As the embodiment of a brilliant yet artificial fire, a light without heat, Undine is an apocalyptic muse who conceals her powers of destruction under an illusory and shifting surface. In writing *The Custom of the Country*, Wharton assumes the role of an "angel of devastation" to write a book of revelation about the monstrous union that threatens to devour the American artist.

FIVE

Pomegranate Seeds

Letters from the Underworld

(The Touchstone and Ghosts)

They fed him up with hopes and air,
Which soon digested to despair,
And as one cormorant fed him, still
Another on his heart did bill;
Thus, while they famish him and feast,
He both consumèd, and increased,
And languishèd with doubtful breath,
The amphibium of life and death.
—Andrew Marvell,
"The Unfortunate Lover"

Edith Wharton's last completed story, "All Souls," was finished in February of 1937. Wharton died in August, and later that year "All Souls" was published in a posthumous collection of her ghost stories, appropriately titled *Ghosts*.[1] By the time she wrote "All Souls," the circle of the living had grown smaller for the woman who had dedicated her autobiography to "the friends who every year on All Souls' Night come and sit with me by the fire."[2] Writing on All Souls' Night sixteen years earlier, in 1921, Wharton gave a litany of those she called "all my dead." The list included such friends as Henry James and Howard Sturgis and was headed by her childhood nurse, "my darling Doyley."[3] In 1937, at the age of seventy-five, Wharton faced both the inevitability of her own death and the signs of another war with Germany.

One might read a self-portrait of Wharton at the end of her life in the elderly woman she describes isolated on an estate in rural Connecticut in "All Souls." After having injured her ankle, the woman is mysteriously deserted for a single day by all of her servants; left alone with a plate of stale sandwiches, she finds that the telephone is dead and the electricity is off. The fire has gone out and no one answers her cries. Hobbling with pain down the stairs, the woman hears a disembodied voice in the apparently empty kitchen. It turns out to be a radio, but Wharton makes the point that ghosts and ghostly fears did not disappear with the invention of electricity; indeed, a source of terror in her last years was the voice of Hitler heard on the radio.[4] In "All Souls," the elderly woman feels estranged from her servants; even when questioned, they never explain their departure or even admit their absence. In the years when she could no longer care for herself, Wharton experienced the loss through old age or death of her trusted servants. Like the woman in her story, she found herself more and more amidst a household of strangers. The "Great War" had disturbed hierarchies and unsettled Wharton's familiar surroundings. She described the new world in the preface to her ghost story collection as a "roaring and discontinuous universe" (x).

Ghosts is Wharton's selection of her best ghost stories. Although most of the eleven stories in the collection had been published previously in magazines and anthologies, a surprising number of them were composed toward the end of Wharton's life. In the preface she defines the stories as successful because they treat themes that frightened her; she emphasizes that the teller must be frightened in the telling of the story in order to bring out what she calls the "thermometrical" (xii) response: a cold shiver to the spine of the reader. In "Life and I," her unpublished autobiography, Wharton confesses that "till I was 27 or 8, I could not sleep in the room with a book containing a ghost-story & that I have frequently had to burn books of this kind, because it frightened me to know that they were downstairs in the library!"[5]

Wharton's description of the physical experience of reading ghost stories suggests that her response to this genre was more visceral than her response to other kinds of texts. According to Wharton, the medium of communication for this writing, like the faculty used in the apprehension of ghosts, lies below the conscious intellect in "the warm darkness of the prenatal fluid" (xii). In the preface Wharton also insists that ghost stories need an active and intimate reader; the tale is meant to evoke, build upon, and feed upon the fears of the reader, who must feel the immediacy of someone actually listening to a story-teller. Only through the reader's elaboration and amplification of the narrative through her or his own fears can the latent terror of the text be realized. "When I first began to read, and then to write ghost-stories, I was conscious of a common medium between myself and my readers," Wharton explains, "of their meeting me half way among the primeval shadows, and filling in the gaps in my narrative with sensations and divinations akin to my own" (viii).

This acknowledgment of the peculiar demands of the ghost story genre is unusual for Wharton because it suggests that what she openly attempts in the ghost story is the opposite of what she admires in other kinds of writing— whether novels or treatises on art. When works evoked sympathy and acts of identification, Wharton felt that they encouraged responses from readers which she considered "sentimental undergrowth" (*BG*, 141). This "sentimental vegetation"[6] that Wharton frequently derided occluded the possibility of clar-ity; as we have seen, she preferred a realism which was conveyed through opposition rather than identification. However, while she seeks a formal dis-tance from her reader in her other works, in her ghost stories Wharton seeks basic points of identification. Wharton seems willing to share with her readers her fears of loneliness, isolation, and abandonment.

In this sense, as texts in which Wharton acknowledged an autobiographical investment, the ghost stories can provide clues for understanding Wharton both as a writer and a person. More important, however, the ghost stories (along with Wharton's first work of longer fiction, *The Touchstone*, which I will argue belongs to her ghost story genre) contain her most personal discussion of the place of the "woman writer." In the previous chapters, I examined Whar-ton's fears about women and women writers: the costs of assuming the pose and place of the writer, the dangers of both becoming and having a mother, the horror of both caretaking and infertility, the need to rehabilitate the mother, the siren song of sentimental story, and the feminine aesthetic that threatens to destroy the American artist. We saw also that Wharton was particularly anxious about silence and inarticulateness, as well as the dangers and possibilities of women's speech. In this chapter, I will explore how Wharton's ghost stories reveal her efforts to imagine a voice for the woman writer, to place the woman writer in relation to the unwritten (and in some sense unspeakable) story of women's silence. Through the medium of the ghost story, Wharton peers into (what she calls in the story "Afterwards") the "deep dim reservoir of life" and the "back-waters of existence" that "breed, in their sluggish depths, strange acuities of emotion" (73). Wharton explores in these narratives a repressed story about women who become unquiet ghosts because they cannot have a voice.

Wharton's family had a history of weak lungs; many of her relatives died of tuberculosis. Wharton herself may have inherited some of her difficulties in breathing from the Jones family; she suffered from debilitating hay fever and asthma, which may have been psychosomatic, at least in part. When she lay near death with typhoid fever as a child, Wharton's mother saved her by wrapping her in cold, wet sheets. This image seems almost a poetic reversal of the "cocoon" Wharton describes as the permeable warmth of her childhood nurse, Doyley, the "atmosphere without which I could not have breathed" (*BG*, 26). After the fever, Wharton was haunted by the fear that she would not be able to breathe. In retrospect, she would see the fever as the dividing line at which her secure infancy ended and her terror began. It might also be seen as marking a point of increasing individuation which brought her to identify with her mother, the cold Lucretia Jones, rather than her nurse.

Wharton associated a loss of speech and breath with both the death of her father in 1881 and the death of her dearest friend, Walter Berry, some fifty years later. At death, each had been unable to speak. "Twice in my life," writes Wharton in *A Backward Glance*, "I have been at the death-bed of someone I dearly loved, who has vainly tried to say a last word to me." She continues: "I doubt if life holds a subtler anguish" (*BG*, 88). Wharton thought about her father's "stifled cravings"; she felt with certainty that he was a lonely man, even in life "haunted by something always unexpressed and unattained" (*BG*, 39). Wharton is frightened not only by literal death but also by the metaphorical death represented by voicelessness. These were Wharton's greatest fears, and throughout her life she turned to the ghost story as a medium for their expression. In *Ethan Frome* and *Summer*, Wharton reflected on New England as a dark and unconscious place of beginnings. The ghost stories, however, provided a more immediate form in which she could give voice to her unspoken thoughts and fears. The contemplation of taciturn New Englanders allowed Wharton to dwell on her own sense of inarticulateness and her inability to bridge cultural otherness. In the ghost stories, the fear of inarticulateness becomes more directly a fear of the loss of breath: a fear of being absolutely silenced by either isolation or death.

Ten of the eleven stories in *Ghosts* are concerned with the abandonment and/or imprisonment of a "female" figure.[7] (I place "female" in quotes here because I will suggest that in these stories, as in *Ethan Frome*, the female can be figured by a male character.) The prison of inarticulateness that Wharton fears most deeply, manifested in the theme of women's isolation, is figured throughout her autobiographical and fictional writings in recurrent images of people who are strangled, lose their breath, or simply are silenced. These images recall Wharton's own years of chronic, formless anxieties, what she called "the choking agony of terror."[8] Hers was a breathless fear (by her own account) experienced for many years as she approached closed doors, especially as she returned to the threshold of her mother's house. (R. W. B. Lewis connects this fear to the waiting presence of Wharton's mother.)[9] Wharton feared being trapped in her mother's house, surrounded by the trivial matters she associated with women in general and her mother in particular. Furthermore, as we saw in varying degrees in both *The House of Mirth* and *Ethan Frome*, Wharton's fiction reflects anxieties about growing into a mature woman's body like that of the mother, a body that would draw one into the ritual responsibilities of the female cycle. Wharton feared the power of the mother that could blight the "buds of fancy" (*BG*, 39) and sacrifice full lives to a life of caretaking that would cripple innovation and impede ambition.

Several of the ghost stories dramatize these kinds of fears, focusing in particular on the dangers of social structures that isolate women and trap them in prisons of inarticulateness. "A Bottle of Perrier," "Kerfol," and "Mr. Jones" all combine Wharton's central themes of "female" imprisonment and strangulation. "A Bottle of Perrier" is among Wharton's most frightening depictions of entrapment in place by the landscape of the feminine.[10] This story contains virtually no female characters: the only females ever mentioned, the "two or three charming women . . . chattering and exclaiming" (376), are left on a terrace overlooking the Nile early in the story. The story can be seen, however, as a barely encoded depiction of a psychosexual struggle between men and women.

An American anthropologist named Medford meets an English anthropologist named Almodham and the two men ride "back to Luxor together in the moonlight" (376) before going their separate ways. Almodham invites Medford to visit his home in the desert, and several months later, the young American appears at Almodham's house to accept the Englishman's offer of hospitality. The Englishman is absent; we learn at the end of the story (but suspect much sooner) that he is dead. While he waits, the sick and unsuspecting American is cared for in the ruin of a Crusader's castle by the Englishman's manservant, Gosling, who predicts for a week his master's imminent return from what supposedly was a day's expedition.

In "A Bottle of Perrier," Wharton, who found the source of ghost stories below conscious reason in "the warm darkness of the pre-natal fluid" (vii), writes a story about bad water. Medford, the American, suffering from a recurrent fever and unable to drink wine, requests only water. After his bath, Medford notices "something sick and viscous, half smell, half substance" (396) clinging to his skin. During the course of the story, the water from the only well becomes increasingly worse: it gives off a "sweetish foulish" smell (402). "Gosling" means (among other things) a foolish or callow person, but by the end of the story it turns out that he is a madman; he not only has murdered his master but has left his victim's body in the only well—the single water source in an oasis surrounded by days of desert on all sides. The enclosing walls surround the central well, which, meant to be a source of "purity" and life, has become the receptacle of death. In a style reminiscent of Poe, Wharton describes an erotically charged scene: "An ancient fig tree, enormous, exuberant, writhed over a whitewashed well-head, sucking life from what appeared to be the only source of moisture within the walls" (371). There are specific echoes of Wharton's landscape in *Ethan Frome*—in particular, the "orchard of starved apple trees writhing over a hillside among outcroppings of slate."[11] Yet frozen New England seems less frightening in its infertility than the rotting opulence of the poisoned fecundity of "A Bottle of Perrier."

The place described in "A Bottle of Perrier" at first appears benign. The American Medford finds it especially attractive: "To anyone sick of the Western fret and fever the very walls of this desert fortress exuded peace" (373). It is a sort of psychic womb in which air rather than water is the surrounding medium: "a place . . . to rest in! The silence, the remoteness, the illimitable air! And in the heart of the wilderness green leafage, water, comfort . . . a humane and welcoming habitation" (372–73). The description, however, begins to assume the characteristics of a place of sexuality, particularly feminine sexuality. Like a heart, covered with leafage, offering fertility and comfort and "a humane and welcoming habitation," this seems to be a "human" as well as a "humane" place in which to dwell. We learn that the English tenant had chosen from the fortress's "jumble of masonry . . . a cluster of rooms tucked into an angle of the ancient keep" (375), next to the well which reaches deep into the courtyard below. Adding to this image of internal residence in the female are the openings of the "crimsoned shutters" of the house. The place, in Wharton's description, has become the landscape of the female body.

With its suggestive images of household apertures, "A Bottle of Perrier" echoes another story about bad water: Poe's "The Fall of the House of Usher," particularly the poem within the story in which Roderick Usher tells of the demise of the House of Usher. The third and sixth stanzas of "The Haunted Palace" introduce strangers who look through windows to see life in the kingdom of "The Haunted Palace." "The two luminous windows" of the third verse, obviously a figure for eyes, become the suggestive "red-litten windows" of the sixth verse: "Through the red-litten windows, see / Vast forms that move fantastically / To a discordant melody." The red-lighted windows become linked to the "pale door"—the source of a "rapid ghastly river" of death.[12] In "A Bottle of Perrier," the visiting stranger Medford imagines the watchful gaze of his host at the "crimsoned shutters" of the fortress. Like the story of the haunted palace, "A Bottle of Perrier" records the transformation of the "Crusader's castle" from an innocent place into a cannibalizing landscape reminiscent of the miasmic tarn which in the end consumes the House of Usher.

"A Bottle of Perrier" also tells the story of a devouring landscape where the source of life has become literally a place of death and bodily corruption. The story focuses on the water and the well. The well is visible from the vantage point of the living area in the keep. Yet early in the story Medford looks down from the ladderlike stairs and sees not the well but rather another symbol for female sexuality in a bizarre image of the head of the manservant Gosling rising toward him: "It rose slowly and Medford had time to remark that it was sallow, bald on the top, diagonally dented with a long white scar, and ringed with thick ash-blond hair" (373). As with the "red gash across Ethan Frome's forehead,"[13] Gosling's head may be seen as a graphic displacement of the female genitals, a closed opening analogous to the less specific symbol found in the "whitewashed well-head" (371).

The exuberant water-fed fig, it follows with appropriate symmetry, stands as the symbol for the "master" of the fortress. Medford describes Almodham at the beginning of the story as a "scholar and a misogynist" (371); he contemplates Almodham's conception of himself as a figure of Victorian romance who gradually becomes known through the setting he chooses to live in: Medford imagines him to be defined by this place as "the one who lives in a Crusader's castle." He sees this as a youthful pose that became a "gradual imprisonment" and "slowly stiffened" (377) in middle age. With Poe-like humor, Wharton alludes to the rigor mortis of Almodham's corpse deep at the bottom of the well: in life and death a rigid, phallicized presence. With the mention of "something deeper, darker, too," Wharton mixes metaphors to depict a metaphoric coitus as the master is thrown into the well to consummate the diseased relation between both tree and well, master and servant. Wharton links the writhing tree and the sexuality of the master through Medford's belief that Almodham has chosen this place and life to heal "an old wound, an old mortification, something which years ago had touched a vital part and left him writhing" (377).

The "punctual Gosling," also described as "correct, close-lipped" (401) and as "the quick cosmopolitan man-servant," seems the perfect attendant. He is from Malta, and he speaks a half-dozen desert dialects and what the narrator calls a "palimpsest Cockney" (372), which consists largely of dropped *h*'s. The American thinks of the castle fortress as a place which had encouraged "inertia, mental and moral" (371) in Almodham, a place where "life had the light monotonous smoothness of eternity" (380). Medford had promised to wait a year for Almodham, but he discovers that measures of time are meaningless in such a place: "The silly face of his watch told its daily tale to emptiness. The wheeling of the constellations over those ruined walls marked only the revolutions of the earth; the spasmodic motions of man meant nothing" (380). Gosling—the punctual, the efficient, the quick servant—knows what time it is: he has been at this place continuously for eleven years and five months.

Gosling's identification with the stasis and inertia of the place reinforces his role as the female in the story. Indeed, his story of stasis seems tritely familiar in the history of woman's place: "When he's here he needs me for himself," says Gosling of his absent master, "and when he's away he needs me to watch over the others" (382). As the guardian of the household, Gosling performs his services as ritually and ceremoniously as the mindless cycles of the sun. He says that Almodham had him "chained up 'ere like 'is watchdog" (406). Medford describes Gosling as showing a "dog-like affection" (385), but Gosling's bond represents a tie that goes beyond doglike obedience. He insists that he has a right to leave his master, but he doesn't, enacting what traditionally has been a woman's predicament. Even after he kills his master, Gosling feels compelled to stay. Tied to the round of his daily responsibilities, he becomes a martyr, even in becoming a murderer.

As "watch-dog," Gosling joins together the figures of the "silly face" of the watch and the dog, an inscrutable embodiment of obedience. He is a kind of mad dog whose madness seems to have been brought on by a consciousness of the temporality of the world outside his desert home. He senses himself growing older in the seeming timelessness of the desert cycles. We learn at the opening of the story that Medford is disturbed by the enveloping atmosphere of the landscape: "Awed by his first intimate sense of the omnipresence of the desert, [Medford] shivered and drew back" (371). On another occasion, Medford notices that "through the spell of inertia laid on him by the drowsy place and its easeful comforts his instinct of alertness was struggling back" (386). Medford is trying to waken himself from the Circe-like surroundings where the ancientness of the shifting sands makes a mockery of the hourglass. Gosling has gone awry. He has pulled himself violently out of the cycles of nature into time, and his slight discordance awakens Medford to a sense of something wrong. Medford's "mind reached out on all sides into the enfolding mystery, but it was everywhere impenetrable" (394). Throughout the story there is the lulling sense of being near sleep, disrupted by Medford's growing suspicion of the danger in the surrounding veil of mystery.

Gosling warns Medford that Medford cannot understand the Arabs and that he cannot be taught to understand: "You'd 'ave to 'ave lived among them, sir, and you'd 'ave to speak their language" (386). When Medford responds that he has "travelled among them," Gosling "could hardly conciliate respect with derision in his reception of this boast" (386–87). Stasis has given Gosling the knowledge of this place; he speaks the language of place, using a half-dozen dialects in his daily rounds. We sense that Gosling might have become a kind of "slave" over the years (indeed, workers in the desert historically have had difficulty exercising the so-called right to quit). Almodham originally promised him a month's holiday; in reviewing the injustice done to him when that holiday was taken away, Gosling insists that he should have had six months. At least in this last speech, he seems to have some familiarity with the rights of the English workingman. Even so, in this despotic relation between master and servant, his idea that he should have two weeks vacation for each year is oddly out of place in a story that does not mention pay or any other remuneration.

One can see in "A Bottle of Perrier" some of the preoccupations of *Ethan Frome*. Gosling is trapped by a sense of ritualized responsibility. As with Frome (who attended technical school and has an interest in biochemistry), Gosling's manhood seems to be represented by an interest in modern technology. He wants to visit a technological exposition, and it seems as if his masculinity can become ascendant only if he can get away from an entrapping place. Gosling has come to embody, even in his physical appearance, the mark or "wound" of womankind; and significantly, he has internalized beyond all reason the prima-ry attribute of women's traditional role: the responsibility of the caretaker. While Frome (with his wound and crippled leg and truncated house) may be seen as symbolically castrated, he remains at least to the engineer's eye the great wreck of a man. Gosling himself is a great palimpsest, an inscrutable text of woman, dog, clock, and slave. A man speaking many tongues, he has assumed the power of the snake-haired Medusa, turning his master to stone in the night "peopled by palms of beaten silver and a white marble fig tree" (390). The rigid pose of Almodham in life has passed through rigor mortis to the state of a liquified dissolution, ironically still feeding the greedy fig. In the cloying abundance of the life-sucking fig, Wharton has found a figure for the resilience of the master and an image of patriarchy: the thick, ancient trunk of a tree.

Gosling represents a thoroughly colonized mind; what he wants from Med-ford, at least in part, is a new master. Just as he entraps Almodham's body in the well, Gosling tries to imprison a new master in the castle. He does not capture Medford in order to escape. Paradoxically, the reason Gosling gives for his efforts to imprison Medford is that Medford has been so sympathetic about Gosling's denied holiday. "I've told Mr. Almodham so, agine and agine. He'd never listen, or only make believe to; say: 'We'll see, now, Gosling, we'll see'; and no more 'heard of it. But you was different, sir. You said it, and I knew you meant it—about my 'oliday. So I'm going to lock you in" (392). Gosling wants to serve his captive master obediently because he needs a new master to repair the disrupted ritual of his life; but he also needs Medford because he has been his only sympathetic listener. To such a master he could repeat again and again the story of his madness. Early in the story, Medford imagines Gosling turned by the moonlight into a "white spectral figure, the unquiet ghost of a patient butler who would have died without his holiday" (383). With his mindless patience and his history of colonized intimacy, it is easier for Gosling to kill his master than to leave him. However, even through the act of violence that results in the master's death, Gosling cannot tear himself from the ritual of his life into the assertive individualism that would signify free manhood. Wharton suggests that unquiet ghosts emerge from repressed cravings; those who sacrifice their own needs eventually kill the ones they are caring for, or, in effect, themselves.

At the end of the story, Gosling is "choked" by anguish: "His voice died out in a strangled murmur" (406). We do not know what direction Gosling's madness will take, whether it will become its own prison of guilt, but in the end, the two men stand and stare at each other without speaking. Wharton melodramatically returns to the eroticized scene as "the moon, swinging high above the battlements, sent a searching spear of light down into the guilty darkness of the well" (406). "A Bottle of Perrier," with its eroticized and cannibalistic landscape, is Wharton's vision of the monstrous and murderous feminine. Gosling is caught between "masculine" assertion and "feminine" service but he cannot escape from his feminine role. As a "man-servant," he is threatened with annihilation by the pastoral female timelessness of the desert's cycles. He in turn, assuming the woman's part, becomes deadly for his male masters. The story depicts Wharton's fears about the dangers of stasis and her anxieties about the stagnation she associated with the place of women.

In "Kerfol" and "Mr. Jones," Wharton presents another dramatization of the psychosexual struggle between men and women. In "A Bottle of Perrier" (and indeed in novels such as *Ethan Frome* and *Summer*), women are figured as entrapping and mothers are seen as potentially murderous. These stories depict women as the victims of misogynous masters who dictate and enforce a deadly social isolation. (The feminized Gosling is himself the victim of a despotic master, but in his search for another man to serve he assumes the role of the deadly agent of female entrapment.) In contrast to "A Bottle of Perrier," the silent houses of "Kerfol" and "Mr. Jones" are pictures of domestic order.

Initially, both houses are viewed by their new or prospective owners as silent texts containing stories and histories of past occupants. Yet both of these stories set in the present have visible ghosts—the watchdog of Kerfol and Mr. Jones (who, like Gosling, is also referred to as a "watch-dog" [288]) of Bells. These wraiths lead the house's owners and prospective owners to investigate the reasons for the hauntings. In "Kerfol" and "Mr. Jones," women from the past tell their stories of loneliness and imprisonment. Anne de Cornault of "Kerfol" and her English counterpart in "Mr. Jones," Juliana, Viscountess of Thudeney, were both childless, and both suffered from cruel husbands who kept them imprisoned in houses.

In "Kerfol," a visitor to the Breton region, following his host's advice, goes to look at an old manor house called "Kerfol." The guardian is absent. The narrator is conscious of "the depth of the silence" that makes his gestures seem irrelevant acts to "that great blind house looking down at me, and all the empty avenues converging on me" (150–51). At first the house is described in terms of its accumulation of history, the "sheer weight of many associated lives and deaths"; but the presence of Kerfol indicates more than the psychic accretions of human passage through a particular place. The narrator feels "penetrated by the weight of its silence." The house suggests a "perspective of stern and cruel memories stretching away, like its own gray avenues, into a blur of darkness." The darkness may be the blur in the distance of the receding and indecipherable past, but these avenues converge on a house that has "completely and finally broken with the present" (151).

While spending a day on the grounds of Kerfol, the narrator is watched at a steady distance by a pack of silent dogs. When he returns, he learns that he has seen "the dogs" which have been seen for centuries *and* that "there were no dogs at Kerfol" (179). He then receives from his host a history of the Duchy written in 1702, nearly a century after the events that concern Kerfol and the dogs have taken place. More than the presence of the house, it is the presence of this text which dominates the narrative. The manuscript contains the life story of Anne de Cornault, as it emerges through what is called an "almost literal transcription" of her month-long murder trial.

The narrator decides not to "translate" the old record, because "it is full of wearisome repetitions, and the main lines of the story are forever straying off into side issues." Instead, the narrator rewrites the text, attempting to "disentangle" the narrative and "give it here in simpler form" (159). He claims to have added nothing of his own besides a description of a drawing of Anne de Cornault, but the description of the Baron as "short and broad, with a swarthy face, legs slightly bowed from the saddle, a hanging nose and broad hands with black hairs on them" (160) suggests that (like the narrator of *Ethan Frome*) the narrator's sympathy with the main character in his story leads him beyond the boundaries of the courtroom document into the realm of fiction.

The narrative of Anne de Cornault's trial for the murder of her husband weaves back and forth between Anne's statements to the court and the narrator's account of how the authorities responded to her story. Her audience appears to have been less hostile than incredulous in hearing her story, which to them seems trivial. Anne's own lawyer is said to have "tried several times to cut short her story" out of personal embarrassment. Telling a truth that for her listeners borders on the ridiculous, heretical, or insane, Anne persists in telling her story: "She went on to the end, with a kind of hypnotized insistence, as though the scenes she evoked were so real to her that she had forgotten where she was and imagined herself to be reliving them." Her story is described as a "curious narrative," received with "impatience and incredulous comment. It was plain that the Judges were surprised by its puerility." We hear a tale of life-threatening horror and cruelty, but to the judges the "odd tale" only proved that her husband "disliked dogs, and that his wife, to gratify her own fancy, persistently ignored this dislike" (174).

The "disentangled" story of young Anne de Barrigan begins with her marriage to Baron de Cornault in the early 1600s. Of good stock (although her father has squandered his estate), she is brought from a stone house on the edge of a moor to the grand house of Kerfol. Forty years her senior, the baron is said to have had "fits of gloomy silence" (162) before the marriage. Anne finds her married life lonely—her word, the narrator tells us, was "desolate." She explains that she is "a woman accursed to have no child, and nothing in life to call her own" (162). Then the baron gives her a rare Chinese sleeve dog that appears to her like a "bird or a butterfly" (164). (The ghost of this unusual dog has been seen by the narrator among the silent dogs at Kerfol; it is described as "a large tawny chrysanthemum" [153].) The dog becomes the "nearest thing to a child she was to know" (164). At one point the Baron likens Anne to the tombstone image of his grandmother Juliana lying with her dog at her feet; he tells her that she will have this symbol of faithfulness if she is deserving.

The baron, however, becomes jealous when he learns about a friendship between Anne and a young man, and he strangles her dog and places it, still warm, next to her pillow. Afterwards, the husband strangles four other dogs for which Anne has shown affection. All the dogs, except an old watchdog that he also kills, are placed on Anne's bed with their necks wrenched. Anne attempts to conceal her tenderness for the dogs; she gives them away, hides them in rooms and chests. But no matter how secretive she is, each is summarily strangled. When the young man comes a year later to speak to Anne at midnight, the Baron appears cursing her from the top of the stairs. At this moment the Baron is killed. His body is found with wounds that look like bites, as if it has been torn by sharp instruments. When questioned by the judge, Anne testifies that she recognized the barks of her dead dogs.

The power of "Kerfol" emerges from the constant juxtaposition of the narrator's view of Anne de Cornault's speech and thoughts with the way that her words are apprehended by the listening authorities. Not only are her listeners hostile; they seem to come from another world. Throughout the trial, they translate her words from a male point of view, hearing her story from the Baron's perspective. For instance, her grief over childlessness is seen as "a natural enough feeling in a wife attached to her husband; and certainly [they add] it must have been a great grief to Yves de Cornault that she bore no son" (162–63).

The problem of the unsympathetic jury, the reader who rejects a story because he identifies with the values of a masculine culture in which the female world is foreign or invisible, is explored in a story by Susan Glaspell published one year after "Kerfol" in 1917.[14] In "A Jury of Her Peers," two women have been brought to the house where a murder has taken place to get some clothes for the wife of the victim. While the men on the scene make condescending remarks about the woman's housekeeping, the two women read in the house the story of the wife, who (the women realize) has probably strangled her husband with a rope. As the men look for clues to a motive for the murder, they are blind to the signs of the woman's life. The women read the half-sifted flour and a roughly stitched quilt square as signs of psychic distress. They surreptitiously restitch the quilt square. When they find a torn birdcage and a strangled canary, prepared for burial in a small box, one of them hides the canary in her pocket. It is suggested that although the men are incapable of reading signs that are legible only to women, the men would probably convict the wife on the evidence of this strangled canary. Yet these female judges, this jury of the wife's peers, know that the woman as a girl had sung in the town choir; they recognize the strangled canary as an emblem of the woman's loss of voice and her isolated and childless life. They hide the only evidence of the motive for the crime from the male jury that otherwise finds every part of the woman's life to be meaningless as well as puerile.

The narrative of "Kerfol" implies that Anne's jury, composed of men who accept the baron's right to kill his peasants (he had a peasant hanged for stealing a faggot the day after he killed the first dog), would not have tried Yves de Cornault had he murdered his wife. His wife, who has been locked up and isolated by her near-silent husband, appears to have had the status of a pet—a pet that he just as willingly would have strangled. It is not irrelevant that Wharton herself loved dogs and that for her, as well as for Anne de Cornault, they seem to have taken the place of children. In *A Backward Glance*, Wharton associates her early consciousness of herself as a feeling person with the gift of her first dog. "Kerfol" relates the strangling of the childlike dogs to the woman's prison of inarticulateness. Even after the death of her husband, Anne de Cornault is imprisoned in the keep of Kerfol until she dies many years later. Like the isolated woman in Glaspell's "A Jury of Her Peers," Anne de Cornault has been confined to a life of voicelessness. Each woman is robbed of the solace of animals with whom she seems to share a bond of inarticulateness. (Wharton associates her own deep sympathy with dogs with her realization of the depth of their inarticulateness.)[15] Like "A Bottle of Perrier," these stories are about the revenge of female figures who have been victimized by misogynist and tyrannical masters. However, although the murders of the strangled animals are avenged and the brutal husbands pay for their crimes, the women remain victims. Silenced, they already are as mute as their pets.

The narrator of "Kerfol" is to all appearances male, yet he does become a sympathetic reader to Anne de Cornault's story. "Mr. Jones" also recounts the discovery of a hidden story of a female victim, but here the reader is a woman. Indeed, "Mr. Jones" contains one of Wharton's relatively rare depictions of a female author. The story is about Lady Jane Lynke, an author of travel books that feature sentimental depictions of foreign cities. (Wharton, too, was the author of travel books such as *A Motor Flight through France*.) Lady Jane is known for her spirit of adventure and her ability to find entrances to sights closed to others. In "Mr. Jones," Lady Jane inherits an old house called Bells and decides to change her plans for her life in order to make a home there. First, however, she must confront Mr. Jones, the longtime caretaker of the house, and Wharton's great fear: locked doors.

Although it is named Bells, the house is repeatedly described as "mute" and "silent." From the outset, Lady Jane comments on its "inexorable face" (286). Again and again, she comes into conflict with the orders of Mr. Jones; he is described by his grandniece as being "more dead than living" (292). Mr. Jones has been the absolute, unquestioned authority in the house since the early nineteenth century—apparently for over one hundred years. He corresponds with the previous absentee landlords and sends orders to the servants who never see him. Mrs. Clemm, the housekeeper and Mr. Jones's elderly grand-niece, claims to have seen him once when she was a child.

Mr. Jones is also the keeper of the house's legacy of papers. When Lady Jane and her novelist friend Stramer after some difficulty gain entrance to the muniment room, she finds that a parcel of papers is missing from the otherwise complete record of the house. These papers, it turns out, contain the story of the Viscountess Juliana, whom they already call "Also His Wife" after "the only name on her monument" (302–3). A woman who was deaf and mute and was married for her inheritance, she was abandoned at Bells by her husband (a former owner of the house). Mr. Jones, as caretaker of the house, enforced the woman's complete solitude. Her story is contained in the letter she wrote entreating her husband to order Mr. Jones to allow her to visit with neighboring women.

"Mr. Jones" concludes with a description of the body of the strangled Mrs. Clemm. We assume that she was killed by Mr. Jones, who blames Mrs. Clemm for allowing Lady Jane to discover the missing papers. The presence of the Viscountess Juliana's letter to her husband among Mr. Jones's papers suggests that this letter of entreaty, her final plea to her husband to allow her female company, has never been read by anyone besides Mr. Jones. Lady Jane appears to be the first reader besides him to read the story of the woman's imprisonment. She is certainly the first sympathetic reader.

In her isolation, Juliana's prison of muteness and deafness has meant a prison for her mind. The story suggests that like Anne de Cornault in "Kerfol," she also dies childless and alone, with no sympathetic reader for her story. Mr. Jones, of course, stands as a figure of absolute authority. His repression and imprisonment of this mute woman, his attempt to silence her forever by suppressing her writing (her only form of communication), is finally more horrible than Mr. Jones's frightening ghostly presence. What is remarkable, however, is that Wharton chose to give her father's name—Mr. Jones—to this omnipresent and nearly invisible character of authority. As a depiction of patriarchal oppression, the story that bears her father's name gives no indication of the affection Wharton expressed for her father.

Although Lady Jane enjoys the privileges of publication and the courage of an indomitable spirit that forces the discovery of the silent woman's story, she seems to be responsible for precipitating the violent retribution carried out by the patriarchal Mr. Jones. Mr. Jones reasserts his authority by strangling the woman still under his rule, Mrs. Clemm. Mrs. Clemm is said to have "a pursed-up mouth" (290); the *Oxford English Dictionary* lists "fetter, cramp, constriction, confinement" in the etymology of "clem." Victimized by Mr. Jones in a way that literalizes the fate of Juliana, Mrs. Clemm seems to die in the place of Lady Jane, who lives to tell the story.

Consistent with the emphasis on mothers that appears in Wharton's later writings,[16] "Mr. Jones" is in part a meditation on the role of women in the preservation of culture. In "Mr. Jones," besides depicting the suppression of women by patriarchal authority, Wharton considers the meaning of women's "unchronicled lives": lives that have been "piled up like dead leaves" (289). At one point Lady Jane considers the legacy that has been written through bodies and recorded in the material record of the house itself. She imagines what the house has meant to past people: not a "museum, or a page of history, but a cradle, nursery, home, and sometimes, no doubt, a prison." The house, like the dead and the frozen face of the Viscountess's portrait, is mute: "If those marble lips in the chapel could speak! If she could hear some of their comments on the old house which had spread its silent shelter over their sins and sorrows, their follies and submissions!" (289). At this moment in the passage, the narrator stops imagining a spoken message from the marble lips and begins to use terms which refer to the house as a written text.

The house is described as a "long tale, to which [Lady Jane] was about to add another chapter, subdued and humdrum beside some of those earlier annals." Wharton is concerned about the meaning of women's silence, the stories that have remained unspoken or unwritten. She contrasts Lady Jane's freer, more varied life to the "unchronicled lives of the great-aunts and great-grandmothers buried there so completely that they must hardly have known when they passed from their beds to their graves. 'Piled up like dead leaves,' Jane thought, 'layers and layers of them, to preserve something forever budding underneath'" (289). The "dead leaves" are, for Wharton, the mute pages, the frozen whiteness that forms the background for the portrait of the silent, voiceless women of Bells.

The dead women are reduced to mute texts. However, although their muteness maintains the silence of the past, in Wharton's texts this muteness is crying out for a voice. While they are alive, Anne de Cornault and the Viscountess Juliana tell part of their stories through oral testimony, written transcriptions, or letters; but in each instance they are not heard or they are heard by men who find their tragedies meaningless or puerile. The final legacy that Wharton transcribes in the women of Bells can be read in their bodies: blank pages being written over and over again with the same story, framed in beds or graves with life "budding underneath." "Dead leaves" for Wharton are the unread pages of unread lives—the "cold paper and dead words" that Ethan Frome envisions.[17] In both "Mr. Jones" and "Kerfol," Wharton includes a reassuring motif: the discovery of the woman's words, which are read after her death by a sympathetic reader. After giving play to her anxieties throughout the ghost stories, Wharton seems to find a way to master her fears at least partially: these women are rescued from muteness by being read.

Like all of the stories in *Ghosts*, "A Bottle of Perrier," "Kerfol," and "Mr. Jones" are concerned with abandonment and social isolation. Yet these stories in particular are concerned with the suppression of self and voice that is brought about in part by separation from sympathetic listeners. The central characters are stranded socially as well as physically: not only are they ruled by husbands and/or masters, they cannot trust the servants below them in the social hierarchy. For the women of Bells and Kerfol, the servants are the overseers who report or repress their efforts to find sympathetic listeners. Women, like Gosling, are caught in the power dynamics of master and servant; like the "man-servant" Gosling, they cannot tear themselves from their marginal position, even by murder. Each of the characters has been silenced by isolation, condemned to a lonely life under the domination of a powerful master whose repressive influence is not diminished even by his death.

Wharton's tales give voice to these suppressed lives by providing them with listeners, readers of their life stories, but in the end the voices from the past can tell only the story of their repression and unutterable loneliness. The stories may find listeners, but they can only repeat the past tragedy of the completed life. The character of the writer Lady Jane Lynke, who wrests the story of female muteness from a silent house, taking control of the house from the paternal authority of the ghostly Mr. Jones, may represent a partial reprieve from the cycle of repression. Lady Jane Lynke, at least, seems to secure a place for herself in the present as she provides a link to the past. Despite the narrator's playfully deprecatory attitude toward Lady Jane's writing, Lady Jane is presented as a woman who publishes her work. However, by committing herself to the story of the house and a single place, Lady Jane precipitates the death of another woman, who is in a sense punished for her acts of publication. She may gain control of the title to the house but Mr. Jones does not give up control of the house or the title to the story.

In "Mr. Jones," the woman writer, albeit in circumstances that are less than reassuring, serves as the medium for a suppressed story that is authored by a dead woman in a letter. *The Touchstone* depicts a woman writer who sends her letters herself yet also finds sympathetic readers only after her death. Appearing in 1900, *The Touchstone* is the first longer work of fiction that Wharton published. As we saw in Chapter 1, this novella contains one of Wharton's few depictions of a famous woman novelist. Like *The House of Mirth*, this narrative turns on the possession of letters; and in the context of the stories we are considering, we also can recognize it as one of Wharton's ghost stories.

The story of Margaret Aubyn—read as person and personage, woman and monument—displays the anxiety about publishing that is present in Wharton's early fiction. *The Touchstone* presents Margaret Aubyn as a woman whose strong voice makes her publicly revered yet personally unloved. The object of her personal devotion while she is alive, and the recipient of her letters, is a lawyer named Stephen Glennard. He is unable to respond to her love or her intellectual and artistic brilliance; he confesses to himself that "he had been oppressed, humiliated almost, by the multiplicity of her allusions, the wide scope of her interests, her persistence in forcing the superabundance of thought and emotion into the shallow receptacle of his sympathy."[18] Aubyn originally explains to Glennard that she must move to England "to be nearer you" (*T*, 24). Initially the letters did bring her closer, but even her written voice in the letters was too strong, too rich in unfamiliar allusions. Glennard increasingly resents Aubyn because her attention to him reveals his inadequacies as a person and a reader.

Three years after the death of Margaret Aubyn, Glennard anonymously publishes the letters that he had received from her over a period of many years (letters that he barely read when he first received them). Although, like Lily Bart, he is tempted to burn the "packets" (*T*, 14) of letters in a "grate" (*T*, 26), unlike Lily he decides to sell the letters to gain enough money to get married. Glennard uses a friend named Flamel as his emissary and pretends that the man to whom the letters were written is dead. Ironically, however, the point of *The Touchstone* is that the man addressed by the letters never existed. Like the stories of Kerfol and Bells, *The Touchstone* tells the story of a woman's life of personal isolation. Margaret Aubyn, like the Viscountess Juliana and Anne de Cornault, finds her reader only after her death. By publishing the letters, Glennard in a sense mails the correspondence again. (One reader of the published letters describes him as "the letter-box, the slit in the wall through which the letters passed to posterity" [*T*, 70–71].)

The *Aubyn Letters* become the book of the day, to be breathed in the air "like the influenza" (*T*, 67). Before this point Glennard has never really been able to read the letters. A character described as a cynical young man suggests within Glennard's hearing that Aubyn's anonymous correspondent "counted on the public to save him the trouble of reading" the letters (*T*, 69). Glennard himself feels entrapped by a "disadvantageous bargain." He is angry, yet he realizes that his anger is not directed at either Flamel or his wife but rather "against the mute memory to which his own act had suddenly given a voice of accusation" (*T*, 59).

Glennard is awakened to the living presence of the letters, despite hopes that after the passage of time he will become inured to them. He, like the women readers described in *The Touchstone*, must take the words personally, subjectively: he is conscious that he is at least in part the subject of the letters. After reading the letters, his friend Mrs. Touchett says, "It's the woman's soul, absolutely torn up by the roots—her whole self laid bare; and to a man who evidently didn't care; who couldn't have cared" (*T*, 67). Glennard sees the published volumes lying "before him like live things that he feared to touch." Opening a volume of the letters, he shares Mrs. Touchett's sense of the exposure of something living: "A familiar letter sprang out at him, each word quickened by its glaring garb of type. The little broken phrases fled across the pages like wounded animals in the open. . . . It was a horrible sight . . . a *battue* of helpless things driven savagely out of shelter" (*T*, 76; Wharton's ellipses).

Early in the book, the *Aubyn Letters* have become a nightmare for Glennard: a fulfillment of Margaret Aubyn's closing vow that she would be with him always. "His punishment henceforth would be the presence, the inescapable presence, of the woman he had so persistently evaded. She would always be there now. It was as though he had married her instead of the other. It was what she had always wanted—to be with him—and she had gained her point at last" (*T*, 59). As the narrative progresses, Glennard senses himself capable of "subtler perceptions" (*T*, 116); he castigates himself for stupidly rejecting Aubyn. He is driven, despite Aubyn's death, to garner the feeling of her nearness: "Her presence remained the one reality in a world of shadows. . . . he was reliving with incredible minuteness every incident of their obliterated past: as a man who has mastered the spirit of a foreign tongue turns with renewed wonder to the pages his youth has plodded over. . . . It was as though she had bought him with her blood" (*T*, 117). The letters are the emblems of Margaret Aubyn's blood, the "rarest vintage" saved for the ritual of her "hidden sacrament of tenderness" (*T*, 25): her lengthy correspondence with Glennard. In his shame, Glennard visits the cemetery where Aubyn is buried. After requesting some flowers "in the emblematic line" from a florist who has only white flowers ("white azaleas, white lilies, white lilacs"), he scatters the flowers on the grave: "The edges of the white petals shrivelled like burnt paper in the cold" (*T*, 122–23).

The story of *The Touchstone*, in which a living man is consumed by the inescapable presence of a dead woman, anticipates the story of "Pomegranate Seed," which Wharton completed in January of 1931 and collected in *Ghosts* in 1937. In "Pomegranate Seed," a deceased wife (Elsie Corder Ashby) continues to dominate the thoughts of her newly remarried husband through a series of letters which arrive mysteriously through the mail slot. The new wife (Charlotte Gorse Ashby) becomes anxious whenever she enters the doorway that another one of the disturbing letters will be there, just as Glennard dreads that he will find another letter from Aubyn on his hall table. The letters are recognizable because of their faint markings, although the writing is illegible to the new wife. She knows that the letters are from a woman, although the writing has "masculine curves" (325). Only at the end of the story, when the living wife suspects that her husband will not return at the end of the day, does her mother-in-law reluctantly admit that she sees on the nearly blank paper the handwriting of her son's dead wife.

When the mother-in-law looks at the bare place on the wall where the dead woman's portrait used to hang, it suddenly occurs to the new wife that her husband can read the mysterious writing. She tries to get her mother-in-law to admit that she knows the letters are from the dead woman, insisting: "Why shouldn't I say it when even the bare walls cry it out? What difference does it make if her letters are illegible to you and me? If even you can see her face on that blank wall, why shouldn't he read her writing on this blank paper? Don't you see that she's everywhere in this house, and the closer to him because to everyone else she's become invisible?" (366–67).

The title of the story, "Pomegranate Seed," is never explained in the text. Wharton somewhat disingenuously remarks in the preface to *Ghosts* that when the story "first appeared in a magazine, I was bombarded by a host of inquirers anxious, in the first place, to know the meaning of the story's title (in the dark ages of my childhood an acquaintance with classical fairy lore was as much a part of our stock of knowledge as Grimm or Andersen)" (viii–ix). The title, of course, refers to the myth of Persephone, the daughter of Demeter who was stolen from her mother and earth and taken to the underworld. In the version of the myth offered in Book 5 of Ovid's *Metamorphoses* (a favorite source for Wharton), Persephone grows hungry and picks a pomegranate and eats seven seeds of the crimson fruit from the pale rind. Because Persephone has eaten the seeds, Demeter is unable to secure her return to earth and Persephone must thereafter dwell for the months of winter as queen of the realm of the dead. The title of Wharton's story suggests that the letters themselves—those of the late Margaret Aubyn as well as those of the deceased wife—are the seeds of the underworld; once consumed, they call upon their reader to dwell for a season in the underworld with the dead woman writer.

As Wharton rewrites the story of Demeter and Persephone in "Pomegranate Seed," the Persephone figure is at first the husband Ned Ashby, over whose fate the deceased wife, Elsie Corder Ashby, and the living wife, Charlotte Gorse Ashby, struggle. Elsie Corder Ashby, the writer of the letters, is the author of the ties that bind. The middle name of the living wife, Gorse, is the name of a prickly plant sacred to the goddess Demeter, suggesting her association with the maternal figure in the myth. However, Wharton's rewriting of the myth is also a reading of the story of Demeter and Persephone. In "Pomegranate Seed," the seed is singular; it points to Charlotte Gorse Ashby's illicit reading of a single letter—an act that seals the fate of all of the characters at the close of the story. Charlotte Gorse Ashby becomes the Persephone figure at the close of the story as she, instead of her husband, eats the forbidden fruit. Like Lily Bart in *The House of Mirth*, who is transported to the erotic underworld as she reads Bertha Dorset's letter, Charlotte Gorse Ashby opens the letter from the underworld: the letter from her husband's deceased wife. She also reads a letter which calls her to "come" (363) to the underworld. In this sense, Demeter shares with Persephone the experience of the underworld—only her hell is the barren winter of the soul experienced by the abandoned woman on earth. "Pomegranate Seed" links the experience of mother and daughter as it explores a deeper story in this cyclical myth of female replacement.

In addition to these thematic and narrative parallels, Wharton signals the deep connection between "Pomegranate Seed" and *The Touchstone* by giving her story exactly the same title as one of Margaret Aubyn's imaginary novels. *Pomegranate Seed* is the only novel of Aubyn's that is named (*T*, 79). The significance of this detail is suggested by its appearance in yet another text: "Copy," Wharton's story in dialogue form about a successful woman novelist who also has written a book called "Pomegranate Seed." In "Copy," published one year after *The Touchstone* in 1901, Wharton appears to rewrite the story of Margaret Aubyn. In this story, a male poet and a woman novelist both hope to gain seeds for their future writing from the love letters they wrote to each other in the past. Reading their letters from the past is described as "very like unrolling a mummy. . . with a live grain of wheat in it." At the close of the story, the writers are transformed; they burn their letters as a way of destroying the "key" to their "garden"—the "secret garden" that Wharton found in her writing.[19]

In *The Touchstone*, the letters of Margaret Aubyn are described as the emblems of blood; they are a "rarer vintage" which is contrasted with the "dry rind" (*T*, 25) that other writers offer to their friends in personal writing. By the end of *The Touchstone*, Glennard and his wife are said to have been brought closer together by the "seeds of understanding," the fertile silences gained from their shared concern with the letters. With her letters, Aubyn has sown seeds beyond her life on earth; through these previously unread seeds, she becomes an "inescapable presence," the "one reality in a world of shadows" (*T*, 155, 117).

In *The Touchstone* and "Pomegranate Seed," letters from a dead woman gain control of a living man who is at the time preoccupied with the feminine presence of a living woman. The living wife requires financial support, a house, and recreational outings, while the dead woman demands the attention of the desired and distant man through her writings. Wharton tried to imagine an alternative to this scenario in *Hudson River Bracketed*, the novel she published in 1929, the year before she began to write "Pomegranate Seed." With its 1932 sequel *The Gods Arrive*, Wharton ended her career with an almost thousand-page narrative about the American artist. If Wharton began "Literature" in 1914 to write a *Künstlerroman* that unlike *The House of Mirth* and *The Custom of the Country* (and even *Ethan Frome* and "Old Woman Magoun") would not demand the suicide of the potential writer, it was not until the end of her career that she was able to write a story about a young writer who awakens to poetry and lives. In *Hudson River Bracketed*, the writer is a man, but the literary awakening that leads to his first novel takes place under the eyes of a dead woman of letters. Vance Weston finds himself for the first time in a "private library," an event made more remarkable by the fact that "all these books had been a woman's, . . . and she had sat among them, lived among them, died reading them—reading the very one on the table at his elbow!"[20] Entering the library with his cousin, Vance is at first "startled" by the "fact that one of the books lay open, and that across the page was a small pair of oddly-shaped spectacles." Remembering his cousin's "fear of ghosts," Vance glances "about him half apprehensively, as if the reader of that book, the wearer of those spectacles, might be peering at them from some shadowy corner of the room." Indeed, he discovers a portrait of the woman, who is pictured leaning "on a table with a heavy velvet cover, bearing an inkstand and some books—the very table and the very inkstand . . . on which the picture itself looked down" (*H*, 60).

Vance comes to identify the woman in the picture with the young woman who appears "standing in the door" (*H*, 64) as he begins to read the volume of Coleridge that lies open on the dead woman's writing table. In the novel (entitled *Instead*) that he eventually writes about the late owner of the library, Vance imagines her not as "a predestined old maid" but rather as "a creature apt for love" who instead finds "compensation" under "the guise of poetry, dreams, visions . . ." (*H*, 359; Wharton's ellipses). In a sense Vance becomes a novelist after he encounters a ghost: the dead woman of letters who still inhabits the library and even seems to move in and out of her portrait ("as if it were she who had just dropped her book and spectacles, and reascended to her frame as he came in") in a passage between the realms of life and art, the living and the dead. However, for Vance Weston the dead woman and her story are increasingly embodied by the living woman, Halo Tarrant, who in effect becomes his emissary to the "incomprehensible past" (*H*, 61) by helping him to imagine the life of his fictional heroine.

Vance *is* called to the underworld of art by the presiding spirit of a dead representative of literature and the past. At one point in *The Gods Arrive* Halo Tarrant seems to fear this when she decides to open a cabinet and surreptitiously read the "manuscript" that Vance has been working on; she stops because she finds herself feeling like "a jealous woman expecting to find a love-letter." "Why shouldn't there be love-letters in that drawer," she thinks; yet, as if she has been reading *The Touchstone* or "Pomegranate Seed," her fears seem to be less about romantic infidelity than about literary conversation: "If Vance had ceased to talk to her about his work it was because he was talking about it to some other woman. . . . She no longer thought of the novel—what she saw, through those worm-eaten panels, was a packet of letters in a woman's writing."[21] Halo's fears are unfounded; unlike the living wife in "Pomegranate Seed," she is threatened not by the woman of letters in the underworld but rather by a false living muse, Floss Delaney. After abandoning her, however, Vance finally returns from both the fashionable world of Floss Delaney and the underworld of letters to the realm of a living art. At the end of *The Gods Arrive* he finds in the pregnant Halo Tarrant the embodiment of a living muse.

However, this fusion of the figures of Persephone and Demeter, of the underworld of fiction and the living world of an actual life, does not take place when Wharton tries to imagine the fate of the woman writer. In *Hudson River Bracketed*, in which Wharton may be seen to identify with the male novelist as well as both the dead and the living muses, Wharton seems to succeed in joining the roles that divided her throughout her life. As "Pomegranate Seed" and *The Touchstone* suggest, however, Wharton was haunted by conflicting calls within herself, by two worlds which seemed sharply divided. Writing toward the end of her life in her unpublished autobiography, "Life and I," Wharton calls on the Persephone myth to describe her early attraction to writing and the written. She recalls the perceptual world in which words were "visible—almost tangible presences, with faces as distinct as those of the persons among whom I lived. And like Erlkönig's daughters, they sang to me so bewitchingly that they almost lured me from the wholesome noonday air of childhood into the strange supernatural region where the normal pleasures of my age seemed as insipid as the fruits of the earth to Persephone after she had eaten of the pomegranate seed."[22]

Wharton contrasts the "normal pleasures" which are the "insipid fruits of the earth" to the "strange" and "supernatural" world of words and letters whose potency is represented in the pomegranate seeds. "Insipid" means tasteless, but it also suggests a lack of "sapience" or wisdom. The pomegranate seed in contrast is among the forbidden fruits, and like the apple in the first garden, it is associated with secret knowledge. To have eaten this fruit is to acknowledge the pull of the underworld, to prefer the "inescapable presence" in the garden of the dead. This passage recalls the divided world of the "moral tortures" that Wharton describes elsewhere in "Life and I": the conflict between the realm of an invisible God who is associated with truth and reading and the domain ruled by her mother that was devoted to social appearances.[23]

Persephone, for Wharton, is the figure for the woman writer who dwells in the underworld savoring the supernatural fruit of letters and books. In Wharton's version of the myth, Persephone consciously chooses this world over the noonday fertility and nameless repetition of her mother's world, the pastoral earth of Demeter which represents cyclical timelessness and asexual reproduction. Persephone in Ovid's version is raped and stolen from this world by "the monarch of the silent,"[24] who strips her of her flowers before driving her through a crack in the earth to the land of the dead. In celebrating Persephone's life in the underworld, Wharton transforms the sexual assault and abduction into an escape from "the insipid fruits of the earth." Persephone escapes not only from her mother and her mother's pastoral asexuality, but also from the earthly daughters who (in the same myth) are turned into Sirens because they were with Persephone when she gathered the "fatal flowers." We have seen that Wharton alludes to the female local colorists (Jewett and Wilkins) as the "authoresses" of "rose and lavender" pages; as a writer she is wary of "sirens" who may promise a "lost masterpiece in their rainbow veils."[25] The sirens Wharton refers to in her polemical introduction to *Ethan Frome* are the voices of the world of the mother, voices that seem to call her to smash herself against the New England rocks. They call her to sacrifice her life to the female role of caretaker, responsible for weak and querulous dependents.

However, for Wharton, there are two sets of sirens, two sets of daughters with seductive voices. The sirens associated with *Ethan Frome* call for her to sacrifice herself as an individual, to give herself over to a life devoted to a living death. This, for Wharton, is the seduction of the sentimental and the sentimentalists, whose fiction seems to feed on the story of virgin death. These are the sirens that Lily Bart seems to listen to as she chooses death rather than the underworld of eroticism, experience, and letters associated with Bertha Dorset. The other seductive voices are heard in the power of words which Wharton compares in "Life and I" to the lure of "Erlkönig's daughters" who sang to her "so bewitchingly that they almost lured me from the wholesome noonday air of childhood." Here Wharton refers to a myth from another culture's folklore—and more specifically, I think, to an early poem by Goethe, "Erlkönig." In this poem, a young boy riding through the forest with his father is called by the elf king: "You sweet child, come, come with me! We shall play lovely games together, there are flowers of many colours by the water's edge, my mother has many garments of gold." Erlkönig then attempts to lure the boy with the promise of his daughters as attendants: "They will rock you and dance you and sing you to sleep." Although it is the king who calls to lure the boy away from his father, the seduction he offers is based on the lure of the feminine and the maternal.

For Wharton, who links the voices of Erlkönig's daughters to her own love of words and the eating of the pomegranate seeds, the final statement of the elf king might have recalled the abduction of Persephone: "I love you, I am charmed by your beautiful shape; and if you are not willing, I will use force." Just as Persephone calls out for her mother as she is carried off, the boy calls to his father, "Oh father, father, now he's catching hold of me!"[26] At the end of the poem the boy is dead; like Persephone, he may be imagined as a royal consort in a "strange, supernatural region" where there is life after death.

The significance of Persephone in Wharton's private mythology as a figure for the woman artist is underlined by the context of the story in Ovid's *Metamorphoses*. Book 5 presents the story of Persephone along with a series of stories about female voice, songs, and creativity. A large portion of the narrative tells the story of nymphs, boastful women, and the Muses. The section about Minerva and the Muses tells the story of a singing contest in which nine boastful daughters challenge the Muses. One of the daughters sings a song which insults the gods by portraying them as beaten in battle by men. The ravishment of Persephone and the anger of Demeter are narrated in a story within a story, or rather a song within a song which is sung by the Muses. The singing contest itself is seen as one of the several insults that the Muses have to endure. The boastful women, who have no sense of their own lack of singing ability, are turned into magpies: imitators of voices and thieves of sounds who produce only meaningless chatter. Within the song of the muses and the story of Persephone is the story of the Sirens, the innocent daughters who are turned into birds with the faces and voices of women. They were with Persephone gathering flowers when she was abducted, and they have been given wings to search for her. Their beautiful voices are praised as the dower of human song; but they become the illusive and seductive voice of the female irresistibly calling men to their destruction.

That Persephone's story is told in the song of the muse who wins the singing contest over the meaningless chatter of women may (for Wharton) add to Persephone's status as the potentially authentic woman artist. The song of Persephone is for Wharton the story of an escape from sirens who represent both her mother and her female predecessors. Like the local colorists, like Erlkönig's daughters in Goethe's poem, they promise flowers of many colors and garments of gold; but they also threaten to draw her life into the long and anonymous line of women's lives written in flesh and dissipated in the details of survival. As the woman writer, Wharton flees "the insipid fruits of the earth," but as with the luring voices of Erlkönig's daughters and the Sirens, the role of Persephone and the woman writer also presents dangers. In a version of the familiar dilemma of the creative woman who must choose between life and art, Wharton implies that the woman writer, if she sings the song of the "true" muse, must inhabit the underworld; she implies that art, not just realistic art, is under the surface of life and near death. In Wharton's view, she is lured by two kinds of sirens, two kinds of women's voices, two kinds of death: the insipid world of death in life that is represented by the feminine, and the underworld of knowledge that is the only place for the woman writer.

In an uncollected dramatic poem called "Pomegranate Seed," Wharton creates a dramatic dialogue between Demeter, who is said to be "undaughtered," and Persephone, who is said to have an "estranging darkness" on her brow after her experience in the underworld. Persephone "fears the sound of life that thunders in her unaccustomed ears"; estranged from the world of her mother, she argues against the world of nature, with its "path winding deathlessly to death." Persephone has "eaten of the seed of death" and can no longer "sit within the doorway of the gods and laughing spin new souls along the years." Persephone insists on choosing the world of experience and knowledge over the world of the mother. At the end of the poem, Demeter acknowledges the difference between herself and the daughter who has "eaten of the seed of death"; "stand off from me," she tells Persephone, "Thou knowest more than I."[27]

Although the poem "Pomegranate Seed" presents the points of view of both mother and daughter, it reads in part as a defense of Persephone's acceptance of her place in the underworld—a choice that for Wharton is related to the world of writing. In 1913 she wrote to her publisher, "Plus je vais, more and more it becomes the essential thing for me that anyone who writes should be able to say 'Gods of heaven and Gods of hell have I looked on face to face, and adored them.'"[28] Wharton's definition of the necessary experience of the writer is drawn from Apuleius's *The Mysteries of Isis*, which she quotes at greater length in the planning notebook for her unfinished novel, "Literature": "I trod the confines of death and the threshold of Proserpine; I was swept around all the elements & back again; I saw the sun shining at midnight in purest radiance; *Gods of heaven & Gods of hell I saw face to face & adored them*."[29] For Wharton, "anyone who writes" must cross the threshold of Persephone; and in particular, the woman writer must eat of the pomegranate seed.

In these terms, all of Wharton's works of fiction may be seen as ghost stories. For Wharton, the woman writer stripped of her flowers and virginal innocence is Persephone trying to speak from the dead. "A Bottle of Perrier," "Kerfol," "Mr. Jones," "Pomegranate Seed," and *The Touchstone* reveal a pattern which suggests the power of the suppressed voice of women. "A Bottle of Perrier" represents the monstrous and murderous feminine: Gosling, like Ethan Frome, bearing the mark and the wound of womankind, stands as a figure for the female principle of death. He represents the ritualized world of the mother that Wharton views as a living death. The other stories, including *The Touchstone*, tell the story of women writers trying to be Persephone. As they tell of women silenced, mute, isolated, or estranged in death, these stories revolve around written texts that provide women with a voice with which they can speak from the grave. Each woman tells a story that has been suppressed; each through her written voice finds a sympathetic reader who in effect enables her to come back from the underworld. These letters from the underworld are like pomegranate seeds that draw the living reader to dwell with the absent woman in the realm of the dead. These ghost stories suggest the options available in Wharton's view for women in general and women writers in particular. The woman who writes is like Persephone, speaking as a ghost from the other side.

As Wharton prepared her last book for publication in 1937, she might have faced the ironic possibility that when *Ghosts* appeared she herself would be a ghost: speaking posthumously, as it were, from the grave. Through the inclusion of "Pomegranate Seed," the story written toward the end of Wharton's life, *Ghosts* alludes to Wharton's first work of longer fiction, *The Touchstone*, as well as to the poem in which she gives voice to Persephone. One can imagine Wharton at the end of her life musing over *The Touchstone*, her story of the deceased author of *Pomegranate Seed*, reviewing the fate of the woman writer. Like Persephone, the woman writer is not fated to dwell among the living. Her voice may have the power to speak from the grave, but she, too, must repeat the woman's story of death in life.

Notes

Introduction: The American Persephone

1. Cited in Cynthia Griffin Wolff, *A Feast of Words: The Triumph of Edith Wharton* (New York: Oxford University Press, 1977), 205. See Edith Wharton, *Hudson River Bracketed* (New York: Appleton, 1929), 541.

2. Edith Wharton, planning notebook for "Literature," unpublished manuscript, Wharton Collection, Beinecke Rare Book and Manuscript Library, Yale University, New Haven, Conn.

3. R. W. B. Lewis, *Edith Wharton: A Biography* (New York: Harper and Row, 1975), 495. Judith Fryer also notes the importance of the "Demeter-Persephone" myth for Wharton in *Felicitous Space: The Imaginative Structures of Edith Wharton and Willa Cather* (Chapel Hill: University of North Carolina Press, 1986), 194, 366. In a chapter in *After the Fall: The Demeter-Persephone Myth in Wharton, Cather, and Glasgow* (which I became acquainted with while this book was in press) Josephine Donovan presents an informative and suggestive survey of the Persephone-Demeter motif in Wharton's works. See *After the Fall: The Demeter-Persephone Myth in Wharton, Cather, and Glasgow* (University Park: Pennsylvania State University Press, 1989), 43–83. For Donovan, "The Demeter-Persephone myth is singularly relevant to the historical transition that occurred in middle-class women's culture in the late nineteenth century in the Western world. It allegorizes the transformation from a matricentric preindustrialist culture—Demeter's realm—to a male-dominated capitalist-industrialist ethos, characterized by growing professionalism and bureaucracy: the realm of patriarchal captivity" (2). Although Donovan takes a different approach and arrives at different conclusions, the evidence she presents confirms the importance of the figure of Persephone for Wharton, as well as its relevance to the problem of female identity.

4. See Edith Wharton, *The Touchstone* (New York: Scribner's, 1900), 79; Edith Wharton, "Copy," in *Collected Short Stories of Edith Wharton*, 2 vols., edited with an introduction by R. W. B. Lewis (New York: Scribner's, 1968), 1:276; Edith Wharton, "Pomegranate Seed," in *Ghosts* (New York: Appleton-Century, 1937), 321–67; Edith Wharton, "Pomegranate Seed," typescript of poem, Wharton Collection, Beinecke Rare Book and Manuscript Library, Yale University, New Haven, Conn. For a more extensive discussion of the figure of Persephone, see Chapter 5.

5. Elizabeth Ammons, *Edith Wharton's Argument with America* (Athens: University of Georgia Press, 1980).

6. Cited in Lewis, 126, from a letter James wrote to Mary Cadwaller Jones in August

1902. James reports that he is sending Wharton a copy of his *Wings of the Dove*, which he describes as "rather long winded," and expresses his desire "to get hold of the little lady and pump the pure essence of my wisdom and experience into her."

7. Henry James, reprinted as "On *The Reef*: A Letter," in *Edith Wharton: A Collection of Critical Essays*, edited by Irving Howe (Englewood Cliffs, N.J.: Prentice Hall, 1962), 150. For more of the tendency to see Wharton as a disciple of James, see Lewis, 88–89. For a critique of the comparison of Wharton and James, see Wolff, 134, 422–24. Wolff notes that the habit of viewing Wharton through the work of James has obscured what was "unique (and often best) in *her* work" (424). See also Richard Poirier, "Edith Wharton: *The House of Mirth*," in *The American Novel from James Fenimore Cooper to William Faulkner*, edited by Wallace Stegner (New York: Basic Books, 1965), 117–18.

8. Edith Wharton, *The Letters of Edith Wharton*, edited by R. W. B. Lewis and Nancy Lewis (New York: Scribner's, 1988), 104 (hereafter cited in the text as *L*). For other letters that describe Wharton's relation to America, see letters to Sara Norton—in particular, *L*, 84, 125.

9. Cited in Millicent Bell, *Edith Wharton and Henry James: The Story of Their Friendship* (New York: Braziller, 1965), 147.

10. In 1905, Wharton spent Christmas at the Vanderbilt estate in Asheville, North Carolina, where she was impressed by the vegetation and plantings. "It is so far from everything," she wrote, "that beyond the park, as James said, there is only 'a vast niggery wilderness'" (*L*, 100–101). A year later she traveled as far west as Detroit by night train to attend the opening of the dramatization of *The House of Mirth*; she returned by lake steamer to Buffalo (*L*, 110). Even with these limited views, Wharton knew little of America west of the Appalachians or south of Washington, D.C.

11. Edith Wharton, "Life and I," unpublished autobiography, Wharton Collection, Beinecke Rare Book and Manuscript Library, Yale University, New Haven, Conn., 20 (hereafter cited in the text as LI).

12. Edith Wharton, *A Backward Glance* (New York: Appleton-Century, 1934), 119 (hereafter cited in the text as *BG*).

13. Diana Trilling, "*The House of Mirth* Revisited," in *Edith Wharton: A Collection of Critical Essays*, edited by Irving Howe (Englewood Cliffs, N.J.: Prentice Hall, 1962), 103.

14. Blake Nevius, *Edith Wharton: A Study of Her Fiction* (Berkeley: University of California Press, 1953), 24–25.

15. See Nevius, 24–25.

16. Edith Wharton, "The Great American Novel," *Yale Review* 16 (1927): 649.

17. Cf. Henry James, "The Question of Our Speech," in *The Question of Our Speech, The Lesson of Balzac: Two Lectures* (Boston: Houghton, Mifflin, 1905), 45.

18. See Lewis, 309; Wolff, 163–64; and Ammons, 76.

19. Cited in Fred Lewis Pattee, *The Feminine Fifties* (New York: Appleton-Century, 1940), 110.

20. For Wharton's discussion of her mother's prohibition of reading novels, see *A Backward Glance*, 65.

21. Edith Wharton, *Fast and Loose: A Novel by David Olivieri*, edited by Viola Hopkins Winner (Charlottesville: University Press of Virginia, 1977), 121, 118. See Viola Hopkins Winner, "Convention and Prediction in Edith Wharton's 'Fast and Loose,'" *American Literature* 42 (1970): 55.

22. Edith Wharton, *French Ways and Their Meaning* (New York: Appleton, 1919), 102.

23. *French Ways and Their Meaning*, 102; Lewis, 25.

24. Edith Wharton and Ogden Codman, Jr., *The Decoration of Houses* (New York: Scribner's, 1897), 29–30.

25. Edith Wharton, *The Age of Innocence* (1920; reprint, New York: Scribner's, 1970), 335–36.

26. *The Age of Innocence*, 358.

27. Unpublished notes, Wharton Collection, Beinecke Rare Book and Manuscript Library, Yale University, New Haven, Conn.

28. *The Age of Innocence*, 46.

29. See Lewis, 308–9; and Ammons, 57–77. Shortly after the publication of *Ethan Frome* in 1911, Wharton wrote to Morton Fullerton: "If I didn't feel the irresistible 'call' to write I should give up the last struggle for an individual existence & turn into a nurse & dame de compagnie for Teddy, because, after all my experiments & efforts, I have found no solution to the problem between doing this & breaking altogether" (L, 261).

30. R. W. B. Lewis's introduction to *The Collected Short Stories of Edith Wharton*, 1:xvi. In his biography of Wharton, Lewis describes the phrase "real life" in "Life and I" as a "euphemism" for her nascent "vital eroticism" (25).

31. *The Age of Innocence*, 360.

32. Edith Wharton, *The House of Mirth* (1905; reprint, New York: Scribner's, 1963), 318.

33. Edith Wharton, "The New Litany," unpublished poem, Wharton Collection, Beinecke Rare Book and Manuscript Library, Yale University, New Haven, Conn.

34. Edith Wharton,"Margaret of Cortona," in *Artemis to Actaeon and Other Verse* (New York: Scribner's, 1909), 26.

35. *Artemis to Actaeon*, 15. This phrase is taken from the lines, "so that the poor flesh,/Which spread death living, died to purchase life!" in the poem "Vesalius in Zante." See Chapter 2 for a discussion of Wharton's poems.

Chapter 1: Women and Letters (The House of Mirth)

1. Cynthia Griffin Wolff, *A Feast of Words: The Triumph of Edith Wharton* (New York: Oxford University Press, 1977), 109–11. For more on the "Art Nouveau woman," see Judith Fryer, *Felicitous Space: The Imaginative Structures of Edith Wharton and Willa Cather* (Chapel Hill: University of North Carolina Press, 1986), 55–61, 75–80, 91. See also Cynthia Griffin Wolff, "Lily Bart and the Beautiful Death," *American Literature* 46

(1976): 16–40; and Patricia Meyer Spacks, *The Female Imagination* (New York: Avon Books, 1975), 324–25. Elaine Showalter, citing *A Feast of Words*, calls *The House of Mirth* "a fictional house of birth for the woman artist," and she concludes her essay by contrasting Lily's death to Wharton's survival as an artist: "The death of the lady is thus also the death of the lady novelist, the dutiful daughter who struggles to subdue her most powerful imaginative impulses" ("The Death of the Lady [Novelist]: Wharton's *The House of Mirth*," *Representations* 9 [1985]: 134, 147). See also Judith Fetterley, "'The Temptation to Be a Beautiful Object': Double Standard and Double Bind in *The House of Mirth*," *Studies in American Fiction* 5 (1977): 199–211. For a related discussion of women's *Künstlerromane*, see Rachel Blau DuPlessis, *Writing Beyond the Ending: Narrative Strategies of Twentieth-Century Women Writers* (Bloomington: Indiana University Press, 1985), 84–104.

2. See R. W. B. Lewis, *Edith Wharton: A Biography* (New York: Harper and Row, 1975), 86–87; and Wolff, *A Feast of Words*, 63–64. Wharton wrote to her publisher Edward Burlingame in 1898: "—As to the old stories of which you speak so kindly, I regard them as the excesses of youth. They were all written 'at the top of my voice,' & The Fullness of Life is one long shriek.—I may not write any better, but at least I hope that I write in a lower key, & I fear that the voice of those early tales will drown all the others: it is for that reason that I prefer not to publish them" (Edith Wharton, *The Letters of Edith Wharton*, edited by R. W. B. Lewis and Nancy Lewis [New York: Scribner's, 1988], 36).

3. Edith Wharton, *The Collected Short Stories of Edith Wharton*, 2 vols., edited with an introduction by R. W. B. Lewis (New York: Scribner's, 1968), 1:180 (hereafter cited as *C*).

4. See Lewis, 87.

5. See Viola Hopkins Winner, "Convention and Prediction in Edith Wharton's 'Fast and Loose,'" *American Literature* 42 (1970): 51; and *C*, 440n. "April Showers" begins by quoting the final line of *Fast and Loose* (changing only the names): "'But Guy's HEART slept under the violets on Muriel's grave.'" In "April Showers," this is the "beautiful ending" of a story that the girl Theodora has authored (*C*, 189). The title of the novel written by Mrs. Fetherel in "Expiation" is also *Fast and Loose* (*C*, 440).

6. See Edith Wharton, "Copy," *C*, 276; Edith Wharton, *The Touchstone* (New York: Scribner's, 1900), 79; "Pomegranate Seed," in Edith Wharton, *Ghosts* (New York: Appleton-Century, 1937); and Edith Wharton, "Pomegranate Seed," typescript of poem, Wharton Collection, Beinecke Rare Book and Manuscript Library, Yale University, New Haven, Conn. The connection between the title in "Copy" and Wharton's ghost story "Pomegranate Seed" has been noted by Robert L. Coard, "Names in the Fiction of Edith Wharton," *Names* 13 (1965): 4. For a fuller discussion of these works, see Chapter 5. For a discussion of Wharton's view of the professional woman author, see Amy Kaplan, "Edith Wharton's Profession of Authorship," *English Literary History* 53 (1986): 433–57.

7. *The Touchstone*, 25.

8. *The Touchstone*, 35–36.

9. *The House of Mirth*, 21–22. Further citations, unless otherwise noted, will refer to this text. For more on the intricacies of plot in the novel, see Gary H. Lindberg, *Edith Wharton and the Novel of Manners* (Charlottesville: University Press of Virginia, 1975).

10. Wharton's *tableau vivant* scenes are clearly related to the *tableau vivant* scenes in Goethe's *Die Wahlverwandtschaften* (*Elective Affinities*, translated by Elizabeth Mayer and Louise Bogan [South Bend: Indiana University Press, 1963], 185–89). The episode in which Luciane's portrayal of a Ter Borch painting is interrupted by a spectator who "shouted the words which we sometimes write at the end of a page: '*Tournez, s'il vous plaît!*'" (187) suggests the importance in Lily's performance of *reading* the *text* of a *tableau vivant*. Other relevant literary models include Gwendelon's *tableau vivant* of Hermione from *The Winter's Tale* in *Daniel Deronda* and the private theatricals performed in *Mansfield Park*. For extensive discussions of these scenes, see David Marshall, *The Figure of Theater: Shaftesbury, Defoe, Adam Smith, and George Eliot* (New York: Columbia University Press, 1986), 196–205; and "True Acting and the Language of Real Feeling: *Mansfield Park*," *Yale Journal of Criticism* 3 (1989): 87–106. For more on the question of painting, theatricality, and the novel, see Marshall, *The Surprising Effects of Sympathy: Marivaux, Diderot, Rousseau, and Mary Shelley* (Chicago: University of Chicago Press, 1988). Both David Marshall's work and his conversation have encouraged me in my reading of Lily Bart's representation of "Mrs. Lloyd."

11. Walter Benn Michaels also has found it significant that Lily is writing in the *tableau vivant* of Mrs. Lloyd. He suggests that "it may well be that Lily herself is only a stand-in for another person who is impersonating her, the person of the writer" (*The Gold Standard and the Logic of Naturalism* [Berkeley: University of California Press, 1987], 240–41). As Michaels notes, the significance of a preoccupation with acts of writing is explored in another context by Michael Fried in *Realism, Writing, Disfiguration: On Thomas Eakins and Stephen Crane* (Chicago: University of Chicago Press, 1988).

12. *Mrs. Lloyd*, exhibited at the Royal Academy in 1776, commemorates the marriage in 1775 of Joanna Leigh to Richard Lloyd, although it may have been painted before their actual wedding. For a helpful account of the painting, see the catalog entry by David Mannings in *Reynolds*, edited by Nicholas Penny (London: Royal Academy of Arts, 1986), 275–76.

13. See Rensselaer W. Lee, *Names on Trees: Ariosto into Art* (Princeton: Princeton University Press, 1977).

14. William Shakespeare, *As You Like It*, in *The Complete Works* (Baltimore: Penguin Books, 1969), 3.2.5–10; *The Poems of Andrew Marvell*, edited by G. A. Aitken (New York: Scribner's, 1899), 98–99.

15. Torquato Tasso, *Jerusalem Delivered*, translated by Edward Fairfax (New York: Capricorn Books, n.d.), 135. The literary and artistic traditions that Reynolds drew upon are discussed in Mannings's catalog description of *Mrs. Lloyd*, 275–76. See also Lee, passim.

16. Before the presentation of the *tableaux vivants*, under the "splendours of the Venetian ceiling" that Gerty Farish has been told is "by Veronese," Gerty says, "Did you

ever see such jewels? Do look at Mrs. George Dorset's pearls—I suppose the smallest of them would pay the rent of our Girls' Club for a year" (129). In the context of the doubling played out between Lily and Bertha, one can imagine Tiepolo's *tableau* of conspicuous consumption as a portrait of Bertha that Lily chooses not to enact.

17. For a discussion of Artemisia Gentileschi's *Self-Portrait as the Allegory of Painting*, see Mary D. Garrard, "Artemisia Gentileschi: The Artist's Autograph in Letters and Paintings," in *The Female Autograph: Theory and Practice of Autobiography From the Tenth to the Twentieth Century*, edited by Domna C. Stanton (Chicago: University of Chicago Press, 1987), 81–95.

18. For the early titles of *The House of Mirth*, which include "A Moment's Ornament," see Lewis's introduction to *The House of Mirth*, x.

19. These images also anticipate the scrapbook Mrs. Heeny keeps of Undine's exploits in Edith Wharton, *The Custom of the Country* (New York: Scribner's, 1913), 582. See Chapter 4 for a discussion of the significance of these scraps of paper.

20. See Lewis's introduction to *The House of Mirth*, xiv, and Coard, 1.

21. For readings that stress the economic relations and the problem of exchange in the novel, see Wai-Chee Dimock, "Debasing Exchange: Edith Wharton's *The House of Mirth*," *PMLA* 100 (1985): 783–92; Michaels, 225–44; and Wayne W. Westbrook, "Lily-Bartering on the New York Social Exchange in *The House of Mirth*," *Ball State University Forum* 20 (1979): 59–64. For a relevant discussion of *The Custom of the Country*, see Elizabeth Ammons, *Edith Wharton's Argument with America* (Athens: University of Georgia Press, 1980), 97–124.

22. Jane Tompkins observes: "The power of the dead or the dying to redeem the unregenerate is a major theme of nineteenth-century popular fiction and religious literature" (*Sensational Designs: The Cultural Work of American Fiction, 1790–1860* [New York: Oxford University Press, 1985], 127–28). See also Ann Douglas on the "domestication of death" in *The Feminization of American Culture* (New York: Avon, 1977), 240–72; and Wolff, "Lily Bart and the Beautiful Death," 39.

23. "The heart of the wise is in the house of mourning; but the heart of fools is in the house of mirth" (Ecclesiastes 7:4).

24. "Literature," unpublished manuscript, Wharton Collection, Beinecke Rare Book and Manuscript Library, Yale University, New Haven, Conn., 55.

25. Wharton's lifelong friends, the Rutherfords, called her by the nickname of "Lily" from the time she was a child. See Lewis, 39.

26. Susan Gubar writes that the word "is Lily's dead body; for she is now converted completely into a script for his edification, a text not unlike the letters and checks she has left behind to vindicate her life. . . . Lily's history, then, illustrates the terrors not of the word made flesh but of the flesh made word" ("'The Blank Page' and the Issues of Female Creativity," in *The New Feminist Criticism: Essays on Women, Literature, and Theory*, edited by Elaine Showalter [New York: Pantheon Books, 1985], 298–99).

27. For an extensive discussion of this, see Chapter 5.

28. Unpublished notes for *The Age of Innocence*, Wharton Collection, Beinecke Rare

Book and Manuscript Library, Yale University, New Haven, Conn.

29. "Pomegranate Seed," in *Ghosts*, 325.

30. There may be another portrait by Reynolds that is suggested in the novel. Charles Augustus Trenor, who owns an estate called Bellomont, recalls in name and actions an eighteenth-century nobleman painted by Reynolds: Charles Coote, Earl of Bellomont. According to David Mannings, Lord Bellomont was known as "the Hibernian Seducer" (Penny, 261).

31. "The Oresteia," unpublished cycle of poems, Wharton Collection, Beinecke Rare Book and Manuscript Library, Yale University, New Haven, Conn.

32. Sophocles, cited in *New Larousse Encyclopedia of Mythology* (New York: Hamlyn, 1959), 166.

33. See Aeschylus, *Oresteia*, translated by Richard Lattimore (Chicago: University of Chicago Press, 1973). For a different reading of the mythological allusions in these scenes, see Josephine Donovan, *After the Fall: The Demeter-Persephone Myth in Wharton, Cather, and Glasgow* (University Park: Pennsylvania State University Press, 1989), 60–61.

34. See Christine Dowing, *The Goddess: Mythological Images of the Feminine* (New York: Crossroads, 1981), 182.

35. For this version of the sacrifice of Iphigenia, see Alexander S. Murray, *Classic Guide to the Ancient World* (New York: Crescent Books, 1988), 290. Showalter writes: "Whereas childbirth and maternity are the emotional and spiritual centers of the nineteenth-century female world, in *The House of Mirth* they have been banished to the margins. Childbirth seems to be one of the dingier attributes of the working class; the Perfect Lady cannot mar her body or betray her sexuality in giving birth" (138). As Showalter notes, the names of Wharton's characters recall the characters in Elizabeth Oakes Smith's 1854 novel, *Bertha and Lily*. In this feminist novel, Bertha is the mother and Lily is the daughter who "'will be an artist, an orator'" (cited in Showalter, 139). Spacks sees Lily's hallucination of the child in her arms as "an escapist fantasy of motherhood" (310). Cf. Susan Gubar, "The Birth of the Artist as Heroine: (Re)production, the *Künstlerroman* Tradition, and the Fiction of Katherine Mansfield," in *The Representation of Women in Fiction*, Selected Papers from the English Institute, 1981, edited by Carolyn G. Heilbrun and Margaret R. Higonnet (Baltimore: Johns Hopkins University Press, 1983), 19–59. Also relevant is Margaret Homans, *Bearing the Word: Language and Female Experience in Nineteenth-Century Women's Writing* (Chicago: University of Chicago Press, 1986). For more on the question of virgin death and the embodiment of the mother, see Chapter 3.

36. Emma tastes an "affreux goût d'encre" after she takes the poison. Charles eventually finds "les lettres de Léon" hidden in Emma's desk, along with the "portrait de Rodolphe . . . au milieu des billets doux bouleversés" (Gustave Flaubert, *Madame Bovary* [Paris: Garnier Frères, 1971], 322, 354).

Chapter 2: The Woman Behind the Door (Ethan Frome)

1. Cited in R. W. B. Lewis, *Edith Wharton: A Biography* (New York: Harper and Row, 1975), 234.

2. Ibid., 217. See also 217–38.

3. Ibid., 234.

4. Edith Wharton, *Artemis to Actaeon and Other Verse* (New York: Scribner's, 1909), 7. Further citations of poetry in this chapter will refer to this text and will be indicated by *A*.

5. *Butler's Lives of the Saints*, edited by Michael Walsh (San Francisco: Harper and Row, 1985), 54–55.

6. Edith Wharton, *The Letters of Edith Wharton*, edited by R. W. B. Lewis and Nancy Lewis (New York: Scribner's, 1988), 75 (hereafter cited as *L*).

7. See Andreas Vesalius, *De humani corporis fabrica librorum epitome* in *The Epitome of Andreas Vesalius*, translated by L. R. Lind (New York: Macmillan, 1949).

8. Actaeon is torn apart by hounds that "throng him on every side and, plunging their muzzles in his flesh, mangle their master under the deceiving form of the deer" (Ovid, *Metamorphoses*, translated by Frank Justus Miller [Cambridge: Harvard University Press, 1984], 1.141).

9. Cynthia Griffin Wolff notes that, like *Ethan Frome*, Wharton's ghost story "The Eyes" also has both a first-person narrator and a fiction within a fiction (*A Feast of Words: The Triumph of Edith Wharton* [New York: Oxford University Press, 1977], 156–59).

10. Edith Wharton, *Ethan Frome* (New York: Scribner's, 1922), 27. Further page references following citations in the text, unless otherwise noted, will refer to this edition.

11. Edith Wharton, *A Backward Glance* (New York: Appleton-Century, 1934), 296 (hereafter cited as *BG*). For more on Wharton's defensiveness, see Chapter 3.

12. Cited in Lewis, 160. Wolff links this confession to Wharton's early fears: as a child, writes Wolff, Wharton saw animals "as inarticulate, helpless, suffering creatures. . . . they are fearsome because the intensity of need that they represent is fearsome" (21). Judith Fryer, in a note, also links Wharton's confession of her fear of animals to *Ethan Frome* and "Kerfol." See *Felicitous Space: The Imaginative Structures of Edith Wharton and Willa Cather* (Chapel Hill: University of North Carolina Press, 1986), 364 n. 46. In Chapter 5, I offer an extended discussion of "Kerfol" as a story about Wharton's fears concerning the silence and muteness of women and animals.

13. Wolff emphasizes that the story of Ethan Frome is "ultimately" the narrator's "'vision'" (165), speculating that Wharton set out to "write a novel that captures the compulsive quality of vision-making" (184). She links the narrator to the character of Frome he projects, stressing the points of the narrator's identification with Frome. For Wolff, "the tale of Ethan is . . . a terrified expression of the narrator's latent self—his *alter ago*, his 'Winterman'" (183–84). See also Joseph X. Brennan, "Ethan Frome: Structure and Metaphor," *Modern Fiction Studies* 27 (1961): 347–56. Brennan discusses the narra-

tor's sensibility and his authorship of the vision, the fiction within the fiction. He also provides a careful analysis of the images of nature found in both the narrative frame and the narrator's vision. In *The Writing of Fiction*, Wharton warns against naively seeing "the mind of the creative artist as a mirror, and the work of art the reflection in it." "The mirror," she contends, "indeed, is the artist's mind, with all his experiences reflected in it, but the work of art from the smallest to the greatest, should be something projected, not reflected, something on which his [the writer's] mirrored experiences . . . are to be turned for its full illumination" (*The Writing of Fiction* [New York: Scribner's, 1925], 58.)

14. William Faulkner, *Absalom, Absalom!* (1936; reprint, New York: Vintage, 1972), 8. For a relevant account of Faulkner's novel see Robert Parker, *Faulkner and the Novelistic Imagination* (Urbana: University of Illinois Press, 1985), 1.

15. For another discussion of the ellipses in *Ethan Frome*, see Elizabeth Ammons, *Edith Wharton's Argument with America* (Athens: University of Georgia Press, 1980), 62.

16. Planning notebook for "Literature," unpublished manuscript, Wharton Collection, Beinecke Rare Book and Manuscript Library, Yale University, New Haven, Conn.

17. Ammons writes that "in the frozen unyielding world of *Ethan Frome*, there is no generative natural order; there is no mother earth. There is only her nightmare reverse image, the witch figured in Zeena Frome" (63). For Ammons's analysis of *Ethan Frome* as an inverted fairy tale, see 59–63. Ammons also describes the relationship between the barren earth and Zeena as "mother antitheses" (200). Kenneth Bernard emphasizes the imagery of castration in the novel, but he also suggests that the chilled atmosphere is related to Zeena's frigidity. Her sexual coldness is related to the barrenness suggested in the name Starkfield. Bernard comments that "barrenness, infertility is at the heart of Frome's frozen woe." See "Imagery and Symbolism in *Ethan Frome*," *College English* 23 (1961): 182. For the most complete discussion of the imagery of a void that Wharton uses to describe the New England of *Ethan Frome* and *Summer*, see Henry Alan Rose, "'Such Depths of Sad Initiation': Edith Wharton and New England," *New England Quarterly* 50 (1977): 423–39. Rose writes, "In this cultural emptiness, Wharton's imagination was free to range in a manner not duplicated in her cluttered urban world." He argues that in the "barren settings" of New England, Wharton felt "the full extent of the negation, the sense of void" (423–24).

18. Bernard, 184.

19. See K. R. Srinivasa Iyengar, "A Note on 'Ethan Frome,'" *Literary Criticism* 5 (1961–63): 169.

20. See Lewis, 396.

21. Edith Wharton, *Summer*, with an introduction by Cynthia Griffin Wolff (1917; reprint, New York: Harper and Row, 1980), 25 (hereafter cited as *S*).

22. Ammons, 127.

23. Edith Wharton, *French Ways and Their Meaning* (New York: Appleton, 1919), v.

24. Edith Wharton, *Fighting France from Dunkerque to Belfort* (New York: Scribner's, 1915), 153. *Fighting France* also includes a description of exploding shells and "luminous bombs" that is similar to the description of the fireworks scene in *Summer*. In

Fighting France, a flare is described as "a white light opened like a tropical flower." Another "white flower" is said to have "bloomed further down." Along with the "red flash" of "luminous bombs," these white flowers are part of what Wharton calls "those infernal flowers [which] continued to open and shut along the curve of death" (148–49). In the fireworks scene in *Summer*, Wharton writes: "The whole night broke into flower. . . . sky orchards broke into blossom, shed their flaming petals and hung their branches with golden fruit" (147).

25. *Fighting France*, 58.

Chapter 3: Wharton and Wilkins: Rereading the Mother (Summer)

1. Edith Wharton, *Ethan Frome* (New York: Scribner's, 1922), x (hereafter cited as *EF*).

2. Cited in Cynthia Griffin Wolff, *A Feast of Words: The Triumph of Edith Wharton* (New York: Oxford University Press, 1977), 159.

3. Ibid., 159.

4. Cited in ibid., 159. See also *A Backward Glance* (New York: Scribner's, 1934), 296 (hereafter cited as *BG*).

5. Edith Wharton, "Life and I," unpublished autobiography, Wharton Collection, Beinecke Rare Book and Manuscript Library, Yale University, New Haven, Conn., 1–2.

6. Edith Wharton, "The Great American Novel," *Yale Review* 16 (1927): 648.

7. According to R. W. B. Lewis, early reviewers "recognized that *Ethan Frome* was one of Edith Wharton's finest achievements, though some of them found the concluding image too terrible to be borne." The responses to the book were not unlike the responses to *Wuthering Heights* (a book that Wharton names as an inspiration for *Ethan Frome*); some readers seemed to blame the author for the unpleasant tale she told. Lewis describes a review from the *New York Times* which called the novel "an exercise in subtle torture" and a review from the *Bookman* which "could not forgive her cruelty toward both her characters and her readers" (*Edith Wharton: A Biography* [New York: Harper and Row, 1975], 310). Debates about Wharton's knowledge of the region, as well as the question of a class bias in *Ethan Frome*, have continued. See John Crowe Ransom, "Characters and Character: A Note on Fiction," *American Review* 6 (1936): 273–75; and Alfred Kazin, "Edith Wharton," in *Edith Wharton: A Collection of Critical Essays*, edited by Irving Howe (Englewood Cliffs, N.J.: Prentice Hall, 1962), 93. Ransom insists on the distance of this woman author from the concerns of a poor man such as Ethan; he argues that Wharton's use of "a special reporter" and a "peculiar chronological method" suggests "an author wrestling with an unaccustomed undertaking, uneasy of conscience" (273–74). Ransom asserts that a man from Ethan's background would not have thought of alimony. Kazin insists that *Ethan Frome* was not "the granite 'folk tale' *in esse* its admirers have claimed it to be. She knew little of the New England common world, and perhaps cared even less." Noting the work's origin as a French language exercise,

Kazin writes: "She wanted a simple frame and 'simple' characters. The world of the Frome tragedy is abstract. She never knew how the poor lived in Paris or London; she knew even less of how they lived in the New England villages where she spent an occasional summer" (Kazin, 93). Nancy R. Leach concedes that "Mrs. Wharton was aware of certain aspects of New England life, but she was not a native and her writing cannot help betraying this" ("New England in the Stories of Edith Wharton," *New England Quarterly* 30 [1957]: 95). Abigail Hamblen writes: "Mrs. Wharton's writing usually reveals a woman of great common sense and perceptiveness, careful to avoid any appearance of vanity or presumptuousness. Thus it seems strange that she considers herself an authority on the manners and morals of the hill-people of Massachusetts." As evidence of Wharton's lack of familiarity with her subject, Hamblen cites the Congregationalist prohibition against dancing, "particularly dancing in the church building. . . . It is, bluntly, impossible that Mattie Silver could have gone to a dance held in the Starkfield meeting house, as Mrs. Wharton described in *Ethan Frome*" ("Edith Wharton in New England," *New England Quarterly* 38 [1965]: 240). In *New England: Indian Summer, 1865–1915*, Van Wyck Brooks refers to Wharton as a "summer visitor" in New England (*Literature in New England* [Garden City: Garden City Publishing, 1944], 463).

8. "The Great American Novel," 653.

9. See Lewis, 310. See also Theodora Bosanquet, *Henry James at Work* (London: The Hogarth Essays, n.d.), 266.

10. Wharton writes in the introduction to *Ethan Frome*: "Each of my chroniclers contributes to the narrative *just so much as he or she is capable of understanding* of what, to them, is a complicated and mysterious case; and only the narrator of the tale has scope enough to see it all, to resolve it back into simplicity, and to put it in its rightful place among his larger categories" (*EF*, ix). Earlier in the introduction, she argues that she still feels that the "scheme of construction" that she chose for the novel, a scheme "which met with the immediate and unqualified disapproval of the few friends to whom I tentatively outlined it," was "justified in the given case" (*EF*, vii–viii).

11. According to Blake Nevius, Wharton "accused [these writers] too broadly of viewing their region through 'rose-coloured glasses'" (*Edith Wharton: A Study of Her Fiction* [Berkeley: University of California Press, 1953], 25).

12. Wolff tends to adopt Wharton's own opposition of "depth" and "surface." These authors, she writes, offered "a prettified spectacle of billboard art, a pastoral land seen through awestruck eyes." Wharton, according to Wolff, was more like Browning in seeing through the surface "to discover what was timeless in the human mind" (162). For another account of Wharton's relation to Jewett and Wilkins, see Josephine Donovan, *New England Local Color Literature: A Woman's Tradition* (New York: Ungar, 1983), 44, 105.

13. Nancy R. Leach compares Wharton's work to that of the female regionalists ("New England in the Stories of Edith Wharton," *New England Quarterly* 30 [1957]). For Leach, Wharton "is certainly not a New England writer in the sense that Sarah Orne Jewett and Mary E. Wilkins Freeman are. She does not report dialect, local coloring,

village decorum or tradition with their felicity. Miss Jewett and Mrs. Freeman treated New England life with the deftness that Mrs. Wharton manifested in her stories of New York society; they wrote as 'insiders'" (95). Leach suggests that in addition to Wharton's "occasional contacts with the more rustic natives," she drew on her reading of "Nathaniel Hawthorne, Sarah Orne Jewett, and Mary Wilkins Freeman" (97) as sources for her New England of fiction. In one of the rare critical statements from the last thirty years linking Wharton and Wilkins, she asserts that "Mrs. Wharton's New England is closer in concept to that of Mrs. Freeman's than Miss Jewett's, but she never recreates a New England redolent with the details of daily routine and personal idiosyncrasy that delight the reader of these other women's stories" (95–96). Hamblen argues that Wharton's critiques of the local colorists leave her "open to the charge of being a stranger in a strange land, looking at that land, not, indeed, through pink glasses, but rather from the wrong end of a telescope. Nor could she possibly have read all the stories of *A Humble Romance* and *A New England Nun*, or the bitter novel *Pembroke*; if she had she could never have charged Mary Wilkins with oversweetness. And she certainly could not have been familiar with some of the dun-colored stories of Sarah Orne Jewett" (239). In *Felicitous Space: The Imaginative Structures of Edith Wharton and Willa Cather* (Chapel Hill: University of North Carolina Press, 1986), Judith Fryer contrasts the work of Jewett and Wilkins to that of Wharton and claims that "there is neither passion nor horror in the stories of Sarah Orne Jewett and Mary E. Wilkins" (179). Fryer for the most part is concerned with the differences in these authors' relation to the landscape and women's communities; although she does note some specific stories, she (like Wolff) tends to generalize about the bulk of the work of Jewett and Wilkins rather than considering the significance of individual stories. More recently, Josephine Donovan has argued for the relevance of the local color tradition for authors such as Wharton. In *After the Fall: The Demeter-Persephone Myth in Wharton, Cather, and Glasgow* (University Park: Pennsylvania State University Press, 1989), she writes: "I emphasize the local-color generation of American women writers as influences on Wharton, Cather, and Glasgow because they were their immediate generational predecessors in women's literary history and as realists they were taken more seriously by the twentieth-century writers than were the sentimentalists, who comprised the other major nineteenth-century women's school." In her discussion of the Demeter-Persephone myth, she notes that Jewett and Wilkins were "of paramount importance. Their version of the myth and its contrast to the twentieth-century women's treatment illustrates dramatically the historical cultural change between the generations" (6). For her account of this mythological motif in Wharton's works, which I encountered while this book was in press, see 43–83. See also Donovan, *New England Local Color Literature*.

14. Mary Ella Wilkins replaced her middle name with her mother's name, Eleanor, when she became an author; and after marrying in 1902, she published her work under the name, Mary Eleanor Wilkins Freeman. I have chosen to call her Mary Wilkins in this chapter because this is the name she wrote under for most of her career. It was as Mary Wilkins that she gained her literary reputation, and this is the name that Wharton uses

to refer to her. I single out Wilkins from other New England local color writers and sentimentalists because of the specific textual and biographical connections that (I argue) inform the writing of *Summer*.

15. Wharton describes Charity Royall's increasing awareness of the role in her protected life of a "father." In discussing the symbolic significance of this dichotomy between the animal mother and social life, between the rudimentary mountain world of the mother and the orderly valley world of the father, Sandra Gilbert links the wintry burial of the alcoholic mother Mary in *Summer* to the freezing death of another profligate mother: the opiate-addicted Molly of Eliot's *Silas Marner*. Both stories include the deaths of "unworthy" mothers and the adoption of their young daughters by men who assume the role of father. The death of the mother either makes way for or reaffirms the place of the daughters with the adopted fathers, whom Gilbert recognizes as "cultural fathers." *Summer* involves a separation from and rejection of the "cultural mother," a mother "Mary" who recalls the poles of the archetypal mother as the mother of God and the disreputable Magdalen. Gilbert suggests that through these stories Eliot and Wharton define themselves as literary daughters who bury the mother and are adopted by the world of the literary and "cultural fathers." See Sandra Gilbert, "Life's Empty Pack: Notes toward a Literary Daughteronomy," *Critical Inquiry* 11 (1985): 355–84. Contrasting Wharton's personal and literary stance with nineteenth-century American women writers' "strong allegiance to the maternal line and the female community," Elaine Showalter writes that Wharton belonged to "the more troubled and more gifted countertradition of women writers who were torn between the literary world of their fathers and the wordless sensual world of their mothers" ("The Death of the Lady [Novelist]: Wharton's *The House of Mirth*," *Representations* 9 [1985]: 145–56). Elizabeth Ammons argues that in the 1920s Wharton turns to writing novels that declare "motherhood woman's best and most fulfilling job in life" (*Edith Wharton's Argument with America* [Athens: University of Georgia Press, 1980], 157). For relevant discussions of *The Glimpses of the Moon* (1922), *The Mother's Recompense* (1925), *Twilight Sleep* (1927), and *The Children* (1928), see Ammons, 157–87.

16. Edith Wharton, *The Custom of the Country* (New York: Scribner's, 1913), 280, 73–74.

17. Charles Miner Thompson, "Miss Wilkins—Idealist in Masquerade," *Atlantic Monthly* 83 (May 1899): 666.

18. F. O. Matthiessen, "New England Stories," in *American Writers on American Literature*, edited by John Macy (New York: Horace Liveright, 1931), 404. Born in 1852 in Randolph, Massachusetts, a small town twelve miles west of and a half day's travel to Boston, Mary Wilkins lived until her fifteenth year in a town that already was experiencing the industrial escalation commonly associated with the Civil War and postwar periods. The invention of the McKay stitcher, which mechanized the process of making shoes, totally transformed the only significant industry of Randolph, whose economy was based on agricultural subsistence. The major change in Wilkins's life was not the war but her father's decision (in 1867) to move from her mother's home of Randolph,

with its depressed postwar economy, to the town of Brattleboro, Vermont, where he started a dry goods business. A housewright by trade with no prior experience in shopkeeping, Warren Wilkins hoped that the move into the mercantile economy and into the thriving town of Brattleboro would improve the family's prospects. What can be called the Wilkins family's decline began during these years. Wilkins's business was hurt by the shock sent through the whole retail community by a major fire, a flood, and a large bank embezzlement—all of which added a local dimension to a regionwide economic depression.

Despite her family's financial difficulties, Mary Wilkins, the oldest child, finished high school and even was sent for a year to Mt. Holyoke Seminary for girls (the school which Emily Dickinson had attended almost two decades earlier). From Mt. Holyoke (an institution that Mary Wilkins would later describe as being too concerned with students' souls and not concerned enough with their digestions) she returned to Brattleboro, where she attended the Glenwood Seminary for Girls. Her studies there led to a position in a local school, which (despite her family's economic needs) she left after several months because her temperament was unsuited to teaching children.

The advantages of financially depressed Brattleboro for Mary Wilkins were largely cultural. There was a concert orchestra and a regular lecture series; the town had a reputation for literary interests, as exemplified in the salon of Miss Anna Higginson (T. W. Higginson's sister), which attracted writers and visual artists. Because of this level of literary interest, Brattleboro had a fine bookstore, which was located in the same business block as the Wilkins's dry goods store. Here, as well as from the libraries of neighbors, Mary Wilkins began to read the Elizabethan poets, Dickens, Goethe, and Thackeray. Aside from Poe, the other American authors she read were primarily from within the region: Emerson, Thoreau, Jewett, and Harriet Beecher Stowe. It is likely that between the years of her arrival in Vermont and her success as a published writer at age thirty, Mary Wilkins read many contemporary authors in the literary magazines *Harper's*, the *Atlantic*, and the *Century*. These were among the publications to which she began to send her own stories and poems in the early 1880s.

With the failure of the dry goods business, Mary Wilkins's mother Eleanor increasingly assumed responsibility for support of the family. She took a position nursing an invalid, Pickman Tyler, who was well known as one of the four preaching sons of the American playwright, Royall Tyler. As part of her remuneration, Mrs. Wilkins was allowed to move her entire family (herself, her daughter, and her husband) into the Tyler household. (Mary Wilkins's sister had died the year before, leaving her as the only surviving child in the family). This move has been seen as particularly poignant for Mary Wilkins, since the only romantic interest of her life at that time had been Pickman Tyler's son Hanson, who had left Brattleboro to join the navy. Whatever their earlier relationship had been, Mary Wilkins saved several mementos: his gold ensign's buttons and a photograph that she displayed prominently in the years that followed. What must be seen as a remarkable coincidence in any version of this story, however, is that the young woman who would gain a reputation as the primary realist of Yankee village life was the daughter of a servant in a household whose leading literary figure (Royall Tyler, author of the 1813 play *A Yankee in London*) was known as the originator of the "stage Yankee."

Following the death of her mother, Mary Wilkins moved out of the Tyler household; only months later she published her first poem in a Fall River children's magazine; it was appropriately titled, "The Beggar Princess." Soon afterward she won a cash award in a contest sponsored by a Boston newspaper for her story, "The Shadow Family." The death of her father two years after that of her mother left Wilkins without close relatives. During this period of time Wilkins had become a writer and was recognized on the streets of Brattleboro as having had a poem published in the *Century*. Before Warren Wilkins's death and her decision to return to Randolph, Wilkins had secured her most important means of income; she began to publish regularly in *Harper's*. The publication in 1887 of her first volume of short stories, *A Humble Romance and Others*, established Wilkins at the age of thirty-five as one of the most popular and respected writers in America. For fuller biographical discussions (from which I have drawn much of the information compiled in the brief summary above), see Edward Foster, *Mary E. Wilkins* (New York: Hendricks House, 1956), and Perry D. Westbrook, *Acres of Flint: Writers of Rural New England, 1870–1900* (Washington, D.C.: Scarecrow Press, 1951).

19. Mary Wilkins, seen as a village "original," and Edith Wharton, distinguished as a member of Mrs. Vanderbilt's "four hundred," were not as different as their public personae imply. I do not mean to minimize the differences between them. Mary Wilkins and Edith Wharton came from vastly different class backgrounds, and Wharton could not have known as intimately as Wilkins what Matthiessen called "the sharp angles of life" (404). Yet each woman had to confront similar obstacles in becoming a writer, and for both, their lives in some sense depended on becoming writers. Wilkins's success as an author may have literally saved her from a life as a servant or the peripheral identity of the extra female relative. Wharton's success as a writer saved her from a life as a society matron among other society matrons. By becoming writers both Wilkins and Wharton were able to claim a place for their artistic aspirations. Money, which provided essential income for Wilkins, provided essential recognition for Wharton by justifying her identity as a writer. Publications, which brought social and financial rewards, established their identities as literary personages. Wharton describes this process of writing and publication as giving birth to herself—what she saw as an essential stage in her development of a personality.

Both Wharton and Wilkins were shy women whose books served as introductions to the literary world, announcing their wit to those for whom they otherwise would have been invisible. In their later years as "famous" authors, both Wharton and Wilkins were faced with similar problems and experiences. Each writer experienced late in life an erotic awakening with a younger man. Mary Wilkins was nearly fifty when, in 1902, she married her young man, Dr. Charles Freeman, and moved to New Jersey. About five years later, Edith Wharton (herself in her mid-forties) had what many believe to be her first passionate sexual relationship (despite her twenty-three years of marriage) in an affair lasting several years with a younger writer, Morton Fullerton. Between the time of Wilkins's publication of *The Winning Lady and Others* in 1909 and Wharton's publication of *Ethan Frome* in 1911, both writers began to have serious problems with their husbands. Lewis, who has argued that *Ethan Frome* is one of the most autobiographical books ever written, finds in that novel a subtle meditation on Wharton's life (308–10). She fears being crippled (like Ethan Frome) by her responsibility for two weaker men, her husband and her lover. Wharton might be said to have written *Ethan Frome* as a way of imagining her life without her divorce; in the same manner, Mary Wilkins began to include stories about drunken and abusive men and predatory fathers among her pallid tales of life in suburban New Jersey.

In the years preceding the outbreak of World War I, Wharton was told that her boyish (although older) husband Teddy was an incurable neurasthenic. They were divorced in 1913. In these years Mary Wilkins became increasingly aware of her husband's drinking problems. Charles Freeman entered a sanatorium for his alcoholism in 1914; after a later breakdown he was committed to a mental institution. Both Wharton and Wilkins experienced guilt about their husbands' angry emotional dependence, and both witnessed their husbands' entrapment by debilitating mental illness.

20. See Foster, 89.

21. John Macy, *The Spirit of American Literature* (New York: Boni and Liveright, n.d.), vii.

22. W. L. Courtney, *The Feminine Note in Fiction* (London: Chapman and Hall, 1904), xxxiii. As late as 1940, Van Wyck Brooks noted in *New England: Indian Summer, 1865–1915*: "*Ethan Frome*, good as it was, could not compare with the best of Miss Wilkins. Its plot was factitious, and it had the air of a superior person surveying the squalid affairs of these children of fate" (464).

23. Cited in Lewis, 152.

24. Cited in Foster, 131.

25. Sarah Orne Jewett, *The Country of the Pointed Firs and Other Stories*, edited by Mary Ellen Chase with an introduction by Marjorie Pryse (New York: Norton, 1981), xxvii–xxviii. These terms are pointed out by Chase as examples of Maine dialect. The tragedies in *The Country of the Pointed Firs* and related stories by Jewett are subtle but present nonetheless. Aside from words and phrases that tell of melancholy and isolation, the story of "Poor Joanna" and the mystery surrounding Mrs. Todd's dislike of Mary Harris suggest the tragedies of the book. "Poor Joanna" withdraws from society to live and die alone on Shell Heap Island. Wharton's New England is much closer to the inland world of Mary Wilkins. Wharton's closest connection with Jewett's New England of fiction occurs in Wharton's unfinished work, *The Cruise of the Fleetwing*, which includes a character, Captain Casey, who has been a seafarer. For a discussion of this and two other unfinished novels by Wharton about New England (*Mother Earth* and *New England*) see Leach, 90–98. Leach writes: "Wharton probably selected New England as her locale [for *The Cruise of the Fleetwing*] in order to utilize the sea. In none of the published stories does she write about sailing or the sea" (92).

26. Edward Arlington Robinson, *Untriangulated Stars* (Cambridge: Harvard University Press, 1947), 174–75.

27. Rollin Lynd Hartt, "A New England Hill Town," *Atlantic Monthly* (April 1899), 564, 568.

28. Thompson, 669.

29. Matthiessen, 407.

30. Ibid., 405.

31. Ibid., 412–13. Matthiessen's article (which is primarily about Stowe, Wilkins, and Jewett) contains a comment about Wharton that she attributes to "a literary critic" in *A Backward Glance* (296).

32. Mary Austin's comment appears in "Regionalism in American Literature," *English Journal* 21 (1932): 100.

33. John Crowe Ransom, "Characters and Character: A Note on Fiction," *American Review* 6 (1936): 272.

34. Ransom, 273. See Nevius, 123.

35. In emphasizing Wharton's description of Wilkins as one of her "predecessors," I am aware that the term might evoke Harold Bloom's understanding of literary *precursors*. (See *The Anxiety of Influence* [New York: Oxford University Press, 1973].) Although I am suggesting that Wharton would have seen Wilkins as a representative of a past generation that she associated with a female tradition, and although I am emphasizing the extent to which Wharton would have looked upon Wilkins as a rival, Wharton never would have acknowledged Wilkins as a "strong" precursor in the Bloomian sense. The Oedipal model is complex here, not only because female writers are in question, but also because Wharton wished to identify with the son more than the daughter. As I argue in Chapters 2 and 3, if there is anxiety of influence here, it comes from Wharton's ambivalence about her own critique of the women's culture that she associated with the local colorists. For an early discussion of women's writing that takes into account Bloom's categories, see Sandra M. Gilbert and Susan Gubar, *The Madwoman in the Attic: The Woman Writer and the Nineteenth-Century Literary Imagination* (New Haven: Yale University Press, 1979), 3–104. Finally, an implicit argument in all of the chapters of this book is that Wharton's fiction is constantly in dialogue with other texts and authors. Wilkins is not the only author who comes into play in Wharton's fiction. Writers such as Goethe, Marvell, Ovid, and Wharton herself are present in complicated ways, as well as artists such as Reynolds, Boucher, and Turner.

36. Showalter observes that characters named Lily appear in Wilkins's "A New England Nun" and "Old Woman Magoun" (133).

37. By 1905, the year in which Wharton's novel was published, Mary Wilkins claimed to be no longer reading other people's novels; but Lily Bart of *The House of Mirth* was in the air and like Richardson's *Pamela*, her plight was actively discussed by the novel-reading population as well as the established literati. (Just as village bells in England were said to have rung in celebration of Pamela's marriage, one of Wharton's readers is said to have sent a telegram announcing "Lily Bart is dead" when she read the

final installment of *The House of Mirth*. See Lewis, 152.)

38. The story of the rape of Lucrece begins with a scene of gambling and drinking men who make a bet about who has the most virtuous wife. Lucrece's husband brings the men into his home where Lucrece is spinning. She is proven the most virtuous wife, but later one of the men returns to seduce her. He threatens to ruin her reputation if she does not submit: he says he will kill her and a servant and leave their bodies together. Lucrece is raped, but she tells her own story to her husband and father and then kills herself.

39. For a discussion of gambling and marriage in *The House of Mirth*, see Rachel Blau DuPlessis, *Writing Beyond the Ending: Narrative Strategies of Twentieth-Century Women Writers* (Bloomington: Indiana University Press, 1985), 16–17.

40. For a discussion of the connection between Mary Wilkins and the Tyler family of Brattleboro, see Foster, 32–36 and 42–51.

41. See Constance Rourke, *American Humor: A Study of the National Character* (New York: Harcourt, Brace, 1931).

42. Mary E. Wilkins Freeman, *The Winning Lady and Others* (New York: Harper and Brothers, 1909), 100 (hereafter cited in the text as WL).

43. Edith Wharton, *Summer*, with an introduction by Cynthia Griffin Wolff (New York: Harper and Row, 1980), 7–8 (hereafter cited in the text as S).

44. Ovid, *Metamorphoses*, 2 vols., translated by Frank Justus Miller (Cambridge: Harvard University Press, 1984). Donovan notes the relevance of the Daphne myth to "Old Woman Magoun" (*After the Fall*, 15–16).

45. Wolff's introduction to *Summer*, xii–xiii.

46. "Life and I," 18.

47. For a brief but relevant discussion of "Old Woman Magoun," see Julia Bader, "The Dissolving Vision: Realism in Jewett, Freeman, and Gilman," *American Realism: New Essays*, edited by Eric Sundquist (Baltimore: Johns Hopkins University Press, 1982), 190–91.

48. Several important works have discussed and debated the concept of a women's culture. See Caroll Smith-Rosenberg, "The Female World of Love and Ritual: Relations Between Women in Nineteenth-Century America," *Signs* 1 (1975): 1–30; Nancy F. Cott, *The Bonds of Womanhood: "Women's Sphere" in New England, 1780–1835* (New Haven: Yale University Press, 1977); and *The Feminization of American Culture* (New York: Avon, 1977). Also relevant is Nina Auerbach, *Communities of Women: An Idea in Fiction* (Cambridge: Harvard University Press, 1978). In speaking of a women's culture in this chapter, I am not assuming an empirical category that exists throughout time. Rather, I am interested in a particular representation by Wilkins of a set of mores, traditions, and concerns that separates women from men and cuts across class lines. The bonds forged between women in New England included the rituals of birth and death, the caring for the sick, and the laying away of the dead.

49. Edith Wharton, unpublished draft of *Summer*, Wharton Collection, Beinecke Rare Book and Manuscript Library, Yale University, New Haven, Conn.

50. In the draft version of this passage, Wharton has crossed out the word "street-walker" and replaced it with the word "woman."

51. Nevius, 170. See also Chapter 2, n. 24.

52. Harriet Beecher Stowe, *The Pearl of Orr's Island* (Hartford: Stowe Day Foundation, 1979), 103.

53. Annie Fields, ed., *Life and Letters of Harriet Beecher Stowe* (Boston: Houghton Mifflin, 1897), 285–88. See also 205–301.

54. For discussions of Wharton's treatment of incest, see Lewis, 524–48; Wolff, 303–8, 415; Gilbert, 368–78; Ammons, 133–34.

55. See Lewis, 398.

56. Margaret Ferguson has suggested that in giving Lily the apple in this garden, Maria Mason plays the role of Satan as well as Eve, the first mother. For a relevant discussion of the potential subversiveness of Wilkins's work, see Elizabeth A. Meese, "Signs of Undecidability: Reconsidering the Stories of Mary Wilkins Freeman," in *Crossing the Double-Cross: The Practice of Feminist Criticism* (Chapel Hill: University of North Carolina Press, 1986), 19–38.

57. Speaking in another context of *Summer* as "an inversion of the Demeter-Persephone myth," Fryer notes that "Lawyer Royall's trip up the Mountain to rescue the baby daughter of a drunken convict and rear her like a Christian was, from his description, like a journey to the underworld" (194). In the schema that I have been discussing in *Summer*, as the home of the mother and the place where Charity goes when she becomes a mother, the mountain represents the world of Demeter; yet this winter world of death is also a type of underworld. (For further discussion of this, see Chapter 5.) Writing of the "countertradition of women writers who were torn between the literary world of their fathers and the wordless sensual world of their mothers," Elaine Showalter notes that these "two lines of inheritance are generally represented in the literary history of American women writers by the spatial images of the father's library and the mother's garden" (146).

58. "Life and I," 6.

Chapter 4: *The Devouring Muse* (The Custom of the Country)

1. Henry James, reprinted as "On *The Reef*: A Letter," in *Edith Wharton: A Collection of Critical Essays*, edited by Irving Howe (Englewood Cliffs, N.J.: Prentice Hall, 1962), 150. To take only two more recent characterizations of *The Reef*, Elizabeth Ammons calls *The Reef* "Jamesian" in *Edith Wharton's Argument with America* (Athens: University of Georgia Press, 1980), 61; and Sandra Gilbert calls it "perhaps the most Jamesian of [Wharton's] novels" in "Life's Empty Pack: Notes toward a Literary Daughteronomy," *Critical Inquiry* 11 (1985), 365.

2. Edith Wharton, *Ethan Frome* (New York: Scribner's, 1939), vii.

3. Edith Wharton, *A Backward Glance* (New York: Scribner's, 1934), 125 (hereafter cited in the text as *BG*).

4. Edith Wharton, *The Custom of the Country* (New York: Scribner's, 1913), 75. All further citations, unless otherwise noted, will refer to this text.

5. Edith Wharton, "The Banished God," unpublished manuscript, Wharton Collection, Beinecke Rare Book and Manuscript Library, Yale University, New Haven, Conn. The title "The Wandering God" is crossed out.

6. Edith Wharton, *Hudson River Bracketed* (New York: Appleton, 1929), 231–32.

7. Edith Wharton, "Literature," unpublished manuscript, Wharton Collection, Beinecke Rare Book and Manuscript Library, Yale University, New Haven, Conn.

8. Edith Wharton, unpublished manuscript, Wharton Collection, Beinecke Rare Book and Manuscript Library, Yale University, New Haven, Conn.

9. Edith Wharton and Ogden Codman, Jr., *The Decoration of Houses* (New York: Scribner's, 1897).

10. Ibid., xxi.

11. Ibid., 29–30.

12. Ibid., 198.

13. In "The Muse's Tragedy," Mrs. Anerton describes the poet Rendle in pursuit of a woman in Switzerland, writing her letters "about his theory of vowel combinations—or was it his experiments in English hexameter? The letters were dated from the very places where I knew they went and sat by waterfalls together and he thought out adjectives for her hair" (*The Collected Short Stories of Edith Wharton*, 2 vols., edited with an introduction by R. W. B. Lewis [New York: Scribner's, 1968], 1:76).

14. Edith Wharton, *The Writing of Fiction* (New York: Scribner's, 1925), 85.

15. For discussions of the question of theatricality in eighteenth- and nineteenth-century novels, see David Marshall, *The Figure of Theater: Shaftesbury, Defoe, Adam Smith, and George Eliot* (New York: Columbia University Press, 1986); *The Surprising Effects of Sympathy: Marivaux, Diderot, Rousseau, and Mary Shelley* (Chicago: University of Chicago Press, 1988); "True Acting and the Language of Real Feeling: *Mansfield Park*," *Yale Journal of Criticism* 3 (1989): 87–106. See also Chapter 1 for discussions of the *tableau vivant* scenes in *The House of Mirth*.

16. In *Language and Woman's Place* (New York: Harper and Row, 1975), Robin Lakoff discusses aspects of women's speech that, she argues, differ in expression and content from men's speech. Among these are women's use of adjectives, unusual words to denote colors (such as "mauve"), sewing terms, and the inclusion of a tag question or stress on final words in sentences—words that would be conveyed in print with italics. Sally McConnell-Ginet criticizes Lakoff for resorting to stereotypes in "Our Father Tongue: Essays in Linguistic Politics," *Diacritics* 5 (1975): 44–50. In *The Custom of the Country*, however, Undine and Mrs. Spragg display all of the speech characteristics that Lakoff identifies; this is part of Wharton's critique of what I am calling a feminine aesthetic.

17. Friedrich Heinrich Karl de la Motte Fouqué, *Undine*, translated by Edmund Gosse (United States: The Limited Editions Club, 1930). La Motte Fouqué's tale was first published in 1811; Gosse's translation, in 1897. For different accounts of the relation

between Wharton and Fouqué, see Thomas L. McHaney, "Fouqué's *Undine* and Edith Wharton's *Custom of the Country*," *Revue de Littérature Comparée* 45 (1971): 180–86; and Richard H. Lawson, *Edith Wharton and German Literature* (Bonn: Bouvier Verlag Herbert Grundmann, 1974), 109–19. I hear in Wharton's Bertha an echo of Undine's double and rival in La Motte Fouqué's tale: Bertalda.

18. Fouqué, 102, 118.

19. This vision of the gradations between light and shadow suggests Johann Wolfgang von Goethe's 1810 treatise, *Theory of Colours*, translated by Charles Lock Eastlake (Cambridge: MIT Press, 1978), especially the sections "Dazzling Colourless Objects" and "Coloured Shadows."

20. The various definitions of "sprag" in the *Oxford English Dictionary* suggest multiple allusions in Undine's family name. Not only is a sprag a piece of wood used to lock or hold a wheel in place; it also is a mining term for a structural support used to hold up the sides and roof of a mining shaft while a seam is being mined. My father, Donald Waid, has used the word in conversation in speaking of "throwing a sprag in the operation"—in the same way that a *sabot* is the wooden shoe that jams a machine in *sabotage*. He traces his knowledge of this word to his father's descriptions of mining practices. As we shall see, these senses are also appropriate for Undine, who not only might be described as a "gold-digger" but is finally a kind of muse of extraction, ruthlessly emptying as well as destroying the Marvell and de Chelles houses. A sprag also is a type of fish—as one might expect of an undine.

21. Ammons, 119.

22. The phrase "divers et ondoyant" is from Montaigne: "C'est un sujet merveilleusement vain, divers et ondoyant que l'homme." It appears in the essay "Par Divers Moyens On Arrive à Pareille Fin" (*Essais* [Paris: Garnier, 1946], 6).

23. *The Writing of Fiction*, 73.

24. See *New Larousse Encyclopedia of Mythology*, introduction by Robert Graves (London: Hamlyn, 1959), 186.

25. On his extended visit to the United States to gather material for *The American Scene*, James gave two lectures to the 1905 graduating class of Bryn Mawr College. Wharton heard James read one of these lectures, "The Lesson of Balzac," as they sat before a fire early in 1905. The other lecture, "The Question of Our Speech," must have been shared with Wharton around the same time. Whether she read the lecture or had it read to her by the author, her intimacy with "The Question of Our Speech" is confirmed by her use of it in *A Backward Glance*, where Wharton repeats James's image of the English language as an oil cloth that is being tramped over and soiled in daily usage by immigrants (*BG*, 51). See R. W. B. Lewis, *Edith Wharton: A Biography* (New York: Harper and Row, 1975), 143–44.

26. Henry James, "The Question of Our Speech," in *The Question of Our Speech, The Lesson of Balzac: Two Lectures* (Boston: Houghton, Mifflin, 1905), 39, 41, 43.

27. Millicent Bell, *Edith Wharton and Henry James: The Story of Their Friendship* (New York: Braziller, 1965), 147.

28. Edith Wharton, "The Great American Novel," *Yale Review* 16 (1927): 648.

29. Edith Wharton, *Hudson River Bracketed* (New York: Appleton, 1929), 128. See Edith Wharton and Robert Norton, eds., *Eternal Passion in English Poetry* (New York: Appleton-Century, 1939).

30. See G. A. Aitken's introduction to Andrew Marvell, *The Poems of Andrew Marvell, Sometime Member of Parliament for Hull* (New York: Scribner's, 1898), xxi. All citations of Marvell's poems will refer to this edition and will be indicated by *M*.

31. See Aitken's introduction to Marvell, xl–xlii.

32. In "Names in the Fiction of Edith Wharton," *Names* 13 (1965), Robert L. Coard notes that "Marvell evokes the shade of Andrew Marvell the poet, thus emphasizing poor Ralph Marvell's sensitive temperament and literary ambitions" (7–8). Judith Fryer, in a discussion of the pastoral and *The Custom of the Country*, mentions that the image of Ralph Marvell's sea-cave "suggests Andrew Marvell's 'The Garden,' where 'delicate solitude' is preferred both to 'rude' society and to a luscious vegetable abandonment to sensuality" (*Felicitous Space: The Imaginative Structures of Edith Wharton and Willa Cather* [Chapel Hill: University of North Carolina Press, 1986], 107).

33. I have no proof that Wharton owned or knew "The Muse's Library" edition with the cover I am describing; however, it was published by Wharton's publisher, Scribner's, and it was one of the only editions available that speaks of the Popple family. What convinces me finally that Wharton had this cover illustration in mind (and perhaps even on her writing table) is the uncanny resemblance between the illustration and the scenes and details from *The Custom of the Country* that I have been describing. Obviously, my interpretation of Wharton's use of Andrew Marvell's poems does not depend on her having used this particular edition.

34. Edith Wharton to Robert Grant, Wharton Collection, Beinecke Rare Book and Manuscript Library, Yale University, New Haven, Conn. In "Life and I," Wharton writes of her early reading: "I plunged with rapture into the great ocean of Goethe. At fifteen I had read every word of his plays and poems" (unpublished autobiography, Wharton Collection, Beinecke Rare Book and Manuscript Library, Yale University, New Haven, Conn., 31). See Johann Wolfgang von Goethe, *Der Triumph der Empfindsamkeit*, in *Goethes Dramatische Dichtungen* (Leipzig: Inselverlag, 1920), 610–59. The monologue is sometimes published independently as *Proserpina: Ein Monodrama*. For other indications of Wharton's continued interest in and reading of Goethe, see Edith Wharton, *The Letters of Edith Wharton*, edited by R. W. B. Lewis and Nancy Lewis (New York: Scribner's, 1988), 72, 194, 264–266, 391, 435, 526.

35. George Henry Lewes, *The Life of Goethe* (London: J. M. Dent & Sons, 1938), 251. I quote from Lewes's *Life of Goethe* not only because it provides a convenient description of Goethe's play but also because it, too, may be a source for *The Custom of the Country*, in particular for Wharton's portrait of Ralph Marvell. Lewes quotes a description by Heinse of the young Goethe with "his heart full of feeling, his soul full of fire, and eagle-winged" (175). Lewes tells of the young poet who became involved in the "elegant society of the banker's house" and was seduced by the charms of a pretty but frivolous young woman. Unlike Marvell, Goethe went to Italy after he renounced his love and the

life of "the glare of the chandelier . . . driven in endless dissipation from concert to ball" (187). Wharton, of course, was very interested in both George Eliot and Lewes (see Cynthia Griffin Wolff, *A Feast of Words: The Triumph of Edith Wharton* [New York: Oxford University Press, 1977], 106–7), as well as Goethe. *The Life of Goethe* was reprinted in 1908 and 1911 with an introduction by Havelock Ellis. In "The Pelican," Mrs. Amyot's lecture on Goethe is "manufactured out of Lewes's book" (*The Collected Short Stories of Edith Wharton*, 1:91). See also Lawson, 83–108.

36. Lewes, 250. See also Marvin Carlson, *Goethe and the Weimar Republic Theatre* (Ithaca: Cornell University Press, 1978), 31.

37. Lewes, 250.

38. Robert Rosenblum, *Transformations in Late Eighteenth-Century Art* (Princeton: Princeton University Press, 1974), 52.

39. Michael Fried, *Absorption and Theatricality: Painting and Beholder in the Age of Diderot* (Berkeley: University of California Press, 1980), 36.

40. Rosenblum, 51.

41. See Roger-Armand Weigert, *La Tapisserie Française* (Paris: Larousse, 1956), 132–33. Boucher was artistic director of the famous Gobelins tapestry works from 1755 to 1770.

42. Guy Weelen, *J. M. W. Turner* (New York: Alpine Fine Arts Collection, 1981), 11, 115.

43. Cited in ibid., 114.

44. See ibid., 115.

45. See Bell, 147; Lewis, 247, 262.

Chapter 5: Pomegranate Seeds: Letters from the Underworld (The Touchstone and Ghosts)

1. Edith Wharton, *Ghosts* (New York: Appleton-Century, 1937). All further citations, unless otherwise noted, will refer to this edition. For discussions of Wharton's ghost stories, see Margaret B. McDowell, "Edith Wharton's Ghost Stories," *Criticism* 12 (1970): 133–52; Allan Gardner Smith, "Edith Wharton and the Ghost Story," in *Gender and Literary Voice*, edited by Janet Todd (New York: Holmes and Meier, 1980), 149–59; Cynthia Griffin Wolff, *A Feast of Words: The Triumph of Edith Wharton* (New York: Oxford University Press, 1977), 300–301, 307; R. W. B. Lewis, "Powers of Darkness," *London Times Literary Supplement* (June 13, 1975): 644–45; and R. W. B. Lewis, *Edith Wharton: A Biography* (New York: Harper and Row, 1975), 107, 253, 394, 397, 495, 522–23.

2. Edith Wharton, *A Backward Glance* (New York: Scribner's), 1934 (hereafter cited in the text as *BG*).

3. Edith Wharton, "Life and I," unpublished autobiography, Wharton Collection, Beinecke Rare Book and Manuscript Library, Yale University, New Haven, Conn., 15.

4. See Lewis, *Edith Wharton*, 6, 505.

5. "Life and I," 19.

6. Edith Wharton, "The Great American Novel," *Yale Review* 16 (1927): 648; *A Backward Glance*, 233.

7. "The Triumph of the Night" might be said to be the only exception, but even in this story the young man is vulnerable and dies from weak lungs. Patricia Meyer Spacks observes: "All the Wharton novels provide rich imagery of chains, slavery, prison, suffocation" (*The Female Imagination* [New York: Avon Books, 1975], 315).

8. "Life and I," 18.

9. Lewis, *Edith Wharton*, 25. See Wolff, 173.

10. "A Bottle of Perrier," which Louis Auchincloss calls the "masterpiece" of *Ghosts*, is the only story that is not included in the 1973 *Ghost Stories of Edith Wharton* (New York: Popular Library, 1973). (See Louis Auchincloss, *Edith Wharton* [Minneapolis: University of Minnesota Press, 1961].) Wharton writes in *A Backward Glance* of a critic who was offended by "The Lady's Maid's Bell," arguing that "it was hard to believe that a ghost created by so refined a writer as Mrs. Wharton would do anything so gross as to ring a bell!" (126). In "A Bottle of Perrier" Wharton has refined the art of the disgusting story.

11. Edith Wharton, *Ethan Frome* (New York: Scribner's, 1939), 19.

12. Edgar Allan Poe, *Great Short Works*, edited by G. R. Thompson (New York: Harper and Row, 1970), 226–28.

13. *Ethan Frome*, 4.

14. Susan Glaspell, "A Jury of Her Peers," in *American Voices, American Women*, edited by Lee Edwards and Arlyn Diamond (New York: Avon Books, 1973), 359–81.

15. For a discussion of Wharton's fears concerning animals, see Chapter 2. See also Lewis, *Edith Wharton*, 160; Wolff, 21; and Judith Fryer, *Felicitous Space: The Imaginative Structures of Edith Wharton and Willa Cather* (Chapel Hill: University of North Carolina Press, 1986), 364 n. 46.

16. See Elizabeth Ammons, *Edith Wharton's Argument with America* (Athens: University of Georgia Press, 1980), 157–96. For relevant discussions of Wharton's changing view of the meaning of motherhood—and her novels *The Glimpses of the Moon, The Mother's Recompense, Twilight Sleep*, and *The Children*—see Ammons, 157–87.

17. *Ethan Frome*, 130.

18. Edith Wharton, *The Touchstone* (New York: Scribner's, 1900), 25 (hereafter cited in the text as *T*).

19. Edith Wharton, *The Collected Short Stories of Edith Wharton*, 2 vols., edited with an introduction by R. W. B. Lewis (New York: Scribner's, 1968), 1:281, 285. "Copy" also tells the story of "a deserted garden" where the female novelist and male poet used to meet. This garden has become a "public park," a symbol of the publication and therefore the sharing of a private self (285). Wharton's chapter on her writing in *A Backward Glance* is called "The Secret Garden."

20. Edith Wharton, *Hudson River Bracketed* (New York: Appleton, 1929), p. 61. Further references preceded by *H* will refer to this text.

21. Edith Wharton, *The Gods Arrive* (New York: Appleton, 1932), 104–5, hereafter cited as *G*. Vance Weston repeatedly and somewhat melodramatically evokes Goethe's

mythological invention of the "Mothers." He claims to be writing "only for the Mothers" (*G*, 72); he conceives of writing as a way of coming close to the primal forces of origination that the "Mothers" represent. In *The Gods Arrive*, in an epiphany about his art, Weston understands that "you have to go plumb down to the Mothers to fish up the real thing" (*G*, 118). In the penultimate line of *Faust* II, Faust's ascension to the heavens is accomplished through the intercession of "Woman Eternal [Das Ewig-Weibliche]" (Johann Wolfgang von Goethe, *Faust*, translated by Walter Arndt [New York: Norton, 1976], line 12110). In terms of the poem, this figure includes the Virgin Mary, Gretchen, the mysterious "Mothers," and the allusive Helena (whom Faust impregnates). What Faust accomplishes through "Woman Eternal" is accomplished in *The Gods Arrive* through the self-sacrificing Héloïse. Called by the allegorical name and nickname of Halo, this Héloïse represents a female character who is herself the complicated embodiment of the hope for the future of art. At the close of Wharton's sequel, the troubled artist figure Vance Weston assumes a role not unlike that of the repentant Faust at the close of Goethe's sequel. Here, Wharton's Helena figure stands with her hands held in an attitude of prayer. Pregnant with the artist's child, she accepts the prodigal writer as another child under her care. The name of Vance Weston's hometown, Euphoria, may recall the name of the ill-fated child born to Faust and Helena: Euphorion.

Goethe's "Mothers" are at the center of what Mephistopheles names as an "exalted riddle" (line 6213); these "Goddesses sit enthroned in reverend loneliness" (line 6214). As Faust descends to the formless and placeless place of the "Mothers," he is given the "key" (line 6258) that will provide entry after he reaches "the deepest, nethermost shrine" (line 6384). The riddle of the "Mothers," like that of Faust's apotheosis through "Woman Eternal," remains a mystery about the necessary mystery of origins. In *Faust*, the Mothers are beheld as "Formation, transformation, / The eternal mind's eternal recreation, / Enswathed in likenesses of manifold entity; / They see you not, for only wraiths they see" (lines 6287–6290). In an important reading of Wharton's use of Goethe's "Mothers" in *Hudson River Bracketed* and *The Gods Arrive*, Ammons identifies these goddesses with the feared maternal force of the Furies (Ammons, 195–96). The formless figures who are capable of seeing only ghosts also are related to the Persephone that Wharton names as the goddess of "the living and the dead." The union of the dead woman who has become a character in a novel and her living descendant who is both the fertile muse and a woman who is not forced to choose between love and literature is suggestive in this context. One might speculate that Wharton once again is rewriting her own troubling fictions about the loneliness of women, the death of art, and the suicides of writers. In her final *Künstlerroman*, Wharton brings the broken figure of the artist to the woman who represents the fusion of the divided worlds of fiction and life. In this sense Halo represents a paradoxical Persephone figure who brings together both worlds. By accepting the roles of mother and muse, by embodying the source of Weston's art, Halo opens the doors to both Wharton's underworld and Faust's heaven. However, the daughter Persephone, this goddess of the underworld, is not herself a writer.

22. "Life and I," 10.

23. Ibid., 3, 7.

24. Ovid, *Metamorphoses*, translated by Rolfe Humphries (Bloomington: Indiana University Press, 1975), 118. Although, as I have suggested in Chapter 2, the thinly veiled descriptions of eroticism in Wharton's poetry emphasize violence and even physical violation, Wharton's rewriting of the Persephone myth seems to repress or erase any notion of rape. Lily Bart enters the underworld in a scene of attempted and resisted rape but Wharton's figuring of the woman writer who must eat the seeds of the pomegranate focus on a willing and willful choice on the part of the woman to enter erotic and literary experience. In this sense a rape does not seem to occur because Persephone seems to choose the realm of the underworld instead of the world of Demeter. Remarkably, the figure of Hades seems to disappear in these descriptions. The call from the underworld seems to come from other Persephone figures: women who already have eaten the seeds of knowledge.

25. *Ethan Frome*, vii. Humphries, 124.

26. Johann Wolfgang von Goethe, *Selected Verse*, translated by David Luke (Baltimore: Penguin Books, 1964), 81–82.

27. Edith Wharton, "Pomegranate Seed," typescript of poem, Wharton Collection, Beinecke Rare Book and Manuscript Library, Yale University, New Haven, Conn., 1, 8, 9, 12, 13. For the published version, see *Scribner's* 51 (March 1912): 288.

28. Cited in Wolff, 205.

29. Edith Wharton, planning notebook for "Literature," unpublished manuscript, Wharton Collection, Beinecke Rare Book and Manuscript Library, Yale University, New Haven, Conn.

Index

Aeschylus: *Eumenides*, 45–46; *Oresteia*, 45–46

Agamemnon, 46–48

Ajax, 151

Ammons, Elizabeth, 4, 79, 145, 213 (n. 17), 217 (n. 15), 223 (n. 1)

Andersen, Hans Christian, 195

Andromeda, 141–42, 145, 147, 150–54, 164

Apollo, 171

Apuleius: *The Mysteries of Isis*, 1, 3, 202

Ariosto, Ludovico: *Orlando Furioso*, 29

Art Nouveau, 17

Athena, 46

Atlantic, The, 92–93, 95

Auchincloss, Louis, 228 (n. 10)

Aurora, 162–63

Austen, Jane, 7

Austin, Mary: "Regionalism in American Literature," 96

Bernard, Kenneth, 213 (n. 17)

Berry, Walter, 97, 133–34, 177

Bloom, Harold, 221 (n. 35)

Botticelli, Sandro, 27

Boucher, François, 29, 168–72; *Pastorale*, 170; *Pastorales et Paysages*, 170; *Le Coucher du Soleil*, 171; *Le Lever du Soleil*, 171

Bourget, Paul, 62

Brontë, Emily, 7; *Wuthering Heights*, 214 (n. 7)

Brooks, Van Wyck, 215 (n. 7), 220 (n. 22)

Brownell, William Crary, 53

Bryn Mawr College, 152

Burlingame, Edward, 208 (n. 2)

Childbirth, 46–47, 59, 104

Chlora, 48, 162–63, 168

Christ, 54–55. *See also* Wharton, Edith—Works—poetry: "Margaret of Cortona"

Circe, 182

Civil War, 115, 217 (n. 18)

Clytemnestra, 46

Codman, Ogden, 9, 133

Coleridge, Samuel Taylor, 155, 197

Coote, Charles, Earl of Bellomont, 211 (n. 30)

Courtney, W. L.: *The Feminine Note in Fiction*, 93

Crane, Hart, 171

Daughters: rebellious, 3, 200–201; burying body of the mother, 81–82, 91, 113–14, 122; sacrifice of, 98, 106, 111, 112, 121, 199–200; threatened by fathers, 100, 102–12, 120; replacement of mother, 104–5, 116, 125, 196, 199; identification with mother, 113–14. *See also* Persephone

Death, 14, 41–42, 57, 60, 69–70, 104–5, 109–12, 119–23, 147, 175, 177, 181–95, 197, 200–203; in relation to underworld, 43–46, 48, 59, 78, 111, 196, 199–202, 223 (n. 57), 229 (n. 21), 230 (n. 24); in life, 72, 76–79, 200, 201, 202–3; lure of, 79. *See also* Suicide

Delilah, 172

Demeter, 47, 78, 111, 195–96, 198–202, 205 (n. 3), 223 (n. 57), 230 (n. 24)

Description, 9, 131, 133, 136, 144–45, 224 (nn. 13, 16). *See also* Feminine aesthetic

Divorce, 129, 132, 149, 164, 167, 169

Donovan, Josephine, 205 (n. 3), 216 (n. 13), 223 (n. 57)

Douglas, Ann, 210 (n. 22)

Doyle, Arthur Conan, 93–94

Dunne, Finley Peter: "Mr. Dooley," 6

Ecclesiastes, 41

Eliot, George, 7, 8, 21, 227 (n. 35); *Daniel Deronda*, 209 (n. 10); *Silas Marner*, 217 (n. 15)

Eumenides, 46

Fallopius, Gabriel, 56, 58. *See also* Wharton, Edith—Works—poetry: "Vesalius in Zante"

Fates, 110

Fathers: violence threatened by, 18, 19, 98–112, 119–20, 125, 190, 200, 220 (n. 19); benevolence of, 83, 108, 112, 114–16, 118; authority of, 106, 109, 110–11, 115, 120, 189–92

Faulkner, William: *Absalom, Absalom!*, 63–64

Feminine aesthetic, 9, 11, 17, 89, 131, 138, 143, 154, 156, 170, 177; lure of, 129–31, 134, 140–48, 153, 160–64, 172, 198

Flaubert, Gustave: *Madame Bovary*, 48, 94, 119, 211 (n. 36)

Foster, Edward, 219 (n. 18)

Freeman, Dr. Charles, 219–20 (n. 19)

Freeman, Mary Wilkins. *See* Wilkins, Mary

Fried, Michael, 170, 209 (n. 11)

Fryer, Judith, 205 (n. 3), 216 (n. 13), 223 (n. 57), 226 (n. 32)

Fullerton, Morton, 13, 53, 60, 220 (n. 19)

Furies, 45–46, 229 (n. 21)

Gentileschi, Artemisia: *Self-Portrait as the Allegory of Painting*, 30

Ghost stories, 3, 202–3; experience of reading, 175–76, 179; as expression of Wharton's fears, 175–78, 184, 191; autobiography in, 175–78

Gilbert, Sandra, 217 (n. 15), 223 (n. 1)

Glaspell, Susan: "A Jury of Her Peers," 187–88

God, 3, 10–11, 109, 112, 114, 125, 199, 202

Goethe, Johann Wolfgang von, 155, 167; *Wilhelm Meister*, 8; "Erkönig," 14, 199–201; *Der Triumph der Empfindsamkeit*, 167–68; *Die Wahlverwandtschaften*, 209 (n. 10); *Theory of Colours*, 225, (n. 19); *Proserpina: Ein Monodrama*, 226 (n. 34); *Faust*, 228–29 (n. 21)

Gowing, Lawrence, 171

Goya, Francisco de, 27

Grant, Robert, 9–10, 167

Greuze, Jean–Baptiste, 170

Grimm, Jakob, 195

Gubar, Susan, 43, 210 (n. 26)

Hades, 46, 230 (n. 24)

Hamblen, Abigail, 215 (n. 7), 216 (n. 13)

Harte, Bret. 6

Hartt, Rollin Lynd: "A New England Hill Town," 95

Hawthorne, Nathaniel, 6–7, 90, 216 (n. 13); *The Blithedale Romance*, 7; "Ethan Brand," 7; *The Scarlet Letter*, 93–94

Higginson, T. W., 93

Hitler, Adolf, 175

Howells, William Dean, 94

Incest, 94, 95, 106–8, 118

Iphigenia, 46–47

James, Henry, 4–6, 53, 90, 93, 129, 152–54, 172, 175; *The American Scene*, 5; *Hawthorne*, 6; *The Aspern Papers*, 18; "The Question of Our Speech," 152–53; *The Wings of the Dove*, 206 (n. 6); "The Lesson of Balzac," 225 (n. 25)

Jewett, Sarah Orne; 8, 11, 61, 88, 90–91, 94–95, 97, 199; *The Country of the Pointed Firs and Other Stories*, 220 (n. 25)

Jones, Lucretia, 6, 7, 10–11, 53, 125, 177, 178, 199; distaste for Stowe, 8

Jove, 142

Judith, 172

Kauffmann, Angelica, 27

Kazin, Alfred: criticism of *Ethan Frome*, 214–15 (n. 7)

Künstlerroman, 17, 197, 229 (n. 21)

La Motte Fouqué, Friedrich Heinrich Karl de: *Undine*, 140–41

Leach, Nancy, 215 (n. 7), 215–16 (n. 13)

Letters, 18–22, 24–26, 29–45, 47–49, 77, 123–25, 138–39, 147, 154, 189, 191–98, 200

Lewes, George Henry: *The Life of Goethe*, 167–68, 226–27 (n. 35)

Lewis, R. W. B., 3, 8, 13, 53, 178, 207 (n. 30), 214 (n. 7), 220 (n. 19)

Lewis, Sinclair: *Main Street*, 155

Lincoln, Abraham, 77, 115

Lives of the Saints, The, 54

Local color, 8, 9, 87–91, 94, 97, 115, 119–22, 136, 143, 170, 199, 215 (nn. 11, 12), 215–16 (n. 13). *See also* Jewett, Sarah Orne; Sentimentalism; Wilkins, Mary

Lucrece, rape of, 99, 222 (n. 38)

Macy, John: *The Spirit of American Literature*, 93

Margaret of Cortona, 54. *See also* Wharton, Edith—Works—poetry: "Margaret of Cortona"

Marlowe, Christopher, 155

Marriage, 17, 23, 31, 99, 103–4, 108, 118, 130, 144–45, 150–52, 166–67, 169, 186, 189, 193–94

Marshall, David, 209 (n. 10), 224 (n. 15)

Marvell, Andrew, 155–66, 168; "The Garden," 29, 156, 158–61; "Upon Appleton House," 51; "The Nymph Complaining for the Death of Her Faun," 85; "The Mower, against Gardens," 127; "Advice to a Painter," 155; "To His Coy Mistress," 155; "The Gallery," 156, 161–66, 168; "The Unfortunate Lover," 156–58, 164, 173; *The Poems of Andrew Marvell* ("Muses' Library" edition), 160–61

Matthiessen, F. O.: "New England Stories," 93, 95–96

Mayeaux, Henri: *La Composition décorative*, 132–33

Medusa, 152–53, 183

Melodrama, 43, 99

Melville, Herman, 6; "Bartleby the Scrivener," 30

Men: division between women and, 8, 18, 104, 106–7, 120–22, 124, 131, 179, 184; castration, 59, 74, 169, 183, 213 (n. 17); wounds of, 74–75, 77, 78, 169, 181, 183, 187; as predators, 98, 122, 145; instability of, 99; violence of, 99–101, 114, 179, 182–90, 220 (n. 19); compared with animals, 101, 103, 107, 110–12, 114, 182–85; weakness of, 106; power to control women's lives, 106, 110, 115; misogyny of, 181, 184, 188; jealousy of, 186–87. *See also* Fathers

Michaels, Walter Benn, 209 (n. 11)

Milton, John, 20

Minerva, 101, 123, 200

Montaigne, Michel de, 148, 225 (n. 22)

More, Hannah, 21

Mothers: world of, 3, 4, 20, 190–91, 199, 201–2; power of, 36; and motherhood, 47, 98, 113–14, 115, 122; body of, 81–82, 91, 113–14, 115, 122; death of, 81–82, 113; failure of, 91, 117–18, 122; violence of, 95, 113, 117, 119, 120–21, 125, 184; law of, 109–10; in heaven, 109–12, 125; repetition of by daughter, 110, 112–14, 116, 125, 196, 94. *See also* Childbirth; Daughters; Demeter; Fathers

Muses, 101, 200–201

Nation, 7

Nevius, Blake, 6, 7, 91, 215 (n. 10)

New England: in fiction, 7, 75, 78–79, 81–83, 87–92, 94–97, 112–13, 115, 118, 178, 179

New York society, 5, 6, 11; in Edith Wharton's fiction, 59, 92, 96, 134–38, 151–55

Norton, Charles Eliot, 94

Norton, Robert, 155

Norton, Sara, 59, 206 (n. 8)

Omar Khayam, 26

Orestes, 45, 46–47

Ornamentation, 9–11, 61, 132–34, 138–40, 144–49, 169–70; of society, 1, 134–38, 151, 153, 166–67; and women, 9, 11, 17, 48, 120–22, 130–31, 134–40, 143–51, 153–55, 163–66, 172; of language, 132, 134, 151–54

Ovid: *Metamorphoses*, 101, 195, 199–203, 212 (n. 8)

Painting, 17, 18–19, 23, 27–30, 37–43, 48–49, 145, 165, 168–72, 209

(nn. 10, 11), 209–10 (n. 16), 211 (n. 30), 224 (n. 15)

Paris, 12, 78, 79, 99, 115; in Wharton's fiction, 138–39, 166, 169

Pegasus, 141–42, 159, 164

Persephone, 3, 4, 14, 44, 46–48, 78, 89, 111, 167, 195–96, 198–203, 205 (n. 3), 223 (n. 57), 229 (n. 21), 230 (n. 24)

Perseus, 141–42, 152

Phaedrus, 131

Poe, Edgar Allan, 179, 181; "The Fall of the House of Usher," 106, 180

Pomegranate seeds, 3, 12, 13, 14, 44, 77, 111, 195–96, 199–200, 202–3, 230 (n. 24)

Prometheus, 141–42, 156, 161, 164

Proserpine. *See* Persephone

Pygmalion, 142

Racine, Jean: *Phèdre*, 94; Wharton compared with James, 129

Ransom, John Crowe, 96: "Characters and Character," 96–97; criticism of *Ethan Frome*, 214 (n. 7)

Realism, 8–9, 89–92, 94, 95–97, 176, 218–19 (n. 18)

Revelation (Bible), 127, 172

Reynolds, Sir Joshua, 211 (n. 30); *Mrs. Lloyd*, 27–30, 37–39, 42–43, 48–49

Richardson, Samuel: *Pamela*, 221 (n. 37)

Robinson, Edward Arlington, 95

Rose, Henry Alan, 213 (n. 17)

Rosenblum, Robert 170

Ruskin, John: *Modern Painters*, 171

Sand, George, 21; *Consuelo*, 8

Schopenhauer, Arthur, 167

Scribner's, 53, 87, 129, 160

Scylla, 153

Sentimentalism, 7–8, 12, 19, 20, 27, 32, 36, 41, 43, 90, 110, 112, 115, 119–20, 125, 136, 167, 168, 176–77,

188, 200, 210 (n. 22)

Shakespeare, William: *As You Like It*, 28; *Romeo and Juliet*, 39, 42; *Othello*, 42, 151; *The Winter's Tale*, 209 (n. 10)

Showalter, Elaine, 208 (n. 1), 211 (n. 35), 217 (n. 15), 223 (n. 57)

Silence, 32–33, 61–69, 71, 75–77, 79, 88, 92, 177, 184–85, 188–89, 196; and ellipses, 68–69. *See also* Women

Sirens, 88–89, 111, 129, 131, 140, 153, 156, 177, 199–201

Smith, Elizabeth Oakes: *Bertha and Lily*, 211 (n. 35)

Spacks, Patricia Meyer, 211 (n. 30), 228 (n. 7)

Stowe, Harriet Beecher, 8, 41, 115; *The Pearl of Orr's Island*, 115

Sturgis, Howard, 175

Suicide, 14, 17, 18, 22, 29, 34–43, 48, 72, 75–77, 98–99, 104, 111, 122, 131, 150, 165, 168–69, 197

Tableau vivant, 17, 23, 27–31, 37–43, 48–49, 209 (n. 10), 209–10 (n. 16), 224 (n. 15)

Tasso, Torquato: *Gerusalemme Liberata*, 29

Thetis, 171

Thompson, Charles Miner, 92–93, 95–96

Thresholds, 14, 48, 102; between life and death, 3, 76, 101; of doorways, 67–71, 76, 102, 104, 150, 178, 194; of sexual maturity, 100–103, 123; of heaven, 125

Tiepolo, Giambattista, 29; *Cleopatra*, 29, 210 (n. 16)

Tiepolo, Giandomenico, 29

Titian, 27

Tolstoy, Leo: *Anna Karenina*, 94

Tompkins, Jane, 210 (n. 22)

Trilling, Diana, 6

Turner, Joseph Mallord William, 171–72; *Angel Standing in the Sun*, 171–72; *Undine Giving the Ring to Massaniella, Fisherman of Naples*, 171–72

Twain, Mark: *Innocents Abroad*, 6

Tyler, Elesina, 99

Tyler, Hanson, 218 (n. 18)

Tyler, Pickman, 99, 218 (n. 18)

Tyler, Royall (friend of Wharton), 99

Tyler, Royall (playwright), 99–100, 219 (n. 18)

Undines, 145, 152, 171. *See also* La Motte Fouqué, Friedrich Heinrich Karl de

Van Dyck, Sir Anthony, 27

Venus, 162–63

Veronese, Paolo, 27

Vesalius, 56, 58; *De humani corporis fabrica librorum epitome*, 56, 58, 60. *See also* Wharton, Edith—Works—poetry: "Vesalius in Zante"

Waid, Donald, 225 (n. 25)

Watteau, Jean-Antoine, 27

Westbrook, Perry, 219 (n. 18)

Wharton, Edith: fear of silence, 3, 177–78; fear of suffocation, 3, 177–78; place in society, 4, 11, 199, 219 (n. 19); in New York, 4, 12, 92; American citizenship, 4–5; life in France, 4–5, 62, 78, 79–81, 99, 115, 129; compared with Henry James, 4–5, 93, 129; sense of exile, 4–6, 13, 96; and America, 5, 11–12, 13, 59, 62–63, 78–79, 92, 97, 131, 206 (nn. 8, 10); marital problems, 5, 13, 129–30, 220 (n. 19); concern over deterioration of English language, 6; childhood reading, 6, 7, 167, 171, 195; and American literary tradition, 6–7, 90–93; relation to literary predecessors, 7, 11, 90–94, 97–99, 118; eroticism, 8, 13, 44–49,

53–59, 74, 75, 77–78, 94, 117, 123, 179–80, 184, 196, 200; defensiveness about knowledge of New England, 8, 61, 64, 78, 81, 87–91, 94, 96–97, 214–15 (n. 7), 215–16 (n. 13); fear of caretaking, 13, 177; love letters of, 53; use of first-person singular, 53–54, 59, 60, 212 (n. 9); fear of animals, 62, 188; *House of Mirth* compared with Hawthorne's *Scarlet Letter*, 93; and World War I, 79–83, 99, 115, 130, 175; introductions to *Ethan Frome*, 87–89, 199; research for *The Fruit of the Tree*, 90; membership in National Institute of Arts and Letters, 93; fear of mother's doorway, 102, 178, 189; *The Reef* compared with Racine, 129; sells house in New England, 129; childhood nurse, 175, 177; fear of abandonment, 176; death, 177; affection for father, 190; nicknamed "Lily," 210 (n. 25); compared with Browning, 215 (n. 12)—Works:

—nonfiction: *A Backward Glance*, 5–6, 9, 12, 13, 61, 79, 81, 87–89, 96, 133, 151, 175, 177, 188, 225 (n. 25), 228 (nn. 10, 19); *The Decoration of Houses*, 9, 132–33, 170; *Fighting France from Dunkerque to Belfort*, 80–81, 213–14 (n. 24); *French Ways and Their Meaning*, 8, 180; "The Great American Novel," 89–90, 155, 176; *A Motor Flight through France*, 188; *The Writing of Fiction*, 136, 151, 213 (n. 13)

—novels and novellas: *The Age of Innocence*, 12–13, 14, 44, 60; *The Custom of the Country*, 3, 7, 11, 26, 37, 42, 53, 60, 92, 94, 122, 129–72, 197, 210 (n. 19); *Ethan Frome*, 3, 7, 11, 13, 60–83, 87–92, 96–97, 122, 129, 178, 179, 181, 183, 184, 186, 191, 197, 199–200, 202, 214–15 (n. 7), 215 (n. 10), 220 (nn. 19, 22); "Fast and Loose," 7, 20; *The Fruit of the Tree*, 9–10, 90; *The Gods Arrive*, 197–98, 228–29 (n. 21); *The House of Mirth*, 3, 7, 11, 14, 17, 19–49, 59, 77, 93, 94, 98–99, 111, 122, 178, 192–93, 196, 197, 200, 206 (n. 10), 221–22 (n. 37), 230 (n. 24); *Hudson River Bracketed*, 3, 130, 155, 197–98; *The Reef*, 4–5, 60, 129; *Summer*, 3, 11, 60, 61, 62, 78–83, 87–92, 96–100, 102–4, 112–19, 122–25, 178, 184, 213–14 (n. 24); *The Touchstone*, 3, 20–21, 43, 176, 192–94, 196–98, 202–3; *The Valley of Decision*, 4

—poetry: "Artemis to Actaeon," 53, 56–57, 58; *Artemis to Actaeon and Other Verse*, 3, 53–61; "Eumenides," 46; "Life," 53–58, 63, 74, 76; "Margaret of Cortona," 14, 53, 54–55, 56, 57, 58, 74, 77; "Orpheus," 51; "Pomegranate Seed," 20, 201–2; "Vesalius in Zante," 14, 53, 55–56, 57–60, 62, 69, 70, 71–72, 77

—stories: "Afterwards," 177; "All Souls," 175; "April Showers," 20; "A Bottle of Perrier," 178–84, 188, 191, 202; "Copy," 20–21, 31, 43, 196, 228 (n. 19); "Expiation," 20; "The Eyes," 212 (n. 9); "The Fullness of Life," 17, 208 (n. 2); *Ghosts*, 3, 175, 178, 191, 194–95, 203; *The Greater Inclination*, 17, 19; "His Father's Son," 21; "Kerfol," 178, 184–89, 191, 193, 202, 212 (n. 12); "The Lady's Maid's Bell," 228 (n. 10); "The Lamp of Psyche," 17, 19; "The Letters," 21; "Mr. Jones," 21, 44, 178, 184–85, 188–92, 193, 202; "The Muse's Tragedy," 17, 18–19, 20–21, 224 (n. 13); "The Pelican," 19–20, 227 (n. 35); "Pomegranate Seed," 3, 20, 21, 43–44, 194–98, 202–3; "The Portrait," 17–18, 19; "The Triumph of the Night," 178 (n. 7)

—unpublished manuscripts: "The Banished God," 130, 131; *The Cruise of the Fleetwing*, 220 (n. 25); "Life and I," 5, 10, 13, 53, 125, 175–76, 178, 198–99, 200, 226 (n. 34); "Literature," 1, 3, 41, 130–31, 197, 202; "The New Litany," 14; "The Oresteia," 46; "The Rhythmical Structures of Walt Whitman," 130–32

Wharton, Edward (Teddy), 13, 129, 220 (n. 19)

Whelen, Guy, 171

Whitman, Walt, 6, 130–31, 132, 134; "Out of the Cradle Endlessly Rocking," 41

Wilkins, Eleanor, 99, 216 (n. 14), 218–19 (n. 18)

Wilkins, Mary, 8, 11, 61, 88, 90–112, 199; "Old Woman Magoun," 91, 98–100, 102–12, 114–23, 125, 197; biography, 92, 99–100, 216–17 (n. 14), 217–19 (n. 18), 219–20 (n. 19); *A Humble Romance and Others*, 92–93, 95; as contemporary and rival of Wharton, 93; *A New England Nun and Others*, 93; compared with *The Scarlet Letter*, 94; *Pembroke*, 94, 95; *The Winning Lady and Others*, 98, 100, 104, 121, 220 (n. 19); "The Joy of Youth," 100–104; "Little–Girl–Afraid of–A–Dog," 101, 103; "Eliza Sam," 103

Wilkins, Warren, 121, 217–18 (n. 18)

Willis, N. P., 20

Wolff, Cynthia Griffin, 17, 28, 48, 87, 91, 102, 206 (n. 7), 212 (nn. 12, 13)

Women: as writers, 3–4, 7, 8, 14, 17, 19, 45, 47–49, 110, 116–21, 123–25, 176, 188, 192–93; culture, 13, 106, 110, 190–91, 222 (n. 48); objectification of, 17, 98, 105, 108, 111, 149; as muse, 18–19, 20, 33–34, 122, 131, 140, 143, 145–48, 164, 172, 201; repetition or doubling of, 24–25, 31, 33, 45–46, 70–75, 80–83, 104–6, 110, 112–13, 196, 199; revenge of, 31, 33, 34, 46, 59–60, 76, 79–80, 188, 190, 199; silence and inarticulateness of, 32–33, 34–35, 38, 40, 49, 64, 67–69, 71, 73–74, 76, 79, 124, 177–78, 188–92, 202; sacrifice of, 41–42, 45–47, 55, 56, 98, 104, 106, 112, 122, 199–200; infertility of, 47, 60–61, 69–70, 73–78, 83, 106, 111, 185–88; marriage, 47–48, 99; fertility of, 59, 60, 76, 79–80, 199; speech of, 69, 74, 83, 95, 109, 119–21, 123, 152–54, 177, 178–79, 187, 191, 201; abortion, 78, 113, 117, 122; pregnancy, 79–82, 82, 98, 105, 110, 113–14, 117, 123–25, 198; compared with animals, 82, 91, 104, 107, 112, 113, 122, 125, 186, 188; violation of, 98–99, 104–8, 110, 120, 188, 199–203; powerlessness of, 106, 115, 120–21; obedience of, 107–9, 182, 184, 186; vulnerability of, 108, 148; prostitution, 113–14; artifice of, 122, 131, 143, 148, 151, 162, 168; as source of death, 122, 184–87, 191, 201, 202; emptiness of, 149, 154–55, 163, 167–68; isolation of, 178, 185–86, 189, 191–92, 196, 202; as caretaker, 183, 187, 199; literary tradition of, 190–20. *See also* Daughters; Feminine aesthetic; Men; Mothers

Wordsworth, William, 72